Computational Philosophy of Science

Computational Philosophy of Science

Paul Thagard

A Bradford Book
The MIT Press
Cambridge, Massachusetts
London, England

First MIT Press paperback edition, 1993

© 1988 Massachusetts Institute of Technology

This book was set in Palatino by Asco Trade Typesetting Ltd., Hong Kong, and printed and bound by Halliday Lithograph in the United States of America.

Library of Congress Cataloging-in-Publication Data

Thagard, Paul
  Computational philosophy of science/Paul Thagard.
    p. cm.
  "A Bradford book."
  Bibliography: p.
  Includes index.
  ISBN 0-262-20068-6 (HB), 0-262-70048-4 (PB)
  1. Science—Philosophy. 2. Psychology. 3. Artificial intelligence. I. Title.
  Q175.T479 1988   501—dc19   87-21892

For Ziva

Contents

Preface

To some ears, "computational philosophy of science" will sound like the most self-contradictory enterprise in philosophy since business ethics. On the contrary, central philosophical issues concerning the structure and growth of scientific knowledge can be greatly illuminated by drawing on ideas and techniques from the field of artificial intelligence. This book uses PI, a computer program for problem solving and induction, to illustrate the relevance of computational ideas to questions concerning the discovery, evaluation, and application of scientific theories.

The first part of the book is concerned with computational models of scientific thinking, and should appeal to those interested in artificial intelligence and cognitive psychology as well as to philosophers. Later chapters turn to more traditional philosophical issues, concerning the relation between how reasoning is done and how it ought to be done, truth, the justification of scientific methods, and the difference between science and pseudoscience. Some of the general conclusions about the nature of scientific method are applied to the particular fields of psychology and artificial intelligence. The book concludes with a highly speculative chapter concerning what computational models might add to our understanding of two key aspects of the process of inquiry: the interrelations of theory and experiment, and the importance of group rationality in science.

I have tried to make this book accessible to an interdisciplinary readership by clarifying philosophical and computational terms as they arise. To provide background for readers of different fields without interrupting the argument, appendix 1 contains four tutorials providing essential philosophical, computational, and psychological introductions. Each chapter concludes with a summary of its most important claims.

The book is offered in the hope that it will be read without arbitrary categorizations of what is philosophy, artificial intelligence, or psychology, and in the conviction that an understanding of scientific reasoning can only come through interdisciplinary cooperation.

Acknowledgments

This book has depended on the assistance of many people and institutions. It was begun when I was an Associate Professor of Philosophy at the University of Michigan-Dearborn, and I am grateful for the freedom provided there by my colleagues. Much of the work was done while I was also associated with the Cognitive Science Program at the University of Michigan, Ann Arbor, which provided support of many kinds. The book has been completed using the excellent facilities of the Cognitive Science Laboratory at Princeton University, where I am now doing interdisciplinary research as part of the Human Information Processing Group.

In the period during which many of the ideas of this book were being developed, I was fortunate to collaborate with John Holland, Keith Holyoak, and Richard Nisbett on our 1986 book: *Induction: Processes of Inference, Learning, and Discovery*. Some of the themes developed here were sketched in a preliminary way there. I am particularly indebted to Keith Holyoak, since the processing system PI, whose philosophical implications and applications are discussed at length here, is a collaborative project with him. I am grateful to Richard Nisbett for first acquainting me wth work in cognitive psychology, and to John Holland for supervising my M.S. in computer science.

Earlier drafts of this book received valuable comments from Paul Churchland, Robert Cummins, Daniel Hausman, Stephen Hanson, Gilbert Harman, Ziva Kunda, Richard Nisbett, and Ian Pratt. I am especially grateful to Lindley Darden for detailed comments on two separate drafts.

Over the years that this book developed, I have been grateful for the support of the National Science Foundation, the Sloan Foundation, the Systems Development Foundation, the Basic Research Office of the Army Research Institute for Behavioral and Social Science, and the McDonnell Foundation.

Some sections of this book derive from previously published articles. I am grateful to the respective publishers for permission to use the following material.

Section 1.4 and tutorial D draw on "Frames, Knowledge, and Inference", *Synthese*, 64, pp. 233–259, 1984. Copyright © 1984 by D. Reidel Publishing Company.

Some parts of section 4.4 are included in "The Emergence of Meaning: How to Escape Searle's Chinese Room", *Behaviorism*, 14, 139–146, 1986.

Sections 5.2, 5.3, 5.4, and 5.6 draw on "The Best Explanation: Criteria for Theory Choice", *Journal of Philosophy*, 75, pp. 76–92, 1978.

Chapter 6 is a revised version of "Against Evolutionary Epistemology", in P. Asquith and R. Giere, eds., *PSA 1980*, vol. 1, East Lansing, Philosophy of Science Association, 1980, pp. 187–196.

Chapter 7 is based on "From the Descriptive to the Normative in Psychology and Logic", *Philosophy of Science*, 49, pp. 24–42, 1982.

Sections 9.3 and 9.4 are taken from "Resemblance, Correlation, and Pseudoscience", in Marsha P. Hanen, Margaret J. Osler, and Robert G. Weyant, eds., *Science, Pseudo-science, and Society*, Waterloo, University of Waterloo Press, 1980, pp. 17–27.

Section 10.2.1 is taken from "Parallel Computation and the Mind-Body Problem," *Cognitive Science*, 10, pp. 301–318, 1986.

Thanks to Greg Nowak and Greg Nelson for helping with proofreading.

Computational Philosophy of Science

Chapter 1

Computation and the Philosophy of Science

Epistemology without contact with science becomes an empty scheme. Science without epistemology is—insofar as it is thinkable at all— primitive and muddled.
(Albert Einstein, 1949, pp. 683ff.)

1.1. A New Approach

Philosophy of science and artificial intelligence have much to learn from each other. The central questions that can benefit from a multidisciplinary investigation include

1. What are scientific theories?
2. What is scientific explanation and problem solving?
3. How are theories discovered and evaluated?
4. How do theoretical concepts become meaningful?
5. What are the roles of theorizing and experimentation in the process of scientific inquiry?
6. How can descriptive studies of how science is done be relevant to normative judgments about how it ought to be done?

This book presents an integrated set of answers to these questions within a computational framework. Here is a preliminary sketch of what is proposed in later chapters.

1. Theories are complex data structures in computational systems; they consist of highly organized packages of rules, concepts, and problem solutions.
2. Explanation and problem solving are computational processes mediated by the rules, concepts, and problem solutions that can constitute theories.
3. The discovery and evaluation of theories are subprocesses that are triggered in the context of explanation and problem solving.
4. Theoretical concepts are meaningful because of their generation

by discovery processes and because of their connections with other concepts.

5. Theorizing and experimentation play complementary roles in scientic inquiry, with neither dominant.

6. Descriptive studies of how science is done can provide an essential contribution to the determination of how science ought to be done.

Fleshing out these vague claims will proceed in later chapters. To substantiate them, I shall describe an artificial intelligence program for problem solving and induction, showing how its operation helps to illustrate the processes by which scientific theories are constructed and used. I shall argue that richer philosophical accounts of scientific problem solving, discovery, and justification can be developed using the resources of artificial intelligence than are possible with the traditional techniques of logic and set theory. I do not pretend to have solved the numerous difficult problems concerning such topics as explanation and justification that are addressed here; but I do hope to show that a computational approach offers ideas and techniques for representing and using knowledge that surpass ones usually employed by philosophers. Before launching into computational details, I want to situate the enterprise I am calling "computational philosophy of science" in relation to more familiar fields.

1.2. *Artificial Intelligence, Psychology, and Historical Philosophy of Science*

Artificial intelligence (AI) is the branch of computer science concerned with getting computers to perform intelligent tasks. In its brief three decades of existence, AI has developed many computational tools for describing the representation and processing of information. Cognitive psychologists have found these tools valuable for developing theories about human thinking. Similarly, computational philosophy of science can use them for describing the structure and growth of scientific knowledge.

To a large extent, then, the concerns of AI, cognitive psychology, and computational philosophy of science overlap, although philosophy has a greater concern with normative issues than these other two fields. We must distinguish between descriptive issues, concerning how scientists do think, and normative issues, concerning how scientists ought to think. Cognitive psychology is dedicated to the empirical investigation of mental processes, and is interested in normative issues only to the extent of characterizing people's departures from assumed norms (see Nisbett and Ross, 1980, for a recent survey). Similarly, artificial intelligence understood as cognitive modeling can confine itself to the descriptive rather than the normative. AI, however, is also sometimes concerned with improving on the performance of people and therefore can be interested in what is optimal and normative.

SHEARER VIVA   15/10/18

Presentn

   → Project ... Geoscience perspective !!!

s/w ⟶ primary tool

Design by users ... Not
        ⇓
   Hypothesis → simplify UI ⎫ Alternative
                              ⎬ UI flow
|User| has overall control!   ⎭ capability ...

Legacy ...? Effort to change?

How real is This ...?
        └ 'Team'

For philosophy of science, discussion of normative questions is inescapable, although we shall see in chapter 7 that descriptive and normative issues are intimately related.

Current research in AI divides roughly into two camps, which have colorfully been characterized as "neats" and "scruffies". The distinction is based largely on attitudes toward the importance of formal logic in understanding intelligence. The neats, such as John McCarthy (1980) and Nils Nilsson (1983), view logic as central to AI, which then consists primarily of constructing formal systems in which logical deduction is the central process. In contrast, scruffy AI, represented, for example, by Marvin Minsky (1975) and Roger Schank (1982), takes a much more psychological approach to AI, claiming that AI is more likely to be successful if it eschews the rigor of formal logic and investigates instead the more varied structures and processes found in human thought. Using the computer programmers' term for a complex and unsystematically put together program, Minsky remarks that the brain is a "kluge". A third influential approach to AI, the production systems of Newell and Simon (1972), falls somewhere between the neat and scruffy camps. Psychologists range from neats who emphasize the role of logic in thinking (Braine, 1978; Rips, 1983) to scruffies who deny that logic is at all central (Johnson-Laird, 1983; Cheng et al., 1986).

Philosophy also has its neats and scruffies. No one was ever neater than the logical positivists, who used the techniques of formal logic to analyze the nature of theories and other key problems. It is therefore not surprising that formally inclined philosophers are displaying a growing interest in such AI endeavors as algorithmic analysis and logic programming (Glymour, Kelly, and Scheines, 1983). But this trend reflects the relation only of neat AI to neat philosophy of science. Since any computer implementation requires formalization, which was the hallmark of the logical positivists, one might suppose that any artificial intelligence approach to the philosophy of science would fall within the positivist camp. This conclusion, however, sorely underestimates the intellectual resources of artificial intelligence.

In the 1950s and 1960s, philosophy of science saw a rebellion against logical positivist accounts of science, led by such writers as Hanson (1958) and, especially, Kuhn (1970b). (For a sketch of developments in the philosophy of science, see tutorial A in appendix 1.) Critics argued that the positivists' emphasis on formal models had led them farther and farther away from the practice of actual science. Many philosophers of science have since adopted a methodology that avoids formalization, instead giving less precise descriptions of the methods of scientists based on historical case studies. Kuhn, for example, drew heavily on such examples as Lavoisier's theory of oxygen and Einstein's theory of relativity to back his account of the growth of science.

Historical philosophy of science has contributed to a much more rich and subtle account of the nature of science than could be developed within the framework of the logical positivists. But it has lacked one of the most appealing features of the positivist program: analytical rigor. Kuhn described scientific revolutions as the surpassing of one paradigm by another, but the central concept of a paradigm was left notoriously vague. Similarly, Laudan's (1977) influential work on science as a problem-solving activity never said much about the nature of problem solving.

These gaps can be filled in by computational philosophy of science, which this book places at the intersection of scruffy AI and historical philosophy of science. By offering detailed computational analyses of the structure and growth of knowledge, I hope to show that postpositivist philosophy of science can have some rigor in its scruffiness.

Hanson and Kuhn both made use of ideas from gestalt psychology in developing their alternatives to logical positivist accounts of science. Computational philosophy of science is even more closely tied with psychology, by virtue of the link between scruffy AI and current cognitive psychology, which increasingly employs computational models as theoretical tools. These three fields can collaborate in developing a computational account of how human scientists think. Many researchers in philosophy of science and artificial intelligence would prefer to leave psychology out of the picture, and science may indeed someday be performed by computers using processes very different from those in humans. But for now, at least, science is a human enterprise, and understanding of the development of scientific knowledge depends on an account of the thought processes of humans. Hence computational philosophy of science overlaps as much with cognitive psychology as it does with scruffy AI. Even its normative prescriptions about how science ought to be done should take human cognitive limitations as starting points, according to the view developed in chapter 7.

Computational philosophy of science and much of current cognitive psychology employ computational models, but why? In the next section I shall sketch the methodological advantages of using computer programs for understanding thinking.

1.3. Why Write Programs?

There are at least three major gains that computer programs offer to cognitive psychology and computational philosophy of science: (1) computer science provides a systematic vocabulary for describing structures and mechanisms; (2) the implementation of ideas in a running program is a test of internal coherence; and (3) running the program can provide tests of foreseen and unforeseen consequences of hypotheses. Current cognitive psychology is permeated with computational notions, such as search, spreading activation, buffer, retrieval, and so on. The birth of cognitive psychology in the 1960s depended on the computer metaphor that provided for the first time a precise means of describing rich internal structures and processes. In the 1970s, the interdisciplinary field of Cognitive Science brought together researchers from diverse fields, all concerned with understanding the nature of mind, having in common primarily the hope that computational models would help.

The computational analysis of mind depends on these correspondences:

Thought	Program
Mental structures ———	Data structures
Processes ———————	Algorithms

Behaviorists argued that any speculation about the contents of mind was metaphysical baggage, but the computer made it possible to be concrete about postulated mental structures and processes, even if the problem of verifying their existence remained difficult. A program can be understood as a set of data structures along with a set of algorithms that mechanically operate with the data structures. The structures can be very simple—say, just a list of elements such as (**1   2   3**). Or they can become much more complex as in the list processing language LISP, where it is easy to create structures that consist of organized lists embedded within other lists. Algorithms—well-defined procedures—can then be written that operate on those data structures, creating new ones. (For a quick introduction to the role of data structures and algorithms in programming, see tutorial C.)

Similarly, the currently most developed and plausible view of mind postulates internal mental structures or representations accompanied by processes for using those representations (Gardner, 1985). By writing programs that have data structures corresponding to the postulated representations and algorithms corresponding to the postulated processes, we can develop detailed models of mind. To be run on a computer, a program has to be explicit, and the exercise of working out the coordinated structure and processes will normally lead to the development of a richer and more complex model than unaided speculation would provide. Much can be learned about a scientific domain by attempting to analyze it within a complex representational scheme. Moreover, chapter 2 argues that the computational approach makes available richer data structures than would otherwise be considered. Philosophers in particular have tended to restrict their deliberations to a narrow set of structures—sentences or propositions—and a narrow sort of process—deduction. As we shall see, there is a lot more to computation than deduction, making possible the investigation of less constrained processes, such as those underlying scientific discovery.

Because mental processes are postulated to be computational, the computer is potentially an even more powerful tool for psychology than it is for such fields as economics and meteorology that use *weak* simulations in contrast to psychology's *strong* simulations. In a weak simulation, the computer functions as a calculating device drawing out the consequences of mathematical equations that describe the process simulated. A computer can valuably simulate a business cycle or a hurricane, but no one contends that it *has* an economic depression or high winds. In a strong simulation, however, the simulation itself resembles the process simulated. For example, a wind tunnel used to study the aerodynamics of cars is a strong simulation, since the flow of air over the car in the tunnel is similar to the flow of air over the car on the highway. In contrast, a computer model of the car's aerodynamics would only be a weak simulation. Whereas for most fields computers will only provide weak simulations, psychology has the possibility of strong simulations, if the computational theory of mind is correct.

Of course, merely characterizing data structures and processes in computational terms does not tell us how the mind operates. But even getting the program to run provides a test of sorts. Some noncomputational psychologists tend to assume that anything can be programmed, but this is no more credible than the assumption of some computer scientists that any psychological data can be got by a clever experimenter. To run, a computer program has to have at least a coherent interrelation of structures and algorithms. In addition, the threat of combinatorial explosion puts a severe constraint on the realizability of programs: if the program requires exponentially increasing time to run, it will quickly exhaust the resources of the most powerful computers. So developing a computer simulation provides a valuable test of the internal coherence of a set of ideas.

A psychological model should be more than internally coherent: we want it to account for experimental data about how people think. But sometimes, if a model is complex, it is not easy to see what its consequences are. Cognitive models, like many models in the social sciences, often postulate many interacting processes. The computer program enables a researcher to see whether the model has all and only the consequences that it was expected to have. Comparison of these consequences against experimental observations provides the means of validating the model in much greater detail than pencil-and-paper calculations might allow. Computational philosophy of science can benefit from the same model-forming and model-testing benefits that AI provides to cognitive psychology.

1.4. Psychologism

Thus computational philosophy of science is intimately tied with cognitive psychology and artificial intelligence. If the cognitive sciences suggest a revision of standard views of the structure and growth of knowledge, one would expect those views to have immediate epistemological significance. But since the split between philosophy and psychology in the second half of the nineteenth century, most philosophers have developed epistemological views in complete independence from the work of empirical psychologists. The mingling of philosophical and psychological discussions was branded as "psychologism".

The most principled reason for philosophers' fear of an association with psychology is that the normative concerns of philosophy will be diluted or abandoned. Consider the following argument against psychologism, akin to ones offered by Frege (1964) and Popper (1972). Epistemology, the argument runs, is as unconcerned with psychology as is logic. Psychology describes what inferences people do make, but logic is concerned with what inferences people *should* make, with the normative rather than the descriptive. Similarly, epistemology is the normative theory of objective knowledge, and need not take into account what psychology determines to be the nature of the belief systems in individuals. Propositions, or sentences expressing them, can be conclusions of arguments and can be written down in books for public scrutiny. To examine the structure of individual belief systems would only be to encourage a kind of subjectivism that abandons the traditional noble concerns of epistemology—justification and truth—for a vapid relativism. (Relativism is the philosophical view that truth is relative and may vary from person to person or time to time, with no objective standards.)

However, a concern with psychology need not engender epistemological skepticism. Haack (1978) recommends a *weak psychologism*, according to which logic is prescriptive of mental processes. This position is distinguished from both antipsychologism, which is the Frege/Popper view that logic has nothing to do with mental processes, and *strong psychologism*, the view that logic is descriptive as well as prescriptive of mental processes. ("Weak" and "strong" here have no connection with their use in the last section concerning simulation.) Weak psychologism uses empirical psychology as a starting point, since it presupposes an empirical account of the mental processes about which to be prescriptive. But it goes beyond mere description of actual mental processes to consider what sorts of inferential practices are normatively correct. Hence weak psychologism can escape the charge of relativism that is the chief motivation for resistance to admitting the relevance of psychology to epistemology. Escape requires, however, an account of how descriptive empirical matters are relevant to but do not fully answer prescriptive questions.

Knowledge is both private and public, inhabiting the brains of particular thinkers, but also subject to intersubjective communication and assessment. Weak psychologism aims to capture both these aspects. The real test between weak psychologism and antipsychologism consists in seeing which framework can develop a comprehensive and rich account of human knowledge. This book can be viewed as a computationally oriented attempt to describe some possible results of a weak psychologistic research program. Kindred attempts include the naturalistic epistemology of Quine (1969), the genetic epistemology of Piaget (1970), the epistemics of Goldman (1978, 1986), and the evolutionary epistemology of Campbell (1974). The last of these is criticized in chapter 6.

I share with such authors the view that philosophical method should be more akin to theory construction in science than to the sort of conceptual analysis that has been predominant in much twentieth-century philosophy. No precise analyses of individual concepts will be offered, because there are grounds for doubting whether such analyses are to be had (see sections 2.3.1 and 4.4), and because the larger enterprise of describing systematic connections among such processes as explanation and hypothesis formation is much more interesting.

1.5. Overview

Exploration of computational philosophy of science begins in the next chapter, with a discussion of the basic structures and processes relevant to an understanding of scientific knowledge. The artificial intelligence program PI provides a concrete example of how knowledge can be organized and used in problem solving. Chapter 3 then develops a computational account of the nature of scientific theories and explanations. Chapter 4 describes how abductive inference can be computationally implemented, providing an account of several kinds of scientific discovery. It also discusses how new concepts can be formed and acquire meaning. In chapter 5, I develop an account of theory evaluation as inference to the best explanation and describe its implementation in PI. Chapter 6 uses the ideas about discovery and evaluation of theories developed in earlier chapters to criticize the Darwinian model of knowledge development offered by evolutionary epistemologists. The next three chapters shift concern to normative matters. Chapter 7 develops a model for reaching normative conclusions from descriptive considerations, and the model is applied in chapter 8 to the problems of justifying inference to the best explanation and defending scientific realism. Chapter 9 discusses the normative problem of distinguishing science from pseudoscience. Finally, in chapter 10 I offer some speculative suggestions about what computational philosophy of science may be able to contribute to questions concerning the relation of theory and experiment and the role of group rationality in science. I have added three appendices to fill in details that would have distracted from the main argument. The first consists of four tutorials providing background information concerning the philosophy of science, logic, data structures and algorithms, and schemas. The second provides a summary of the structure of the computer program PI discussed in chapters 2–5, and the third presents a sample run of PI.

1.6. Summary

Computational philosophy of science is an attempt to understand the structure and growth of scientific knowledge in terms of the development of computational and psychological structures. It aims to offer new accounts of the nature of theories and explanations, and of the processes underlying their development. Although allied with investigations in artificial intelligence and cognitive psychology, it differs in having an essential normative component.

Chapter 2

The Structure of Scientific Knowledge

This chapter begins a computational analysis of scientific knowledge by discussing how such knowledge can be represented and used in computer programs. Artificial intelligence provides a new set of techniques for representing different parts of the scientific corpus, including laws, theories, and concepts. To present concretely the need for complex representations of these essential ingredients of scientific knowledge, I shall describe PI, a running program for problem solving and induction.

2.1. Structure and Process

In the last chapter, we saw that that there are good reasons for the dramatic influence of computational ideas in psychology. From artificial intelligence, psychology has gained a new stock of ideas concerning representations and processes, as well as a new methodology of testing ideas using computer simulation. This and later chapters will exhibit similar reasons for a computational approach to epistemology and the philosophy of science.

The case for the epistemological relevance of computation rests on a simple but extremely important point: Structure cannot be separated from process. We cannot discuss the structure of knowledge without paying attention to the processes that are required to use it. This point is familiar to most practitioners of artificial intelligence, but is new to philosophers, who have in this century had a relatively simple view of the structure of knowledge. Since the pioneering work of Frege and Russell, formal logic has been the canonical way of describing the structure of knowledge. In first-order predicate calculus, a simple atomic sentence such as "Fred is angry" is represented by a predicate and an argument such as $A(f)$. AI use of the predicate calculus is less cryptic, so that the same sentence is represented by **angry (Fred)**. More complex sentences are built up using connectives like **and, or,** and **if-then,** and by quantifiers such as **some** and **all.** For example, the sentence, "All criminals are angry." can be represented as **(for all x)(if criminal(x) then angry(x))**. Predicate calculus has many strengths as a starting point for representing knowledge, but we shall see below that it does not provide sufficient structure for all processing purposes. (Readers in need of a brief introduction to predicate calculus should consult tutorial B.)

In twentieth-century philosophy, the most studied technique for using knowledge is deduction in logical systems, in which rules of inference can be precisely defined. For example, modus ponens is the rule of inference that licenses the inference from **if p then q** and **p** to **q**. But there must be more to a processing system than deduction. If a system is large, assembling the relevant information at a particular time can be highly problematic. In epistemological systems based on logic, a corpus of knowledge is generally taken to consist of all the deductive consequences of a set of statements, even though the set of consequences is infinite. For more realistic systems, it becomes crucial to ask the question, What shall we infer when? So even in a system designed to do deduction, we need processes that take into account what information is available and what rules of inference are appropriate.

In any system designed for learning as well as performance, for acquisition of knowledge as well as its use, nondeductive processes are required. Scientific discovery is multifaceted, requiring diverse processes for generating concepts, forming general laws, and creating hypotheses. Such processes depend, we shall see, on complex representations of concepts and laws.

My concern in this book is with scientific knowledge. Hence the next section will discuss what kinds of structures and processes are most important for characterizing scientific knowledge. Then I shall describe a comprehensive processing system to illustrate in much greater detail how structure and process are interrelated.

2.2. Scientific Knowledge

To represent scientific knowledge, we need to find a formal expression for at least three kinds of information: observations, laws, and theories. Philosophers of science have differed on the relative importance of these aspects in the development of scientific knowledge. On one simple account of how science develops, scientists start by making experimental observations, and then use these to generate laws and theories. On an equally simple and misleading account, scientists start with laws and theories and make predictions that they then check against observations. In most scientific practice, there is rather an interplay of hypotheses and observations, with new observations leading to new laws and theories and vice versa (see chapter 10). To describe the process of science computationally, we need to be able to formalize observations, laws, and theories in structures that can be part of computer programs. In addition, I shall argue that it is also necessary to use a rich representation of scientific concepts. Formalization is necessary but not sufficient for representation, since we could formalize a body of scientific knowledge in predicate calculus or set theory without it being represented in a form that is computationally usable. Formalization and representation must go hand in hand, putting the knowledge into a form that can be processed.

A particular observation that a specimen, call it **specimen27**, is blue can easily be represented in predicate calculus as **blue(specimen27)**. More complex observations concern relations between objects, which predicate calculus can represent by allowing more than one argument. For example, that one specimen is observed to be to the left of another can be represented by **left-of(specimen27, specimen42)**. Relations become even more important if temporal information is also to be added: we can formalize the information that specimen 27 was blue at time t by writing **blue(specimen27, t)**. So predicate calculus appears to be an excellent way of representing observations, particularly about relations. Any representation of scientific knowledge will have to be able to distinguish between x being to the left of y, and y being to the left of x, which predicate calculus does very handily by contrasting **left-of(x, y)** with **left-of(y, x)**.

Science obviously does more than just collect observations. A central aim is to organize observations by means of laws. In physics, these can be highly general, as in the law that any two objects have a gravitational force between them. In the social sciences and in much of twentieth-century physics it is common to speak of *effects* rather than laws, indicating a statistical relation rather than full generality. General laws can naturally be represented by quantified expressions in predicate calculus. For example, the simple law that copper conducts electricity becomes **(for all x)(if copper(x) then conducts-electricity(x))**. It might seem, then, that predicate calculus is all we need for laws too.

But that conclusion neglects the important point about process made above. If all we wanted to do with laws was to use them in logical deductions, then predicate calculus might be fine. But laws have many important additional roles to play. They are discovered using observations, serve to predict new observations, help enormously in problem solving and explanation, and are explained by theories. To function in all these processes, it is useful to give laws a more complex representation such as that used for rules in the system PI discussed below.

From a logical point of view, theories look just like general laws. Newton's theory of gravitation, for example, says that between any two bodies there is a force. This could be represented by the rule, If x is a body and y is a body, then there is a force z between x and y. But theories differ from laws in their origins and explanatory roles. Whereas laws are generalized from observations, theories are evaluated by seeing how well they explain laws (see chapter 5). Moreover, since theories go beyond what is observed

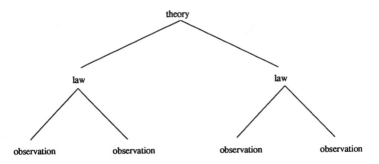

Figure 2.1
Hierarchical organization of observations, theories, and laws.

to postulate entities such as electrons, quarks, and genes, they cannot be discovered in the straightforward empirical way that laws are. Since theories play different roles, they may need a richer kind of representation to function in different processes. We shall need, for example, to keep track of the explanatory successes of a theory in order to evaluate it in comparison with other theories.

The general view of the structure of scientific knowledge that I am proposing here is common in current philosophy of science. It has three layers, consisting of observations, which are generalized into laws, which are explained by theories. In simplest terms, the resulting structure looks like that depicted in figure 2.1. A concrete example is a theory of light, such as the particle theory of Newton or the wave theory that replaced it in the nineteenth century. These theories were intended to explain general laws, such as that light reflects and refracts in certain ways, which were in turn based on particular observations. Psychologists similarly propose theories about how people process information in order to explain experimental effects, which are statistical generalizations from the observed results of the experiments. (Critics of this three-layered view have maintained that all observation is "theory-laden"; see section 5.7.)

Representation of observations, laws, and theories requires the use of predicates like **blue**, **copper**, or **electron**. From the perspective of predicate calculus, there is nothing mysterious about such predicates: they are just marks on paper, simple syntactic units. (Logicians distinguish between syntax, semantics, and pragmatics. Syntax is concerned with the properties that symbols have just by virtue of their form. Semantics concerns the relations of symbols to the world, and pragmatics deals with the use of symbols. See Morris, 1938.) From a semantic point of view, predicates appear to be straightforward, because model theory due to Tarski provides a semantics for predicate calculus in the form of a definition of truth (see tutorial B). Predicates are associated with sets of objects in a domain, interpreted as those objects of which the predicate is true. However, we shall see in chapter 4 that model-theoretic semantics is inadequate as a theory of meaning of scientific predicates.

Scientists are more aware of the value of concepts than logicians. Without appropriate concepts, formation of useful laws and theories is impossible. For example, Einstein and Infeld (1938, p. 133) include the following exclamation in their discussion of the physical concept of a field: "How difficult it would be to find these facts without the concept of a field! The expression for a force acting between a wire through which a current flows and a magnetic pole is very complicated. In the case of two solenoids [coils of wire] we should have to investigate the force with which two currents act upon each other. But if we do this, with the help of the field, we immediately notice the character of all those actions at the moment when the similarity between the field of a solenoid and that of a bar magnet is seen." To understand the importance of concepts in this kind of discovery and in scientific thinking in general, a richer representation of concepts than mere predicates will turn out to be necessary. In particular, chapter 4 will describe how the development of theoretical concepts requires that concepts have a rich internal structure.

2.3. Structure and Process in PI

To be more concrete about the importance of rich representations, I shall now outline an artificial intelligence program called *PI*, which stands for "processes of induction" and is pronounced "pie". PI implements in the programming language LISP a general model of problem solving and inductive inference developed in collaboration with cognitive psychologist Keith Holyoak. The intention in describing PI is not to propose is as a canonical language for doing science; its limitations will be described. Nor is PI claimed to constitute in itself a solution to the host of difficult problems in the philosophy of science concerning explanation, justification, and so on. Rather, I present it as an illustration of how representation and process interact and of how an integrated general account of scientific discovery and justification can begin to be developed within a computational framework. Supplemental descriptions of the operation of PI can be found elsewhere (Holland et al., 1986; Thagard and Holyoak, 1985), and appendices 2 and 3 contain much more detailed information about PI's implementation in LISP.

2.3.1. Knowledge Representation
PI represents particular results of observation and inference by *messages*, which are similar to sentences in predicate calculus and to what are called

"facts" in production systems. A message is a list that includes the following information: predicate, argument, truth-value, confidence, and message-name. For example, the observation that the planet Mars is red is represented by the list **(red (Mars) true 1)**. A similar structure can also represent simple hypotheses. The information that Mars is hypothesized to be devoid of life could be represented by the list **(has-life (Mars) projected-to-be-false .7 hypothesis-26)**. In addition to the obvious truth values **true** and **false**, PI also allows more tentative projected values. The number .7 indicates how confident the system is in the message, while the message name can be used to store additional information, for example, about the evidence for the hypothesis. Thus PI's messages, although starting with a structure derived from predicate calculus, add more information that will play an important role in problem solving and inductive inference.

Laws are represented by rules, which are if-then statements such as **If x is copper then x conducts electricity**. Even more than for messages, it turns out to be useful to add much more structure than a statement in predicate calculus would have. For a start, we want to give rules names to keep track of their successes and failures. Past successes and failures are summed up in a quantity called *strength*, which in PI is a number between 0 and 1. As we shall see below, it is important for problem solving that rules be attached to concepts, so the full profile of the above rule about copper might be

Name:	Rule-22
Data-type:	rule
Concepts-attached-to:	copper
Condition:	If x is copper
Action:	Then x conducts electricity
Strength:	.7
. . .	. . .

LISP programmers will recognize this as a property list of the atom Rule-22. Pascal programmers can think of it as a record with various fields. Basic and Fortran programmers will have to think of it as a more complex kind of array than they are used to. Logicians usually call the condition of a rule its "antecedent" and the action of a rule its "consequent". Complex conditions and actions make possible the representation of mathematical laws. Newton's law $F = ma$ becomes, If x is force and y is mass and z is acceleration, then $x = y$ times z.

Concepts in PI are still more complicated, in that they are represented by rich structures akin to the frames of Minsky (1975). A frame represents a typical kind of object or situation (see tutorials C and D for background). Each of PI's concepts includes information about its place in a hierarchical network of concepts: dogs, for example, are kinds of animals and have collies and Labradors as subkinds, so that the concept of dog has animal as a superordinate and collie and Labrador as subordinates. Moreover, concepts include messages to the effect that various objects fall under the concept. Most important, concepts have attacked to them rules that describe general properties. Here is the representation of the concept of sound that is used in PI's simulation of the discovery of the wave theory of sound:

Name:	sound
Data-type:	concept
Activation:	0
Superordinates:	physical phenomenon, sensation
Subordinates:	voice, music, whistle, animal sounds
Instances:	
Activated-by:	

Rules:

Rule 0:	If x is heard, then x is a sound.
Rule-1:	If x is a sound, then x is transmitted by air.
Rule-2:	If x is a sound and x is obstructed, then x echoes.
Rule-3:	If x is a sound and y is a person and x is near y, then y hears x.
Rule-4:	If x is a sound, then x spreads spherically.
Rule-5:	If x is a sound, then x is a sensation.
Rule-6:	If x is a sound, then x is a physical phenomenon.

The sentential characterization of the rules given above is merely illustrative. Each of the rules here attached to the concept of sound has considerable internal structure. Here is how PI represents Rule-3:

Name:	Rule-3
Data-type:	rule
Concepts-attached-to:	sound
Conditions:	(sound ($x) true)
	(person ($y) true)
	(near ($x $y) true)
Action:	(hears ($y $x) true)
Slot:	person-effect
Status:	default
Strength:	.7
Activation:	0
Old-matches:	nil
Current-match:	nil
Satisfies-goal?:	nil

Projection-status:	nil
Current-value:	0
Action-instances:	nil

The conditions, actions, slot, status, confidence, and strength are all set up by the programmer. The other properties of the rule, from Old-matches on down, are initially empty but get filled in by the program as it proceeds. For example, it is crucial to keep track of old matches—what messages have previously matched all the conditions and led to firing of the rule—to stop the same rule being applied over again in the same inference and preventing other rules from firing. In rule-based systems, this is called "refraction". Satisfies-goal? is used to keep track of whether firing a rule would satisfy a problem's goal, in order to ensure that such a rule will fire. Current-value gets calculated when the conditions of a rule are matched and determines whether the rule will be selected as one of the rules to be fired, taking into account such factors as the strength and degree of activation of the rule. Action-instances are the actions of the rule with variables bound when the conditions are matched against messages. Appendix 2 provides an outline of the LISP functions for firing rules in PI.

Note that rules such as Rule-3 do not constitute a strict analysis or definition of "sound". They express what is typical of sounds, not what is universally necessary and sufficient for being a sound. Dictionaries are of little help in forming such definitions, as the following typical dictionary entry shows (Guralnik, 1976, p. 1360):

> **sound** 1. *a)* vibrations in air, water, etc. that stimulate the auditory nerves and produce the sensation of hearing. *b)* the auditory sensation produced by such vibrations.

In the first place, this definition is highly theoretical, in that it relies on the scientific view that sounds are vibrations. In the second place, it turns out to be quite circular, since the dictionary defines "auditory" in terms of "hearing", and "hearing" in terms of perceiving sounds. Such circularity is no problem for the account of meaning discussed in chapter 4.

Rules generally specify what is characteristic of typical objects, not what is universally true of them. Through the critiques of Wittgenstein (1953) and Putnam (1975) in philosophy, Rosch (1973) in psychology, and Minsky (1975) in artificial intelligence, the traditional notion of concepts as defined by necessary and sufficient conditions has been discredited. Wittgenstein pointed out that there are no definitions that capture all and only the instances of complex concepts such as "game". Such definitions are rarely to be found outside mathematics. The experiments of Rosch and others showed that peoples' concepts are organized around prototypes: a robin, for example, is a more prototypical bird than an ostrich. Minsky argued that for computational flexibility concepts should be represented as frames that describe typical or idealized instances. Accordingly, the rules in PI provide a rough description of what is typical of sounds, not a definition of them. The traditional notion of concepts as fully defined generates a misleadingly strict account of their meaning, a point that will be important for later discussions of how concepts become meaningful (chapter 4) and of incommensurability of conceptual schemes (chapter 5).

Why does PI use messages, rules, and concepts with so much structure? The justification for complicating these structures is simply to be able to use them in complex processes: they support a far more elaborate and interesting model of problem solving and inductive inference than would otherwise be possible. The question of whether a computational model of thinking must have separate structures corresponding to concepts is controversial, and the important cognitive architectures of Anderson (1983) and Laird, Rosenbloom, and Newell (1986) do not have them. I shall argue that they are an important part of a theory of cognition.

2.3.2. Problem Solving

Problem Solving and Spreading Activation of Concepts   PI's central activity is problem solving. Given a set of starting conditions and goals, it fires rules that will lead from the starting conditions to the goals. Here is PI's simple representation of the problem of explaining why sound propagates and reflects:

Name:	explain_sound
Data-type:	problem
Start:	(sound ($x) true)
Goals:	(reflect ($x) true) (propagate ($x) true)
Problem-type:	explanation
Activation:	1

The solution to such a problem is a sequence of rule firings, in this case leading from the supposition that some $x is an arbitrary instance of sound to the conclusion that it reflects and propagates. Once the system has the wave theory of sound, the explanation can be a straightforward application of the rules that sounds are waves and that waves propagate and reflect. However, deciding what rules to fire depends on many nonlogical issues, such as what rules are available from memory, what rules are strongest in the sense of having the best record of success, and what rules appear to be most relevant to the current situation. (For a detailed discussion of the operation of these factors in rule-based systems, see Holland et al., 1986).

When people solve problems, only some of the relevant information is available to them in memory at any given time. PI models the varying accessibility of elements in the memory of an individual scientist by a process of spreading activation of concepts and rules. At any given time, only some of the total set of concepts are active and only some of the total set of rules are available for firing. Rules are attached to concepts: as we saw, attached to the concept of sound are rules such as that if x is sound and y is some person near x, then y hears x. Also attached to the concept of sounds are messages encoding facts about particular sounds, such as that a particular sound is loud. PI matches all the rules from active concepts against all the messages from active concepts; rules whose conditions are matched then become candidates for firing. Any number of rules can be fired at a time, which simulates parallel processing. (Parallelism is computationally and epistemological important; see chapter 10.) When a rule is fired, the concepts used in its action become active. So if the rule "If x is a dog, then x has fur" is matched by the message "Lassie is a dog", then the new message "Lassie has fur" will be produced, and, equally important, the concept of fur will become active. Hence at the next timestep, new sets of messages and rules about fur will become active. Activation can also spread backward from the goal to potentially useful concepts and rules. In addition, in the current version of PI (in contrast to the version described in Holland et al., 1986), activation spreads automatically up and down the conceptual hierarchy, for example, from sound up to its superordinates sensation and physical phenomenon and down to its subordinates music, voice, whistle, and bang. The process of rule firing and spreading activation of concepts continues until the goals of the problem have been accomplished. This process is summarized in figure 2.2.

PI solves the problem of explaining the propagation and reflection of sound by forming a wave theory of sound. Just how this occurred to the ancient Greek or Roman who first discovered the wave theory of sound is unknown, but fragments from Chrysippus (Samburski, 1973) and Vitruvius (1960) suggest that an association was made between sound and water waves. PI has simulated various ways in which the concept of sound and wave might have become simultaneously active, for example, through associations from sound to music to instruments to strings to vibrations to waves. PI's solution of the problem of explaining why sound propagates and reflects proceeds by rule firings and spreading activation, including activation of the concept of a wave that makes possible formation of the hypothesis that sound is a wave. One chain of associations from sound to wave that has been simulated in PI is depicted in figure 2.3. Rule firings are indicated by arrows, and spreading of activation to subordinates and superordinates is indicated by vertical lines. In this simulation, activation spreads from sound down to its subordinate music, and down again to instrumental music. Then the rule that instrumental music is played by an instrument fires, and stringed-instrument is activated as a subordinate of instrument.

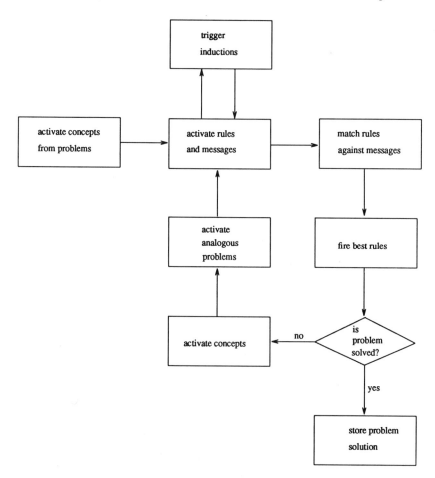

Figure 2.2
Problem solving in PI.

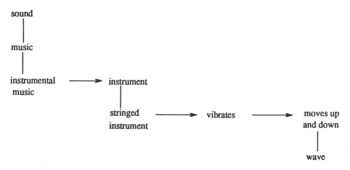

Figure 2.3
Spreading activation from sound to wave.

Two rules then fire: stringed instruments vibrate, and what vibrates moves up and down. Finally, the link that waves are a kind of moving up and down leads to activation of the concept of a wave. See appendix 3 for a fuller description of PI's run on this example. Clearly, this is only one of many chains of association that might have occurred when the wave theory of sound was initially discovered by the ancient Greeks. Moreover, in a more realistic simulation, many other activations and rule firings would also occur simultaneously with the ones just described. Nevertheless, the simulation gives some idea of how an association between sound and wave might occur during an attempt to explain why sound propagates and reflects.

Analogical Problem Solving   Problem solving can be greatly facilitated by the use of past successful problem solutions. Keith Holyoak and I have adapted PI's mechanism of direct spreading activation to provide an analysis of how old problem solutions can be used to solve new problems (Holyoak and Thagard, 1986). The two key questions in analogical problem solving are (1) How, while solving a problem, does one retrieve relevant existing problem solutions? (2) How, once a relevant problem solution is found, does one exploit the analogy between them? In PI, directed spreading activation provides similar answers to both these questions.

We now have running a highly simplified simulation of the ray problem of Duncker (1945). The ray problem consists of figuring out how to use a ray source to destroy a tumor inside a patient, when radiation at full strength will destroy flesh between the source and the tumor, leading to the death of the patient. Subjects have great difficulty coming up with a solution to this problem (Gick and Holyoak, 1980, 1983), but their performance is greatly improved when they are first told of an analogous problem. The fortress problem consists of trying to figure out how an army can capture a fortress when a frontal attack by the whole army is impossible. One solution is to split up the army and have it attack the fortress from different sides. This solution suggests an analogous solution for the ray problem, leading to irradiation of the tumor with lower intensity rays from different directions.

Our current simulation models analogical problem solving in the following steps. First, the base problem (here the fortress problem) must be solved, and its solution stored by association with the concepts mentioned in its problem description. The solved fortress problem, for example, is represented by the following structure:

Name:	capture_fortress
Data-type:	problem
Start:	(army (obj_1) true)
	(fortress (obj_2) true)
	(road (obj_3) true)
	(between (obj_3 obj_1 obj_2) true)
Goals:	(capture (obj_1 obj_2) true)
	(destroyed (obj_1) false)
Activation:	1
Concepts-attached-to:	(army fortress roads between capture destroyed)
Rules-used:	rule_1_army, etc.
Effectors:	(split (obj_1) true)
	(move-separately-to (obj_1 obj_2) true)

Second, solution of the target problem (here the ray problem) is attempted. This begins directed spreading activation in two directions: forward from concepts mentioned in the starting conditions of the target problem by rule-firing, and backward from the concepts mentioned in the goal conditions. Third, this process of rule-firing leads to activation of concepts to which the fortress problem has been attached. Figure 2.4 shows one possible path of activation that PI has been used to simulate. Here an association from ray to shoot to shoot-bullet to gun to weapons to fight to conflict to battle to army leads to activation of the concept **army**. Some of these associations are by firing of rules, such as that rays can shoot, while others are by subordinate/superordinate relations, for example, from fight to its superordinate conflict and down to another subordinate, battle. Thanks to PI's simulated parallelism, at the same time an association from the goal of destroying the tumor leads from destroy to defeat (since one way of destroying something is to defeat it) and then to conquer and capture. Since the stored solution of the fortress problem is attached to the newly activated concepts of army and capture, it gradually accumulates

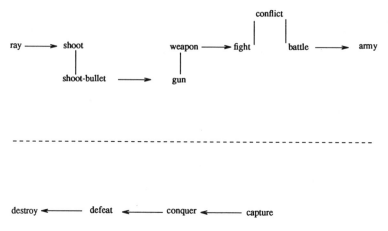

Figure 2.4
Spreading activation from the ray problem to the fortress problem.

activation. When its degree of activation exceeds a threshold, PI triggers an attempt to exploit the analogy in more detail.

Exploitation of an analogy requires noticing correspondences between the two problem solutions and figuring out how to use key steps in the first problem solution to suggest a solution to the target. The fourth step, then, is to set up a mapping between the two problem solutions that highlights the analogous components. PI derives this mapping from the record of spreading activation, since it notices what concepts were responsible for the activation of any newly activated concept. It is therefore able to trace back from **army** to determine that it was activated by **ray**, establishing that the ray source in the ray problem and the army in the fortress problems are analogs. Of course, the activation path to **army** involved other concepts too, but **ray** is the only concept that was activated as part of the target problem description.

Establishment of the analogous components makes possible the fifth step, performing analogous actions in the target problem. PI stores with a problem solution a list of "effectors", the actions that were projected to be performed that led to the solution of the problem. In the fortress problem, the effectors were the splitting up of the army and its moving separately to the fortress. Using the already established mapping, PI then determines that a solution to the ray problem might be found by accomplishing the two subgoals of splitting up the ray and moving its components separately to the target. At this point, the attempt to solve the ray problem by the standard processes of rule-firing and spreading activation is resumed. Now the new sub-goals provide a decomposition of the previously ill-structured ray problem. The analogy with the fortress problem does not provide a complete solution to the ray problem, but it does suggest potentially key steps in its solution.

After PI solves a problem analogically, producing one solution using a previous one, it constructs an analogical *schema*, which is an abstraction from the two previous solutions (for an introduction to the psychological notion of a schema, see tutorial D). Since the fortress problem has contributed to a solution to the ray problem, PI examines the statement of the two problems to see what they have in common. Using the rules stored with the concepts of the respective problems, it attempts to derive an abstract version of the two problems. In the fortress and ray problems, there is enough similarity to produce the following structure:

Name:	capture-fortress/destroy-tumor
Data-type:	problem schema
Start:	(force ($x) true)
	(target ($y) true)
Goals:	(overcome ($x $y) true)
Effectors:	(split ($x) true)
	(move_separately_to ($x $y) true)

This structure is then associated with the relevant concepts, such as **force**, and is available for future analogical problem solving. The schema, however, is potentially much more usable than the two problems from which it was formed, since it will be easier to map a new concrete problem to this abstraction than to the fortress or ray problems. Any new problem whose concepts sufficiently activate the concepts of force, target, and overcome will be be able to exploit the possible solution of splitting the force.

The processes just described simulate many of the experimental results of Duncker (1945) and of Gick and Holyoak (1980, 1983). Holyoak and Thagard (1986) describe how this model can account for such experimental results as the effectiveness of hints in problem solving, the efficacy of problem schemas, and the fact that structural similarities (ones that play a causal role in determining solutions) are more important than surface similarities in analogical transfer.

Extralogical Processes   A logician will naturally ask, Why bother with all this spreading activation? Why not just take the logical consequences of current beliefs and add them to the set of beliefs? We have already seen that no finite memory could handle such a procedure. A system must not clutter up a finite memory with useless facts. Still, one might argue that it would be more elegant to consider, at each timestep, *all* of the messages and rules stored in memory. The computational problem with this suggestion is simply that there are too many of them in a large system such as a human being. What appear to be limitations on human memory—our inability to think of all relevant matters at a given time—may in fact be crucial to thinking, since we would not be able to draw any conclusions at all if we were overwhelmed with information. A problem-solving system must have the capacity to *focus* attention on inferences that past experience shows to provide likely avenues of solution. In PI, the spreading activation mechanism is intended to show how problem solving can be focused on relevant rules and promising analogies.

It should now be clear why concepts have to be so complex. They play in PI the crucial role of spreading activation, determining what information is available at any time as they become active or cease to be active through decay if they are not used. They organize together various messages and rules. Their role in analogical problem solving is central, both for finding useful analogies by spreading activation and for exploiting them using activation traces.

In chapter 3, I argue that we cannot understand theories and explanations in science without taking into account the kind of complex processes of problem solving and learning that PI is being used to study. If this is correct, then the computational analyses given above are of more than psychological interest, being equally essential for philosophical understanding of scientific knowledge.

Thus PI needs complex data structures in order to be able to implement processes that effectively control problem solving and induction. Contrast logic programming, using the language Prolog (Clocksin and Mellish, 1981). For many applications, Prolog is useful because of its logic-like syntax and its deduction mechanism. Expressions in Prolog are similar to ones in predicate calculus, although they must also be understood as programming instructions. For example, the statement "All copper conducts electricity" is represented in Prolog as **conducts-electricity (x)** ← **copper (x)**. Procedurally, this has the interpretation, If you want to show that something conducts electricity, first show that it is copper. For example, if the data base contained the assertion **copper(specimen47)** and the system were asked if **conducts-electricity(specimen47)**, it would use the above rule to deduce that indeed specimen 47 conducts electricity. Deduction is by a resolution theorem prover: Prolog conjoins the negations of the expression to be proved with the set of expressions already asserted and tries to derive a contradiction. If a contradiction is derived, then the assertion in question is considered proven and is added to the data base.

It is earier to write reasoning programs in Prolog than in LISP because the inference machinery is already in place. A resolution theorem prover can of course be written in LISP, or any other programming language, but Prolog has the advantage of providing the programmer with an inference mechanism from the start. However, for producing cognitive models of the sort needed for computational philosophy of science, the advantage is illusory. Feigenbaum and McCorduck (1983, p. 122) maintain, "The major successes of AI have come from mastering the methods by which knowledge can be used to control the search for solutions to complex problems. The last thing a knowledge engineer wants to do is to abdicate control to an 'automatic' theorem-proving process that conducts massive searches without step-by-step control exerted by knowledge in the knowledge base. Such uncontrolled searches can be extremely time-consuming." PI uses complex data structures like concepts and rules to provide greater control to its problem solving and inductive processes than a simple deductive system could have.

Of course, since Prolog is a full programming language as well as a deductive engine, it can be used to produce data structures and processes much like those that PI employs in LISP. At that point, however, any resemblance between Prolog and logic has been lost and its deductive theorem-proving mechanism has ceased to play a serious role in the cognitive model being developed.

The justification given so far for PI's spreading activation mechanism is both psychological, in that it mimics human memory access to some extent (see Holland et al., 1986, chapter 2), and computational, in that it is necessary to limit and focus problem solving. An even stronger computational argument arises from the nature of induction. The restricted activation of concepts, rules and messages turns out to be crucial for directing and constraining the making of inductive inferences.

2.3.3. Induction

I argued above for the necessity of constraining deduction to control what deductive inferences get made when. Constraints are even more essential for inductive inference, that is, inference to conclusions that do not follow necessarily from what is already known. Induction is inherently riskier than deduction, since it can lead to conclusions that are not only useless but false. At least in deduction, what follows from true premises has to be true, whereas induction unavoidably involves a kind of leap. You may have observed myriad instances of copper conducting electricity, but generalizing that all copper conducts electricity still introduces uncertainty.

It might seem less than optimal to design a system that restricts attention to only a fraction of all the information stored in memory. In discussions of induction, philosophers such as Carnap (1950) and Harman (1973) have advocated total evidence conditions, according to which one's inductive inferences should take into account all evidence relevant to the conclusion. Such a requirement is clearly computationally unfeasible, since it would require a comprehensive search through all information stored. We need more practical means of bringing relevant information to bear.

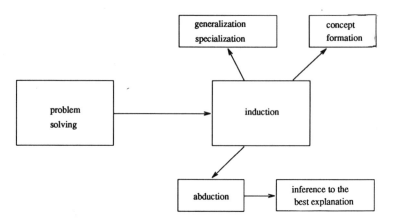

Figure 2.5
Problem solving and induction in PI.

Moreover, in making inductions, we do not want to be concerned only with reaching well-warranted conclusions: we want to produce rules that will be useful for future use in problem solving and explanation. I could, for example, induce that all the tiles on my ceiling have between 1,000 and 2,000 specks on them, but why bother? Similarly, you are unlikely to be devoting much time to generalizing about the number of lines or words on each page of this book. Induction should take into account the goals of the system. (See Holland et al., 1986, chapter 1, for a fuller discussion of the pragmatics of induction; compare the discussion in Harman, 1986, of the importance of interests in reasoning.)

Hence PI only performs induction in the context of problem solving. At each step in an attempted problem solution, PI monitors the currently active list of messages, rules, and concepts. Thus no inductive inferences will be made that are not relevant to the current problem-solving situation. Depending on the current state of activation, PI triggers attempts at various kinds of inductive inference, currently including generalization, abduction, and concept formation; see figure 2.5, which supplements figure 2.2.

I shall treat generalization very briefly, since it is discussed at length elsewhere (Holland et al., 1986, chapter 8). If PI's list of active messages includes the information that some object falls under two concepts, then the attempt is made to see if this holds generally. For example, the messages **(copper (specimen14) true 1)** and **(conducts_electricity (specimen14) true 1)** will trigger attempts to generalize that all copper conducts electricity and that anything that conducts electricity is copper. Additional information stored with the concepts of copper and conducts_electricity are then used to determine whether either generalization is warranted. The attempt to generalize will quickly be terminated if a check of the relevant concepts determines that there are counterexamples to the possible generalization or that the generalization has already been formed. Otherwise, PI considers whether there is enough evidence to warrant the generalization, taking into account both the number of instances in common and background knowledge about the variability of the kinds of things involved. Variability is important in determining how many instances you require before being satisfied that a generalization is acceptable. For example, you will be more willing to generalize from a few instances that a new metal conducts electricity than you will be willing to generalize that a new kind of bird has a particular color, since birds are more variable with respect to color than metals are with respect to electrical properties.

Generalization in PI has much in common with traditional confirmation theory, which analyzes how laws can be confirmed by their instances (Hempel, 1965), but there are also important differences. First, PI does not consider confirmation of laws in isolation, but sees generalization as triggered during the scientific activity of problem solving; this adds a pragmatic, goal-directed component that aids in avoiding the notorious paradoxes of confirmation theory (Holland et al., chapter 8). Second, PI considers not just confirming instances, but also background knowledge about variability. To do this, it requires information stored in concepts concerning superordinate and subordinate relations. Generalization, for example, that crows are black requires knowing that crows are a kind of bird and that black is a kind of color, as well as what other kinds of birds and colors there are (the algorithm that PI uses is sketched in appendix 2). Thus PI's problem-solving and knowledge representation resources take it well beyond what can be done in standard confirmation theory.

Additional kinds of learning—concept formation and abduction—will be discussed in later chapters. Chapter 4 describes the role that abduction plays in forming hypotheses and the importance of concept formation by conceptual combination for the creation of theoretical concepts. The crucial point to keep in mind here is that PI never wastes time trying to form all possible hypotheses or all possible concepts. Abduction and conceptual combination are triggered only when relevant rules and concepts are active. Concentration on what is relevant and important is brought about through control of spreading activation by the process of problem solving.

2.3.4. Limitations of PI

PI has many desirable features of a model of the cognitive processes of scientists, but it also has clear limitations. The simulations run so far have been small, with none using more than 60 rules or concepts, so only a small part of domain knowledge is captured in them: see appendix 3 for an example. A more strenuous test of the model will require simulations that involve formalization of large amounts of domain knowledge, with no preselection of concepts and rules to assure desired solution paths. The current problem solutions employ virtually no knowledge about space, time, and causality, which are important for problem solving and explanation (see section 3.5.2). Some of the mechanisms that PI does employ, such as its particular kind of spreading activation by rule firing and subordinate/ superordinate relations, have yet to be tested by psychological experiments. Its generalization mechanism is only capable of inferring very simple qualitative laws, since it lacks the heuristics for forming mathematical laws found in the BACON program (Langley et al., 1987) and the ability to use domain knowledge to guide the search for rules found in the Meta-DENDRAL program (Buchanan and Mitchell, 1978). PI's implementation of analogical problem solving also needs improvement; a much superior method for mapping from one analog to another has been developed (Holyoak and Thagard, 1987) but has not yet been integrated with PI. Further limitations of PI concerning the discovery and justification of hypotheses will be pointed out in chapters 4 and 5. Nevertheless, PI provides a starting computational framework for investigating questions concerning scientific knowledge.

2.4. *Expressive and Procedural Equivalence*

Despite the above arguments for the importance of concepts in the representation of knowledge, I except that some skeptics will maintain their dispensability on the general grounds that their content can be translated into simpler structures. In the mid-1970s, there was a flurry of activity in artificial intelligence employing Minsky's vague but suggestive frame notion. Hayes (1979) pointed out that there is a natural translation from frame representations to predicate calculus: a frame can be transformed into a conjunction of sentences in predicate calculus, with each sentence representing the information in one slot in the frame. Thus all the information in PI's concepts and rules could be translated into sentences in predicate calculus.

However, the existence of such a translation does not in the least undermine the importance of having rich representations of rules and concepts. Compare two systems of numerals: the Arabic numerals 1, 2, 3 and the Roman numerals I, II, III. If the Roman numerals are augmented with the rather handy numeral 0, there is an obvious translation from Arabic numerals into Roman numerals, so that one might argue that the two are not interestingly different. But consider our algorithms for doing multiplication and long division. We learn at an early age how to divide, say, 46 into 598, along these lines: 46 goes into 59 once, with a remainder of 13, and 46 goes into 138 3 times, so the answer is 13. Compare trying to divide XLIV into DXCVIII. The Roman representation does not lend itself nearly so easily to a simple algorithm for long division. Thus although we might say that Roman and Arabic numerals are *expressively equivalent* because they can be intertranslated and thus have the same content, it would be a mistake to say that they are *procedurally equivalent*, since they are not equally suited for all procedures.

The simple distinction between expressive and procedure equivalence has many applications. Given expressive equivalence between two systems and a procedure in one of them, we can always find a corresponding procedure in the other. But the procedure found may be very inefficient. For Roman numerals, instead of trying to get an algorithm for long division directly, we could simply translate into Arabic numerals, use our familiar algorithm, then translate back. Obviously, however, this process will take much extra time, so it does not challenge the superiority of Arabic numerals. Similarly, the procedures in frame systems can be more efficient for particular kinds of inferences than those found in less specialized logic systems. Any digital computer is computationally equivalent to a Turing machine, which is an extremely simple device consisting of only a tape with squares on it and a head that can write 0's and 1's in the squares. So anything that can be done computationally on a digital computer can be done on a Turing machine. But this fact is not of much interest for understanding intelligence because Turing machines are slow and torturous to program. The design of intelligent systems, whether by natural selection or human engineers, unavoidably takes into account speed of operations. Hence the current wave of research on how parallel architectures for computers can speed up processing is highly relevant for understanding the nature of mind (see chapter 10 and Thagard, 1986).

The distinction between expressive and procedural equivalence is also important for theoretical psychology. Debates have raged over whether the mind employs mental images in addition to propositions, and whether it employs large structures called "schemas" in addition to simpler propositions (see tutorial D). Some theorists have argued that since the content of any image or schema can be translated into propositions, there is no need to postulate the additional structures. But images and schemas might have procedures associated with them that would be much more difficult to perform in a purely propositional system; images, for example, can be rotated or otherwise manipulated in systematic ways. Hence empirical evidence can be found, using factors such as speed of processing and qualitative differences, to support the existence in human thinking of more complex structures like those found in PI's rules and concepts.

2.5. *Summary*

An understanding of scientific knowledge will require the representation of observations, laws, theories, concepts, and problem solutions. For a full description of the roles that these play in such activities as problem solving and discovery, it is necessary to use representations with more structure than a logical model would admit. PI's concepts require much internal structure because of the ways they cluster information together and spread activation through the system during problem solving. The expressive equivalence of two systems does not imply procedural equivalence, and procedural questions are crucial for understanding the development and application of scientific knowledge.

Chapter 3
Theories and Explanations

Scientific theories are our most important epistemic achievements. Our knowledge of individual pieces of information is little compared to theories such as general relativity and evolution by natural selection that shape our understanding of many different kinds of phenomena. We might be tempted to think of ordinary knowledge as changing and growing merely by additions and deletions of pieces of information, but theoretical change requires much more complex global alterations. But what are these entities that constitute the most impressive part of our knowledge?

Researchers in philosophy of science over the past fifty year have employed three different kinds of approaches to the problem of the nature of scientific theories. Following the traditional semiotic classification defined in chapter 2, I shall call these syntactic, semantic, and pragmatic approaches. The logical positivists took scientific theories to be syntactic structures—sets of sentences, ideally given an axiomatic formalization in a logistic system (Hempel, 1965, pp. 182–183). In the past decade, a semantic (set-theoretic) conception of theories has become increasingly popular; this conception abstracts from particular syntactic formulations of theories and interprets them in terms of sets of models, in the Tarskian sense explained in tutorial B. Another recent trend, popular among philosophers with a more historical bent, has been pragmatic in that it considers theories as devices used by scientists in particular context. Philosophers who construe theories pragmatically include Kuhn (1970b), who emphasizes the role of paradigms in historical communities, and Laudan (1977), who stresses the role of theories in solving empirical and conceptual problems.

The next sections describe some of the strengths and weaknesses of these three approaches. I shall argue that a fully adequate account of scientific theories must be pragmatic: formalistic concentration on merely syntactic or semantic features of theories unavoidably neglects some of their essential features. However, the historically oriented pragmatic accounts of Kuhn and others have failed to develop adequate philosophical analyses because they have been unable to add much content to vague notions such as paradigms and problem solutions. A more powerful pragmatic account can be developed using computational ideas. I shall construe a theory as a complex of data structures of the sort described in the last chapter, and argue that the result is practically, historically, and philosophically superior to syntactic and semantic approaches.

3.1. Requirements of an Account of the Nature of Theories

What should we demand of an account of the nature of scientific theories? I propose that an account needs to be adequate at three different but related levels: practical, historical, and philosophical. We want an account that (1) serves to describe the everyday practice of scientists in using theories, (2) accommodates the ways in which theories are developed historically, and (3) gives rise to philosophically satisfactory treatments of such crucial issues in the philosophy of science as the nature of explanation.

To be *practically* adequate, an account must show how theories can function in the diverse ways scientists use them in explanation, problem solving, conceptual development, and so on. Use in these intellectual operations entails that a theory must be a psychologically real entity, capable of functioning in the cognitive operations of scientists. Such functioning is not a purely individual matter, for a theory must be capable of being shared by members of a scientific community and learned by new members. If philosophy of science is to be philosophy *of science* rather than abstract epistemology, it must become psychologistic in that its account of the structure of scientific knowledge recapitulates how knowledge is structured in individual minds. Practical adequacy requires that an account must be broad enough to characterize the uses of both mathematical theories, such as Newton's mechanics, and primarily qualitative ones, such as Darwin's theory of evolution.

To be *historically* adequate, an account must be able to describe how theories develop over time, in a way faithful to the history of science. It must be sufficiently flexible to depict how theories are discovered and undergo conceptual change, while elucidating the notion of sameness of theories. The account must also be capable of describing the dynamic relations among theories, such as reduction or replacement of one theory by another and explanatory competition between theories in the same domain.

To be *philosophically* adequate, an account of the nature of scientific theories must contribute to plausible and rigorous solutions to other central problems in the philosophy of science. Most immediately, an account must suggest an analysis of the nature of scientific explanation. Closely related, we need a detailed treatment of scientific problems and their solutions. We ought to be able to show how a theory can be employed realistically, as purportedly true, but also how it can be construed instrumentally, as a device useful for prediction and other operations. We ought also to be able to give an account of how a theory is confirmed and justified as more acceptable than competing theories. Finally, an account of the nature of theories should suggest an answer to the difficult question of how theoretical terms are meaningful.

3.2. Critique of Prevailing Accounts

To begin the argument that a computational account can be more practically, historically, and philosophically adequate than alternatives, let us briefly review the shortcomings of the positivist, set-theoretic, and Kuhnian accounts.

3.2.1. The Positivist Syntactic Account

Consider first the doctrine of the logical positivists that a theory is an axiomatic set of sentences. Many critics have pointed out that this view has little to do with the ways in which most scientific theories are used. Rigorous axiomatizations are rare in science, and we should be skeptical of maintaining as an ideal what is so rarely realized. Moreover, the utility of achieving full axiomatizations is doubtful, since axiom systems are awkward tools for performing the tasks of problem solving and explanation. Of course, formalization of some sort will be necessary for any computational implementation of scientific knowledge, but it will have to be directed toward procedural issues rather than logical rigor. The emphasis on syntax that is endemic to the view of theories as axiom systems leads to the neglect of semantic considerations crucial to the understanding of conceptual development, and to the neglect of pragmatic considerations that are crucial to justification and explanation. Axiom systems could be said to be psychologically real if we viewed scientists as solving problems by straightforwardly making deductions from sets of propositions, but we saw in the last chapter the need for a much richer approach. In sum, the positivist account is not very practically adequate.

The most influential criticisms of the positivist account have come from historians and historically oriented philosophers (Kuhn, 1970b; Toulmin, 1953; Hanson, 1958). They charge that logical positivists neglected the dramatic extent of conceptual change in the history of science, a neglect stemming in part from the supposition that the meaning of theoretical terms derives from partial interpretation through observational consequences. To mention one example, Kuhn (1970b, pp. 101ff.) argues that the replacement of Newtonian mechanics by Einstein's theory of relativity does not fit the precise model of reduction as deduction of one set of sentences from another. The dynamics of theories are not well represented by the positivist account. Discovery was explicitly excluded as a topic in the philosophy of science by positivists such as Reichenbach (1938), who distinguished between the context of discovery and the context of justification. But we shall see in chapters 4 and 5 that a computational approach can give an integrated account of discovery and justification.

The philosophical adequacy of the positivist account has been called into question by sustained criticisms of the allied views of explanation and confirmation. The deductive-nomological model of explanation, which construes an explanation as a deduction from a set of sentences including laws, has been criticized for failing to provide sufficient or necessary conditions for explanation (see tutorial A for a summary of the deductive-nomological model). Confirmation theory has foundered on the intractable paradoxes of Goodman (1965) and Hempel (1965), which have been given a pragmatic dissolution elsewhere (Holland et al., 1986, chapter 8). I argue in chapter 5 that the justification of scientific theories is better represented by a model of inference to the best explanation than by the hypothetico-deductive model of confirmation, and show how well the computational account of theories meshes with inference to the best explanation. Another major problem with the positivist account concerns the meaning of theoretical terms. It has been challenged concerning the viability of the notion of partial interpretation, and even more fundamentally concerning the tenability of the distinction between theoretical and observational terms. Discussion of the issue of the meaning of theoretical terms will be found in chapter 4.

3.2.2. Kuhn's Paradigms

T. S. Kuhn's notion of a paradigm has replaced the positivist account of theories in many discussions, particularly in the social sciences. Most generally, a paradigm is a conceptual scheme representing a group's shared commitments and providing them with a way of looking at phenomena (Kuhn, 1970b). This notion is flexible enough to have much practical and historical applicability, but it is too vague to help with philosophical problems about explanation, justification, and meaning. Despite a professed desire to avoid total subjectivity, Kuhn has not succeeded in describing how paradigms can be rationally evaluated, or how different paradigms can relate to the same world, or even what it is for a paradigm to be used in solving a problem. Masterman (1970) has distinguished no fewer than twenty-one senses of "paradigm" in Kuhn's writings. No accounts have been given of how paradigms can be discovered or modified. Kuhn's ideas about the structure of scientific knowledge are nevertheless rich and suggestive; later sections of this chapter show how they can be fleshed out in computational terms.

3.2.3. The Set-Theoretic Conception

Recently, a powerful set-theoretic conception of theories has been proposed and developed by several authors (Suppes, 1967; Suppe, 1972, 1977; van Fraassen, 1972, 1980; Sneed, 1971; Stegmüller, 1979). Unlike the positivist and paradigm accounts this conception has not yet received a sustained critical analysis, nor will one be attempted here.

On the set-theoretic conception, a theory is a structure that serves to pick a class M of models (in Tarski's sense—see tutorial B) out of a class of possible models M_p. On the positivist view, we would think of M as those elements of M_p that satisfy the axioms of the theory. But without such specification we can talk generally of a theory as a structure $\langle K, I \rangle$, where K is said to be the core of the theory consisting of the pair $\langle M, M_p \rangle$ such that M is a subset of M_p, and I is the set of models that are intended applications of theory, with I a subset of M_p. A theory construed as such a structure cannot be said to be true or false, but it can be used to make the empirical claim that the models that constitute the intended applications of the theory are among the models picked out by the theory: I is a subset of M.

The set M is characterized through the definition of a set-theoretic predicate P. We define "x is a P" (e.g., "x is a group" or "x is a classical particle mechanics") by stating in informal set theory a series of axioms characterizing those objects that fall under the predicate P. An empirical claim then has the form "a is a P" where a is an intended application.

This approach to the nature of theories does appear to have several advantages over the positivist account. Use of informal set theory rather than formal syntax facilitates the rigorous reconstruction of scientific theories, since the more flexible set-theoretic characterization of a predicate is easier to execute than axiomatization in formal syntax. Moreover, use of set theory avoids the linguistic relativity of having a theory characterized in a specific formal language. (My computational approach similarly does not attach any particular significance to the representation language that PI uses to formalize scientific knowledge. The point of the computational model is not to have a canonical account of scientific knowledge, but only an approximation to what is in the scientist's head: what matters are the data structures, which might be implemented in any number of languages.) Most important, the work of Sneed and Stegmüller suggests that the set-theoretic formalisms can deal more richly with the dynamics of theory development than syntactic ones.

However, we must question whether the elegant formal reconstructions offered by the set-theoretic approach are what is desired in an account of the nature of scientific theories. My primary objection concerns practical adequacy: what is the relation between the model-theoretic structures described above and the cognitive structures employed by scientists? Like the positivist account, the set-theoretic account offers a highly idealized description of theories. Such idealizations may be useful in dealing with isolated philosophical problems, but they hardly serve to characterize theories as used by scientists. A theory should bear some relation to how scientists do research, and the set-theoretic account abstracts too far from conceptual realities. This is especially clear if one looks at less mathematical theories than the examples from physics discussed by Stegmüller and Sneed, such as Darwin's theory of evolution. Of course, mathematical theories are highly important in science, in fields as disparate as population genetics and microeconomics as well as physics. But even in those fields we need a technique of representing conceptual connections that goes beyond set-theoretic formalization. The set-theoretic conception is insufficiently semantic: meaning connections require characterization in more elaborate terms. And it is even worse off than the syntactic conception in failing to suggest an account of such processes as problem solving and discovery, since it says nothing about how parts of models are transformed.

Connected with its practical inadequacy, the set-theoretic account faces philosophical limitations. Its abstraction from pragmatic matters of context and epistemic organization creates large impediments to giving satisfactory treatments of explanation and inference. In particular, the notion of explanation is not captured adequately by set-theoretic isomorphism (cf. van Fraassen, 1980).

3.3. A Computational Account of the Nature of Theories

3.3.1. Rules and Concepts

Chapter 2 described how PI represents knowledge using rules organized by concepts. I now want to show how such structures can contribute to an account of the nature of scientific knowledge that is both reasonably precise and sufficiently rich to account for the various roles of scientific theories.

Focusing on rules alone might suggest that in PI theories are nothing more than syntactic structures akin to the sets of sentences that, according to the logical positivists, constitute scientific theories. Moreover, theoretical problem solving and explanation might be thought to have the straightforward deductive character emphasized by the positivists, since rule firing is at root an application of modus ponens, inference from **if p then q** and p to q. Then we might be tempted say that all that is needed for a computational account of theories is to treat them as rules in a deductive system such as Prolog or a simple production system.

That conclusion, however, would neglect the points made in the last chapter about the importance of concepts in clustering rules together and helping to control the processing of information during problem solving and learning. Concepts would be unnecessary if we could consider all possible deductions from all existing rules, but we have seen that that is not computationally feasible. People seem to have, and programs seem to need, the ability to organize knowledge in ways that allow it to be applied in appropriate situations. Concepts not only organize rules for efficient application; they also organize the storage of problem solutions in ways crucial for analogical problem solving.

Similarly, it would be a mistake to argue as follows: "A computer program is, for the computer on which it runs, a purely syntactic entity, so there is no real difference between any computational account and the syntactic accounts of the logical positivists." Here there is a confusion of levels. Of course a program is a syntactic entity, but processing can be guided by data structures that are best understood in semantic and pragmatic terms. The semantics come from the interrelations of rules and concepts, and from the world (see chapter 4 for a discussion of meaning); and the pragmatics come from the crucial role that goals and context play in determining the course of processing.

To be more concrete, let me describe a simple but important theory, the wave theory of sound, whose discovery has been simulated in PI (see chapter 4). This theory goes back to the ancient Greeks, probably originating with the Stoic Chrysippus (Samburski, 1973), although the first systematic discussion I have been able to find is by the Roman architect Vitruvius around the the first century A.D. (Vitruvius, 1960). Vitruvius used the wave theory to explain several properties of sound that were important for building amphitheaters: sound spreads out from the source, and if it encounters a barrier it can be reflected back, constituting an echo. These facts to be explained are represented in PI by simple rules:

If x is sound, then x propagates.
If x is sound, and x is obstructed, then x reflects.

At first blush, the wave theory of sound might seem to be merely another simple rule, something like

If x is sound, then x consists of waves.

But there are two key respects in which the wave theory of sound differs from the simple rules about sound propagating and reflecting. First, as the discussion of theory evaluation in chapter 5 will make clear, the basis for accepting the wave theory of sound is different from the basis for accepting the other rules, which are derived from observations by generalization. Second, part of the wave theory of sound is postulation of the novel idea of sound waves, which were not observable, so that the concept of a sound

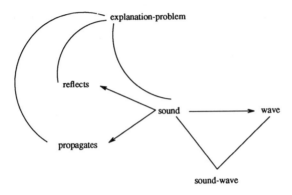

Figure 3.1
Structure of the wave theory of sound.

wave could not be derived from observation. What constitutes the wave theory of sound is thus a complex of rules and concepts.

Equally important, the wave theory of sound includes a record of its past successes—here the successful explanation of why sound propagates and why it reflects. An explanation or solved problem solution may be complicated, but keeping track of it may be immensely useful in the future for solving similar problems. A theory, then, is not an explicit data structure like a rule or concept, but a set of associated structures. For the wave theory of sound, these include

Wave theory of sound:

Concepts: sound, wave.

Theoretical concept: sound-wave.

Rules: If x is sound, then x is a wave.
            If x is sound, then x is a sound-wave.

Problem solution: Explanation of why sound propagates.
                     Explanation of why sound reflects.

Figure 3.1 depicts the complex of interlinked structures that make up the wave theory of sound, after the attempt to explain why sound reflects and propagates has led to formation of the rule that sounds are waves. The new concept sound-wave, formed by conceptual combination (see section 4.3), is a subordinate of the concepts of sound and wave. The new solution of the problem of explaining why sound reflects and propagates is stored with attachments to the concepts of sound, propagates, and reflects.

3.3.2. The Importance of Schemas

In chapter 2, I described how PI forms problem-solving schemas and how this greatly improves problem-solving performance. This facilitation is especially clear for theories, which invariably provide rich explanatory schemas. Remember that the primary function of a theory is to explain different laws, which in turn generalize many observations. A theory will typically involve a narrow set of principles that are applied in similar ways to explain each law, and by extension the particular events that fall under the laws.

Kitcher (1981) describes how theoretical explanation consists of providing unifications of phenomena using problem-solving schemas. He describes how Darwin explained many different phenomena using similar patterns based on evolution by natural selection. Darden (1983, p. 156) has further shown the power of an even more general selection schema, applicable beyond artificial and natural selection, with the following components:

1. An array of variants is generated.
2. Selection of a subset of variants occurs.
3. After selection, the pool of variants is different.

This is a powerful explanatory schema that has been applied in many domains, including the development of knowledge (see chapter 6).

Similarly, Newton explained many phenomena using a schema that Kitcher (p. 517) describes roughly as follows:

1. The force on α is β.
2. The acceleration of α is γ.
3. Force = mass · acceleration.
4. (Mass of α) · $(\gamma) = \beta$.
5. $\delta = \theta$.

To quote Kitcher (1981, p. 517), "The filling instructions tell us that all occurrences of 'α' are to be replaced by an expression referring to the body under investigation; occurrences of 'β' are to be replaced by an algebraic expression referring to a function of the variable coordinates and of time; 'γ' is to be replaced by an expression which gives the acceleration of the body as a function of its coordinates and their time-derivatives; 'δ' is to be replaced by an expression referring to the variable coordinates of the body, and 'θ' is to be replaced by an explicit function of time." This pattern can be instantiated to apply to many different kinds of mechanical phenomena. Kitcher's schema is more mathematically complicated than PI is currently able to handle, but its general function is the same as such problem-solving schemas as the convergence schema that PI derives from its solutions to the ray and fortress problems.

As we saw with the convergence schema, problem schema formation involves a kind of abstraction. Such abstractions are important in scientific explanations, where idealizations are often used. Scientists talk blithely of inclined planes without friction, falling objects without air resistance, and ideal gases. On the view of scientific theories as axiom systems, it can be hard to understand such utterances. But idealization makes sense if one sees a theory as part of a processing system that uses default rules and abstract problem-solving schemas to generate explanations.

The view just described also has the virtue of being compatible with the empirical results of Chi, Feltovich, and Glaser (1981). They found that experts differed significantly from novices in the ways in which they categorized physics problems, and theorized that experts' abilities were a result of their possession of superior problem schemas. Whereas novices tend to categorize problems by surface features, such as "blocks on inclined planes", experts tend to classify according to the major physics principle governing the solution to each problem. During problem-solving experiments, experts take longer to classify problems than novices, but their classifications are much more effective in leading to solutions. Knowledge of physics here obviously goes well beyond knowledge of a set of sentences encompassing the principles of physics, since novices are familiar with those principles too. What novices lack is the procedural knowledge about how and when to apply those principles, knowledge that is most appropriately coded in problem schemas.

3.4. Practical Adequacy of the Computational Account

In the last section, theories were analyzed as complexes of rules, concepts, and problem solutions. The practical adequacy of such an account is best shown by its ability to explain experimental results of problem solving better than alternative models. But it is also interesting to see how the model serves to give an account of more anecdotal phenomena.

To start, let us return to Kuhn's notoriously vague notion of a paradigm. Kuhn (1970b) often used the term "paradigm" to refer to a theory or world-view, as in the Newtonian paradigm. This usage has become widespread, but it is different from the pre-Kuhn understanding of a paradigm as a standard pattern or example, for instance, of a verb declension. In the postscript to the second edition of *The Structure of Scientific Revolutions*, Kuhn regrets using the term "paradigm" both for a scientist's general world-view and for the concrete examples of problem solutions that, Kuhn had argued, were largely responsible for the construction of the world-view. He characterizes this latter conception of paradigms as "the central element of what I now take to be the most novel and least understood aspect" of the book (1970b, p. 187). He offers the term "exemplar" for the concrete problem solutions that he came to see as the "more fundamental" sense of "paradigm" (Kuhn, 1977, p. 298).

Kuhn rejects the common view that students learn a scientific field by learning a theory plus rules for applying it to problems. Rather, they learn a theory *by* doing the problems, solving subsequent problems by modeling them on previous solutions—exemplars. Learning a theoretical formula such as "F = ma" is of minor importance compared to learning the complex manipulations needed to solve various problems about free fall, the pendulum, and so on. Students who claim to know the formulas but to be unable to do the problems are missing the point: knowing the theory is being able to do the problems. By working away at standard problems, students eventually assimilate what Kuhn calls a "time-tested and group-licensed way of thinking" (Kuhn, 1970b, p. 189).

A computational model such as PI can capture both the exemplar and the world-view aspects of scientific practice. PI's mechanisms for solving and storing problems make possible just the kind of analogical problem solving that Kuhn points to. Exemplars are successful problem solutions that are stored with relevant concepts. If much use of such exemplars has taken place, they can be abstracted and stored as problem schemas like the abstraction from the ray and fortress problems described in section 2.3.2. A full-blown conceptual network with many stored problem solutions would constitute a paradigm in Kuhn's larger sense, providing a kind of world-view, a systematic way of approaching problems in the world. The existence of such a network need not remain a vague hypothesis, since they can be simulated in computational models with a sufficiently rich set of data structures, including concepts and problem solutions. It then becomes possible to address more precisely such philosophical issues as the alleged incommensurability of rival theories (chapter 5) and the methodological conservatism of proponents of a theory (chapter 8).

This completes my case for the practical adequacy of the computational approach to scientific theories, although the account of scientific discovery in chapter 4 is also relevant. Historical adequacy is discussed in chapters 4, 5, 6, and 8. The attempt to show that a computational account of theories is more philosophically adequate than alternatives now begins with a discussion of scientific explanation.

3.5. Explanation

Explanation of observed phenomena is one of the most important scientific activities. Much contemporary work in the philosophy of science has concerned providing necessary and sufficient conditions for a scientific explanation. The main focus of this discussion has been Hempel's (1965) powerful deductive-nomological model of explanation, described in tutorial A. I shall not attempt to summarize all the criticisms of that model here, but shall instead develop an alternative conception of explanation consonant with the computational approach to theories outlined above. Since most concepts in natural language are not susceptible to definition in terms of necessary and sufficient conditions, it would be folly to attempt to provide such conditions for explanation. Indeed, the view of concept formation associated with the processing views I have been discussing suggests that conceptual analysis must take the form of characterizing what holds typically of a notion rather than universally.

The term "explanation" is highly ambiguous. Hempel and many others use it to refer to a syntactic *structure* consisting of deductively related sentences including explanans and explanandum. In informal discourse, we often mean by "explanation" a *theory* that figures in an explanation in the Hempelian sense: Newtonian theory is an explanation of the tides. I want to exploit a third sense of the term, in which explanation is not an explanatory structure, nor something that explains, but a *process* of providing understanding. Explanation is then something that people *do*, not an eternal property of sets of sentences. (Note: This sense of "explanation" is to be distinguished from a sense becoming common in AI concerning "explanation-based learning", in which an explanation is a description of how a program achieved some result.)

3.5.1. *Understanding*

Explanation is a process of providing or achieving understanding, but what is understanding? Most generally, to understand a phenomenon is to fit it into a previously organized pattern or context. But this characterization is uninformative without specification of the nature of the patterns and contexts. Much of the plausibility of the deductive-nomological model of Hempel derives from the precise way a logistic system, in which a theory is a set of sentences and explanation is deduction from these axioms, provides a structured and well understood context. We shall see how a computational account can provide richer sorts of structure and context.

On one computational view, to understand an event is to retrieve from memory a knowledge structure that the event instantiates (cf. Schank and Abelson, 1977). To understand a sentence like "John pushed his cart to the checkout counter and took out the soap," a subject must activate a structure (frame, script, schema) that describes typical behavior in a supermarket. The slots in the SUPERMARKET frame are matched with the information provided in the sentence, and then the additional information contained in the frame can be used to answer questions about John's behavior described in the sentence. An adequate program would be able to answer "Why did John take the soap out of his cart?" by applying the knowledge incorporated in the summoned frame, that in a supermarket one typically wheels a cart to a counter, puts the items in the cart onto the counter, and then pays for the items. Deriving an answer to the question is relatively easy computationally once the appropriate frame has been found. The key step in achieving understanding is the procedural one of retrieving a frame that matches the central aspects of the event to be explained. Here, explanation is not by reference to implied laws or unspecified statistical generalizations, but by application of a structure that describes typical occurrences. Understanding is achieved primarily through a process of *locating and matching*, rather than deduction.

This account would be fine if we had precompiled frames for all events to be explained. But it cannot account for our ability to give explanations for unique or unusual events. Suppose we want to explain why John took off all his clothes in the supermarket. The supermarket frame and the undressing frame will not be much help. For increased flexibility, Schank (1982) proposed that knowledge must be organized into smaller structures he calls "memory organization packets". PI gains flexibility by attaching to concepts various rules, which can, once activated, work independently to generate an explanation. Thus PI's explanations involve both matching to a situation, as relevant concepts are activated, and deduction, as rules are fired. This process can be described as the application of a constructed "mental model" to a situation (Holland et al., chapter 2).

3.5.2. Explanation and Problem Solving

In PI, explanation is a kind of problem solving, and description of how the program works should help in showing the relations between these two important scientific activities. A problem is specified by giving its starting conditions and its goals to be accomplished. A problem solution is a set of steps, simulated or actually carried out, that lead from the starting conditions to the goal. In PI, the simplest kind of explanation problem is one in which the goals are not states to be reached, but states known to be true. Nevertheless, the process of rule-firing to generate the goals is the same, with one important difference: whereas in problem solving PI does projected actions, in explanation PI forms hypotheses that can lead to an explanation. To be concrete, imagine that your problem is to help your department chair figure out how to get to Chicago. You can project various actions that will take him or her from your department to Chicago. Structurally, we have

PROBLEM:

  START: N is chair of the Taxidermy Department.

  GOAL: N is in Chicago.

In a more realistic problem, the set of starting conditions would be significantly larger, and the goals would include additional constraints on what would constitute a problem solution.

The analogous explanation would have a similar structure, with an "explanandum"—what is to be explained—instead of the goal:

EXPLANATION-PROBLEM:

START: N is chair of the Taxidermy Department.

EXPLANANDUM: N is in Chicago.

Here you would try to use what you know about N, about your department, and about Chicago to generate an answer to why N is in Chicago. The same general mechanisms of spreading activation and rule-firing that enable PI to figure out how to get N to Chicago will also generate an explanation of why N is there, except that, instead of producing projected actions, the program generates possible hypotheses (such as that N is at a conference) that might provide an explanation. Further discussion of how PI generates hypotheses is in chapter 4.

The structural similarity between explanation and problem solving is clear at the level of explanation of particular facts, such as N's location. But scientific explanation concerns not only particular facts, but also general laws. The sort of explanation and problem solving so far discussed is a significant part of everyday scientific practice, but from a global, epistemic point of view another level of explanation is more important. This is the explanation of general patterns of events, rather than the occurrence of particular events. Such explanation has usually been understood as the deduction of empirical generalizations from axiomatized theories. Kepler's laws of the motions of planets are said to be derivable from Newtonian mechanics; optical refraction is explained by deriving Snell's law from either the wave or particle theories, and so on. Let us return to an example that is simple enough for PI to deal with. The wave theory of sound has to explain the general law that sound propagates, whose simplest expression is a rule with the condition **(sound (x) true))** and the action **(propagates (x) true)**. To explain such a rule is simple. PI creates a problem using an arbitrary object x:

EXPLANATION-PROBLEM:

START: x is sound.

EXPLANANDUM: x propagates.

Thus explanation even of laws can be undertaken in PI by the various mechanisms of problem solving (see section 2.3.2 and appendix 2 for details). It is easy within the computational framework to block trivial explanations, such as that x propagates just because it is sound, or propagates because it propagates.

But there is more to explanation than the discussion of problem solving so far would suggest. To adapt an example from Bromberger (1966), we could assign a student a problem of calculating the height of a flagpole given the length of its shadow, trigonometric formulas, and the law of the rectilinear propagation of light. The student's calculation that the flagpole was n feet high would solve the problem, but it would not *explain why* the flagpole is n feet high. The calculation does not provide us with an understanding of why the flagpole has the height it does.

Such understanding requires more contextual features, and it is easy to see how a system such as PI could provide these. We have much background information about flagpoles, in particular about the *causes* of their construction. Presumably, the *flagpole* concept would contain a rule that flagpoles are manufactured objects. Activating the concept of manufactured objects would make available the rule that designers and factories produce such objects. Hence we would be led by PI's subgoaling process to look for designers and factories that produced the flagpole, and even farther back for an explanation of why the designers planned as they did. The rules about trigonometry and the behavior of light would not normally get activated at all. Setting up the problem with them as part of the starting conditions is a bad joke.

Although it is unlikely that it would produce such a derivation, PI does not currently have the resources to reject a derivation of the height of the flagpole using its shadow as a nonexplanation. Its problem-solving apparatus would, if it had the relevant knowledge and if the appropriate explanation based on human design were not found, arrive at and accept the shadow account. The problem is that PI currently lacks sufficient understanding of causality. As Brody (1972) argues, it is plausible to suppose that what distinguishes real explanations from the flagpole examples and other counterexamples to the deductive-nomological model is the reference to a causal or essential feature. Similarly, Hausman (1982) has argued that causal asymmetries are the key to seeing why the flagpole's height cannot be explained using the length of its shadow: our background knowledge tells us that the heights of flagpoles determine the lengths of shadows, not vice versa. PI needs to be able to acquire a kind of knowledge that it currently lacks, involving high level knowledge of what kinds of things cause what. Acquisition of such "causal schemas" will require an ability to distinguish between accidental generalizations based on mere cooccurrence of things and genuine causal connections. Such performance will require a much deeper understanding of causality than PI or any other AI program currently has, taking into account such factors as temporal priority and patterns of interconnectedness of kinds of events (Hausman,

1984). The advantage of a computational approach over a much more austere syntactic one is that it should be possible to enrich PI to be able to acquire and use such knowledge.

Critics have used the flagpole example to argue that the deductive-nomological model of explanation is too loose, but they have also accused the model of being too strict in always requiring laws. PI can get by with much looser kinds of explanations, since the rules it uses in its explanations need not be general laws: they need only express default expectations about what will happen.

Obviously, the account sketched so far does not even come close to providing sufficient conditions for a good scientific explanation. Theology, astrology, and anything you like can be said to provide explanations in the loose sense of using rules and concepts to generate conclusions. People have conceptual systems for all sorts of mythologies and ideologies, and we want to distinguish the explanations provided by these from the explanations rightly valued in science. However, this task concerns epistemological matters that go beyond the issue of the structure of theories and explanations. I do not think that we can in general distinguish on *structural* grounds between the systems and explanations of science and those of pseudoscience and nonscience. As we shall see in chapter 9, demarcation is a complicated matter of the historical context of a discipline, including the presence of competing theories and the record of the discipline over time. Theology and astrology differ from scientific systems with respect to validation, not structure. A full account of explanation would include a description of the epistemic conditions that a system of concepts and rules have to meet before we honor it as being fully explanatory. Candidates for such conditions include truth, confirmation, and being the best available theory. Chapter 5 shows how these conditions might be applicable to systems such as PI. In this paragraph, I have been using the honorific sense of "explanation" in which we say that only a good (true, acceptable, confirmed) theory explains. The previous discussion was intended to capture the more general sense of "explanation" in which we can talk of a false theory explaining.

I have gone into some detail about explanation to show how a computational account can contribute to philosophical understanding. The attempt to demonstrate the philosophical superiority of a computational account of theories continues in later chapters that consider the processes by which theories are discovered and justified.

3.6. Summary

A scientific theory can be construed as a computational system of concepts, rules, and problem solutions. This construal has several advantages over standard accounts of theories as axiom systems or set-theoretic structures. In particular, we are able to describe how a computational system directs the everyday practice of the scientists in problem solving, using schemas acquired from past problem solutions. In these terms, the complex functions of Kuhn's paradigms can be understood. At a more philosophical level, we are also able to provide a cognitive account of theoretical explanation as problem solving using explanatory schemas.

Chapter 4
Discovery and the Emergence of Meaning

4.1. Introduction

Theories differ from empirical generalizations in that they serve to explain such generalizations and do so by postulating nonobservable entities. Hence theories cannot be discovered directly by observation, since they have concepts that are not found in observation and they are not themselves generalizations of observations. We are thus faced with two severe problems: How can theories be discovered, and how can the concepts they employ be meaningful? This chapter will propose computational answers to both these questions.

Whereas researchers in artificial intelligence and cognitive psychology have mostly concentrated on learning from observations, philosophers of science have long been concerned with the problem of theoretical knowledge. Originally, the logical positivists hoped to reduce theoretical knowledge to epistemologically unproblemic observational knowledge, but the attempt ultimately failed (Hempel, 1965, chapter 4). More recently, there has been much discussion of whether there could be a "logic of discovery". Reichenbach (1938) proposed a sharp distinction between the *context of discovery* and the *context of justification*. He claimed that the philosophy of science should be concerned only with questions of confirmation and acceptance that belong in the context of justification, and that the topic of discovery should be relegated to psychology and sociology. Some philosophers have resisted this restriction (Hanson, 1958; Nickles, 1980a, b), but the relation between justification and discovery has remained unclear.

A description of PI's simulation of both the discovery and the justification of theories will show how discovery and justification blend together, requiring a rejection of Reichenbach's sharp distinction between a *logic* of justification and a *psychology* of discovery. As chapter 1 suggested and chapter 7 argues, there need be no sharp division between logic and psychology. The link between discovery and justification of theories comes through a form of reasoning that Peirce (1931−1958) called "abduction". (Note for nonphilosophers: "Peirce" is pronounced "purse".) Abduction is inference to a hypothesis that provides a possible explanation of some puzzling phenomenon. We shall see how abduction can be both a component in the discovery of hypotheses and a key ingredient in their justification. Later sections in this chapter describe how new theoretical concepts can be formed by PI's mechanisms of conceptual combination. Finally, I shall give a general account of how meaning can emerge in a processing system such as PI.

4.2. Abduction

Most people with an interest in inference have heard of induction and deduction, but Peirce's abduction is not widely known, although a few writers in both philosophy and artificial intelligence have studied it. Yet abduction is a pervasive phenomenon, both in science and in everyday life. Let me start with a simple example. I was recently on a plane to Atlanta, and could not help noticing a group of six young men, obviously traveling together. Three were black, three were white, and they seemed to be vying with each other for who could dress most outrageously. One was wearing a gold lamé jacket with black leather pants and white spats, while another had a Mohawk haircut, army boots, a gold earring in one ear, and a turquoise pair of miniature scissors stuck through the other. With no conscious deliberation, I found myself thinking: this must be a rock band. For that was the obvious explanation of the presence of an interracial group of outrageously dressed young men. Abductively, I formed the hypothesis that they were a rock band and had some confidence in it because of what it explained.

Or consider two events that were widely in the news in February of 1986. When the space shuttle exploded, everyone wanted to know why, and people from NASA experts to TV weathermen began to generate hypotheses about what went wrong. Eventually, evidence mounted that implicated the rocket booster rings as the cause, but in the early stages of the investigation that was only one of many hypotheses that were entertained and served to direct collection of evidence. Similarly, when a woman died in New York State as the result of Tylenol capsules containing cyanide, police and other concerned people quickly generated hypotheses to explain the presence of cyanide in the capsules. Initially, suspicion focused on her boyfriend, with the hypothesis that he had doctored the capsules; but when cyanide was found in other bottles of Tylenol in other locations new hypotheses about the possibility of a company employee with a grudge against the manufacturer were considered.

Hypothesis formation is ubiquitous in everyday life, especially when we form hypotheses to explain the behavior of other people, postulating various motives or states of mind. When our friends are exhibiting unusual behavior, we attribute it to various causes, including their personality, their moods, or events that have recently happened to them. Scientists also frequently form hypotheses to account for puzzling facts such as the motions of the planets or the extinction of the dinosaurs.

As Peirce noticed and as psychologists such as Gregory (1970) and Rock (1983) have subsequently confirmed, abduction plays a role even with relatively simple visual phenomena. Many visual stimuli are impoverished or ambiguous, yet people are adept at imposing order on them. We readily form such hypotheses as that an obscurely seen face belongs to a friend of ours, because we can thereby explain what has been observed.

4.2.1. Discovery or Justification?

Whether abduction is a mechanism for discovery or for justification has been controversial, and Peirce himself changed his mind on the question (Thagard, 1977c, 1981). Before the 1890s, he discussed a form of inference he called "hypothesis", characterized as follows: "Hypothesis is where we find some very curious circumstance which would be explained by the supposition that it was the case of a certain general rule, and thereupon adopt that supposition" (Peirce, 1931–1958, vol. 2, para. 624). Later, however, he replaced hypothesis in his classification of kinds of inference with abduction, which only "furnishes the reasoner with the problematic theory which induction verifies" (ibid., para. 776). Editors of Peirce's works have clouded the transition in his thought by including discussions of hypothesis under the heading of abduction, obscuring his shift from the belief that inference to an explanatory hypothesis can be a kind of justification to the weaker view that it is only a form of discovery.

One major reason for Peirce's transition was that he noticed the clear weakness of the method of hypothesis. Often we can form a hypothesis that explains some puzzling fact, but that should not be accepted because of the possibility of other explanations. Merely having a theory that explains some facts is far from a guarantee of truth (cf. Achinstein, 1971). Hence he decided that what he called induction, in which predictions are made and tested, was the only source of justification. In chapter 5, I shall argue that Peirce's abandonment of what he called the method of hypothesis was unnecessary: what was needed was a richer account of how theories can be justified by what they explain.

The program PI has provided a means of investigating in some detail the interacting processes of discovery and justification of hypotheses, so I shall now explain how abduction works in PI. "Abduction" is becoming an increasingly popular term in artificial intelligence (Pople, 1977; Reggia, Nau, and Wang, 1983; Charniak and McDermott, 1985), but its meaning is being stretched beyond what Peirce intended, to cover various kinds of hypothesis *evaluation* as well as hypothesis formation. PI is also capable of evaluating hypotheses (chapter 5) but here we shall concentrate on mechanisms for generating hypotheses in the first place. Four kinds of abduction have been implemented in PI: simple, existential, rule-forming, and analogical. Simple abduction produces hypotheses about individual objects, such as the rock musicians and the space shuttle. Existential abduction postulates the existence of previously unknown objects, such as new planets. Rule-forming abduction produces rules that explain other rules, and hence is important for generating theories that explain laws. Finally, analogical abduction uses past cases of hypothesis formation to generate hypotheses similar to existing ones.

4.2.2. Simple Abduction in PI

Previous chapters described how PI solves problems by a process of rule firing and spreading activation of concepts. During problem solving various kinds of induction take place. (I am using "induction" in the broad sense of any kind of inference that expands knowledge in the face of uncertainty; abduction, then, counts as a kind of induction.) Crucially, PI does not make all the possible inductions that it might. As Holland et al. (1986, chapter 1) argue, any realistic learning system must be highly *pragmatic*, constraining its inferences to those that have a good chance of being useful to the system. Indeed, systems must even be pragmatic about the deductions that they make, since it is crucial to avoid the combinatorial explosion that unbridled deduction would produce. PI constrains deduction by only considering rules and matches that emanate from active concepts. Similarly, it constrains induction by only focusing on the sets of currently active rules, messages, and concepts. We saw in chapter 2 that PI does not attempt to make all possible generalizations, but only those that are triggered in the context of problem solving.

Similarly, simple abduction is triggered by the current state of activation, taking into account what rules are active as well the active messages. Recall from the last chapter that some problems are explanation problems: their goals consist of finding an explanation for a set of messages. Abduction is appropriate when the system has some message to be explained and there is a currently active rule that would explain it if some additional supposition were made. Suppose you are wondering why a young man, Michael, is dressed outrageously, so that you set yourself the problem of explaining

(dresses-outrageously (michael) true).

An explanation can be found for this puzzling fact if you manage to activate the rule, If x is a rock musician, then x dresses outrageously. Notice that this rule does not have to be universally true; a default expectation will suffice to provide a rough explanation. We are not yet concerned with justifying the hypothesis that Michael is a rock star—that will require more machinery to be introduced in chapter 5. All that matters now is that abduction enables you at least to form for the sake of further evaluation the hypothesis that Michael is a rock musician. PI handles examples such as these by searching through the set of currently active rules for potential explanations of a fact to be explained. Just as Peirce suggested, the form of inference is

> **q** is to be explained.
> If **p** then **q**.
> _____
>
> Therefore, hypothetically **p**.

Putting in this way, however, makes it seem as if nothing new could ever be discovered, since we would have to already have thought of **p** to think that **if p then q**. However, if a general rule is used, some originality is possible. The inference about Michael runs

> **(dresses-outrageously (michael) true .9)** is to be explained.
> If **(rock-musician (x) true) then (dresses-outrageously (x) true)** is a currently active rule.
> _____
>
> **(rock-musician (michael) projected-true).**

Obviously, the hypothesis that Michael is a rock musician was not previously formed, but came to be only as the result of the abduction. More generally, the inference pattern is

> **G(a)** is to be explained, i.e., why a is G.
> If **F(x) then G(x)**, i.e. all F are G.
> _____
>
> Therefore, hypothetically, **F(a)**, i.e., a is F.

The hypothesis that a is F was not previously formed.

PI's simulation of the discovery of the wave theory of sound uses this kind of abduction. We saw in chapter 2 how the attempt to explain an arbitrary instance of sound propagation leads to activation of the concept of wave and hence makes available the rule that waves propagate. Then the following abduction is made:

> **(propagates ($x) true)** is to be explained.
> If **(wave ($x) true) then (propagates ($x) true)** is a currently active rule.
> _____
>
> **(wave ($x) projected-true).**

Here I am including as part of the variable the dollar sign, "$", which indicates in PI that the variable is universal, referring to anything; PI also uses another kind of variable discussed in the next section. The truth value "projected-true" indicates that the hypothesis is to be taken as highly tentative. But there is at least some initial plausibility to the hypothesis that the instance of sound is a wave, since that supposition would explain why it propagates.

Simple abduction in PI encompasses cases more complex than the ones just described, for PI can deal with n-place relations like "loves" as well as 1-place predicates, and will form hypotheses from any number of conditions. If the rule has the form

If A & B & C & D then E.

where E corresponds to a fact to be explained, then all of A, B, C, and D can be hypothesized. For example, if PI had active the rule that if x is a rock musician and on hard drugs, then x dresses outrageously, it would hypothesize both that Michael is a rock musician and on hard drugs. If any of A, B, C, and D are already known, there is clearly no need to hypothesize them, and if one of them them contradicts what is known, the abduction of the rest of the group is blocked. If several hypotheses are abduced together, this fact is noted, because the number of such cohypotheses is important in evaluating hypotheses. Briefly, preferred hypotheses are those that explain many facts and do so without many cohypotheses. Description of how this works in PI and how it applies to important cases of scientific theory evaluation is provided in chapter 5.

The two crucial elements in the formation of a hypothesis are the abstract form of abductive inference, as shown by the above structure, and the role of spreading activation in making available the relevant rule. Abduction can be thought of as a kind of logical inference, but spreading activation has a more purely psychological flavor. But recall that spreading activation in PI is not an uncontrolled, random process like spreading activation in other psychological models, such as that of Anderson (1983). Rather, activation occurs as the result of rule-firing that has a logical component, since firing the rule if A then B, will lead to activation of the concept B. Once again a sharp logic/psychology distinction would obscure more than it reveals.

4.2.3. Existential Abduction

Most discussions of abduction have considered only simple abduction, but there are several additional ways in which explanatory hypotheses can be formed besides the one just described. An important class of inferences involves the postulation of the existence of some previously unobserved thing. For example, Pasteur's investigation of communication of diseases led him to postulate the existence of undetected infectious agents, later identified as viruses. Nineteenth-century astronomers observed that the orbit of Uranus diverged from what was expected from Newtonian mechanics, and correctly hypothesized the existence of Neptune to explain the discrepancy.

In PI, existential abduction operates similarly to simple abduction, using a search through active rules for possible explanations of given explananda. (As tutorial A reviews, in philosophy of science an *explanandum* is something to be explained, and the plural is *explananda*.) In its very simple version of the abduction of the existence of Neptune, PI is given the explanandum

(perturbed (uranus) true).

The attempt to explain it leads to activation of the rule

If (planet ($x) true) & (planet ($y) true) & (near ($x, $y) true) then (perturbed ($x) true).

This says that if one planet is near another, it will have a perturbed orbit. The rule naturally leads to the formation of two hypotheses:

(planet (%y) projected-true)
(near (uranus, %y) projected-true).

These say that there may be some planet near Uranus, where the "%" corresponds to the existential quantifier in predicate calculus, so that "%x" is read "there is an x". Of course, there was no guarantee that there really was a planet near Uranus: a similar abduction that was made about a planet between Mercury and the sun proved erroneous. But forming the hypothesis is often invaluable for suggesting further investigations.

More generally, existential abduction is performed when the conditions of rules include relational predicates that have arguments some of which are not bound using information in the explanandum. Formally, if the problem is to explain why object o has property F, i.e., to derive **(F (o) true)**, then a rule of the form

If (R ($x, $y) true) then (F ($y) true),

which says that if x is in relation R to y, then the y is F, generates the hypothesis

(R (%x, o) projected-true),

that is, that there is some x that has relation R to o. As in simple abduction, PI is capable of performing existential abduction with rules with any number of conditions and n-place predicates.

Other historically important inferences can naturally be understood as cases of existential abduction. In the early history of chemistry, seventeenth-century researchers postulated the existence of phlogiston to explain combustion. Experiments suggested that objects that were burned lost weight, so it was supposed that they contained a substance, phlogiston, that was given up during combustion. The existential abduction to the existence of phlogiston was something like

> Why x lost weight is to be explained.
> If x contains a substance y that is given off, then x loses weight.
> _____
> Therefore, there is some substance y contained in x that was given off from it.

Later more careful experiments using sealed jars determined that in fact objects *gain* weight during combustion, explanation of which suggests the existential abduction that there is some substance (oxygen) that combines with objects during burning. (For more on this case, see Thagard, 1987.)

Existential abduction is also important in metaphysics. Given the task of explaining why the world is complex, and the rule that says that things that have designers that made them are often complex, PI will hypothesize that there is something that designed the world. Chapter 5 will have much more to say about evaluation of hypotheses such as these.

4.2.4. *Abduction to Rules*

So far, I have only been discussing abduction to messages, corresponding to propositions such as that Michael is a rock musician. How then do we get abduction to theories, which are themselves rules? The simple schema above to infer **F(x)** from **if F(x) then G(x)** and **G(x)** does not indicate how we might infer a general rule. Even more problematically, theories sometimes consist of sets of rules, and it is unclear how we can infer a whole set of rules at once by abduction. I shall now describe two ways of using abduction to get rules. The first is problematic and does not seem to play any role in theory formation. In it, we postulate the rule that all A are B to explain why a particular A is B. The second is a combination of abduction and generalization, and we shall see the role that it plays in PI's simulation of the discovery of the wave theory of sound.

Here is the unsatisfactory kind. Consider an apparently straightforward kind of abduction to rules from facts. Suppose you want to explain why Michael dresses outrageously and you already know that he is a rock musician. You might naturally form the hypothesis that *all* rock musicians dress outrageously, because you could then explain why Michael does. The form of inference is then

> Michael dresses outrageously.
> Michael is a rock musician.
> _____
> All rock musicians dress outrageously.

The inference sounds reasonable in this particular case, but adding such a form of inference to PI produced too many weak hypotheses. I introduced a triggering condition that, given a message to be explained and another active message about the same individual, generated an explanatory rule such as the one about rock musicians. The problem arose in larger simulations that too many rules were being generated, producing much clutter. For example, if you know ten additional facts about Michael, say, that he reads mysteries, plays football, watches "Miami Vice" on television, and so on, each will generate a new hypothetical rule. To weed out the overabundance of hypotheses, it is necessary to do just what PI does for generalization: consider counterexamples, number of instances, and variability. But then abduction to rules from facts is redundant, since the rule that it forms can be arrived at more adequately by generalization, to which explanation is irrelevant. Contrary to the claims of Harman (1973, 1986), not all induction is inference to an explanation. One can generalize that all copper conducts electricity by considering examples of copper that conduct electricity along with background knowledge about variability, without worrying directly about explanation. Hence, the general mechanism of abduction to rules from messages has been excised from PI, with no apparent loss since rules about observables can be formed by generalization.

However, abduction to messages can still play an important role in producing new rules. Recall from the last chapter how PI sets out to find explanations of rules of the form **If x is F then x is G**. What PI does is to start with some arbitrary object x that is F and try to explain why x is G. This gets things down to the level of explaining messages, and abduction to other messages can produce other hypotheses about x. Abduction to rules works like this: if PI forms the abduction that the F that is x is also H, because that would explain why is G, it can naturally generalize that all F are H. This is much more restricted than the general abduction to rules that I rejected above, since it is triggered only when there has been explanation of a message by another that contains a universal variable representing an arbitrary instance.

Let me be more concrete by returning to how PI simulates the discovery of the wave theory of sound. As we saw, PI's task of explaining why sound propagates and reflects gets translated into the problem of explaining why an arbitrary x that is sound also has the properties of propagating and reflecting. Activation spreads from the various concepts activated as part of the starting conditions and goals. Once the concept of wave is active, abduction furnishes a possible explanation of why x propagates and reflects, using the mechanism of simple abduction described above. Now we have the messages that x is a wave and that x is sound, with the former produced by simple abduction, so abductive rule formation is triggered and produces: All sounds are waves. See appendix 3 for a full trace of this process.

Thus PI comes up with the theoretical hypothesis that sound is a wave by abduction and abductive rule formation. Later in this chapter I describe a mechanism for forming the theoretical concept of a sound wave, and chapter 5 will discuss how PI evaluates the wave theory of sound in comparison with alternative theories that can also be discovered in the way just described. PI also forms a particle theory of sound by abduction from the rules that particles reflect and propagate.

The discovery of the wave theory of sound depends on noticing an analogy between sound and waves, but the analogy is unusually tight. Abduction produces the hypothesis that sound *is* a wave, not just that sounds are similar to waves. Looser analogies are also important in the formation of hypotheses.

4.2.5. *Analogical Abduction*
The combination of abduction and abductive rule formation just described suffices to form simple, unitary explanatory rules such as that all sounds are waves. But hypothesis formation seems sometimes to be considerably more complex. Sherlock Holmes trying to solve a murder may form a whole complex of hypotheses, not only about who the murderer is but also about the method and the motives. PI models a simple form of such inference, arguing that Moriarty is the criminal because that supposition, along with various rules about the crime, explains the evidence. But Holmes may simultaneously form the hypotheses that Moriarty was the criminal *and* that he had a particular motive. Formation of such complex hypotheses most plausibly derives from analogy: Holmes knows that in similar cases in the past criminals have performed acts with certain kinds of motives.

Varieties of analogical abduction are clearly important in science. Hanson (1961) described how scientists frequently go in search of particular hypotheses knowing that there are certain kinds of hypotheses that are likely to be useful since they have worked in related cases. Once a theory has established itself, scientists frequently want to use similar kinds of explanations. For example, the great success of Newtonian mechanics made most scientists of the eighteenth and nineteenth centuries strive to give mechanical explanations of phenomena. In the cases of abduction described so far, hypotheses have been directly or indirectly generated using the conditions of rules whose actions are relevant to what is to be explained, as when the rule that waves propagate was used to explain why something propagates. Some hypotheses, however, are formed by much greater leaps, using past knowledge. If you are trying to explain a fact that has some similarity to something already explained, you may naturally consider a similar type of explanation. The search for explanations may therefore benefit from analogical reasoning. We shall now briefly review how analogical problem solving operates in PI and then describe how it has been adapted to yield new hypotheses by analogical abduction.

Recall the discussion of analogical problem solving in the last chapter, which described how PI can solve a new problem by applying actions that worked in a former problem solution. Similarly, past problem solutions can suggest complexes of hypotheses that will provide an explanation in a new case. Analogical abduction is like analogical problem solving except that hypotheses are generated instead of subgoals. In PI, if the problem to be solved consists of finding an explanation, the mapping found between analogous problem solutions generates hypotheses for the new explanation problem analogous to those that proved to be explanatorily successful in the earlier problem. These new hypotheses may then lead to a solution to the new problem.

Suppose you are a detective trying to solve a crime involving the murder of a rich woman. You may be reminded of another case in which a rich woman was murdered, and in which the hypothesis that she was murdered by her philandering husband turned out to be true. Because of the similarity of the cases, you may form the hypothesis in the new case that a philandering husband was responsible. Such a hypothesis will be flimsy in the absence of further evidence, but may be invaluable in suggesting what evidence to gather. The form of reasoning here is, Hypothesis H was the right explanation in case C_1 that is like the current case C_2 in many respects, so an analog of H might work in C_2.

The reasoning that led Darwin to discover the theory of evolution by natural selection appears to have been based on analogical abduction. He often cited the analogy with artificial selection by breeding as important for development of his ideas about natural selection (Darwin, 1969, 1958). We can imagine the analogical abduction working roughly as follows. We know that Darwin was familiar with many cases of breeding, in which, for example, new kinds of pigeons and dogs were produced. If asked how a particular breed such as the collie came about, he could use rules derived from previous known cases to suggest that there must have been some breeder or breeders who selected the desired traits until the breed of collie resulted. Darwin made the great leap of seeing that species are similar to breeds, going against the generally accepted view that species were created individually by God. Just as collies arose as the result of breeding, we can generate the analogous hypothesis that the species of dogs also arose through a kind of selection by some unknown agent. This analogical hypothesis needs further development, which Darwin got by another analogy, this time with Malthus' views on human population growth, which suggested how nature could select.

PI's mechanism of analogical abduction has been used to simulate the first part of this reasoning. PI is given a rule summarizing existing knowledge that breeders working with existing breeds that undergo some variation have managed to produce new breeds:

If z is a breed, x is a breeder, y is a breed, y varies, x selects from y, and y becomes z,
then z developed.

When asked to solve problem 1 by explaining the development of the breed collie, PI performs the existential abduction that there was a breeder that selected from another breed to produce collies, producing hypotheses with existential variables:

(breeder (%x) true) (breed (%y) true) (varies (%y) true)
(selects-from (%x %y) true) (becomes (%y collie) true)

Then PI is set problem 2, to explain the existence of a *species*, dog. It does this by a simple abduction using the rule, If x developed, then x exists. Hence PI hypothesizes that the species dog developed. Problem 3 consists of explaining why it developed, but the rule about breeding cannot be used to generate an existential abduction of the sort that explained the development of collies, since the knowledge that dogs are species and not breeds conflicts with what would be hypothesized from the rule. However, the attempt to solve the problem of the development of dogs leads to activation of the analogous problem of the development of collies. As in analogical problem solving, PI uses the trace of spreading activation to determine what is analogous in the two explanation situations. The key step accomplished in the mapping is that **dog** and **collie** are analogous. PI accordingly infers that dogs came about because something selected from a predecessor of dogs, producing the hypotheses

(breeder (%u) true)   (breed (%z) true)   (varies (%z) true)
(selects-from (%u %z) true)   (becomes (%z dog) true)

Whereas in ordinary analogical problem solving analogy is used to construct new subgoals for the current problem based on what worked in the past, analogy in explanation problems is used to construct new hypotheses based on hypotheses that worked in similar problems. In both cases, potentially useful analogs are retrieved by spreading activation and mapped together by the trace of activation between analogous concepts.

Thus analogical abduction can be important for generating hypotheses that involve more substantial leaps than simple, existential, or rule-forming abduction. The latter depend on having relevant rules already formed, whereas analogy can bring into association ideas that produce hypotheses that are much more daring. Such hypotheses will be even more speculative and in need of evaluation than ones that come by simpler methods, but would never have arisen if analogy were not available to provide for a higher degree of creativity.

The recent work at Yale on the Swale project can be understood as an investigation of analogical abduction (Kass, 1986; Leake and Owens, 1986). Swale was a horse who died just a week after winning a major race, and SWALE is a program that finds explanations for his death using stored structures called "explanation patterns". One such pattern concerns the death of Jim Fixx, who died while jogging. The program attempts to explain an anomalous event by retrieving a relevant pattern from memory, but if there is not an exact fit it is capable of "tweaking" the pattern, that is, modifying it to apply more exactly to the current situation. The formation of an explanation to account for Swale's death involves retrieval of an explanation of something similar, just as when PI forms hypotheses by analogy. From preliminary description, SWALE appears sophisticated in its ability to use causal knowledge stored in explanation patterns to suggest appropriate "tweaks", but limited in its capacity to accumulate such causal knowledge and explanatory patterns in the first place.

PI and SWALE represent two approaches to the understanding of analogical hypothesis formation, and undoubtedly others are possible (Falkenhainer, 1987). A major goal of computational philosophy of science must be the development of AI models sophisticated enough to replicate, in much more detail than the simple examples I gave above, the thought processes underlying major discoveries in science. (See also Langley et al., 1987, which, however, is concerned primarily with generalization rather than abduction.) I now turn to the question of whether models such as PI and those that I hope will be developed will constitute a "logic" of discovery.

4.2.6. Logic of Discovery?

Hanson (1958) advanced the claim that abduction constituted a logic of discovery, but later retracted it in favor of a kind of reasoning that suggests only *kinds* of hypotheses (1961). Salmon (1966) argued that there might be a logical component to judging the plausibility of a hypothesis, but not to the actual thinking of it. In place of Reichenbach's proposed distinction between the psychology of discovery and the logic of justification, this suggests the triadic distinction

1. initially thinking of a hypothesis,
2. judging a hypothesis to be plausible,
3. judging a hypothesis to be acceptable.

If PI's operation is at all a good account of scientific thinking, the proposed distinction is seriously deficient, for each step blurs into the next. The distinction between initially thinking of a hypothesis and judging its plausibility will not stand up, since, when PI forms a hypothesis, it does so *because* it would furnish a possible explanation using an established rule. Hence any hypothesis formed has some initial plausibility. Initial thinking depends on spreading activation juxtaposing a fact to be explained with a potentially explanatory rule, but the actual formation of the hypothesis is by an abductive inference that confers at least initial plausibility to it. The hypothesis would not have been formed if it were not a possible explanation: the hypothesis plus the rule used in forming it together can explain some puzzling fact. Additional plausibility is achieved by noticing other evidence that the hypothesis explained, but such noticing is abductive in structure too. Thus formation of hypotheses is far from random, a point pursued further in chapter 6's critique of evolutionary epistemology, and initial thinking blurs into judgment of plausibility.

Critics of the idea of a logic of discovery maintain that there can be no mechanical methods for generating successful discoveries. They have in mind methods such as generating truth tables in propositional logic, where you can be sure that in a finite amount of time it will be possible to determine whether an arbitary proposition **p** is a tautology or not. But we must be wary of what "mechanical" means in such contexts. The problem of deciding whether propositions are tautologies is NP-complete: it is one of a class of problems that appear to be intractable in that they require exponentially increasing time as the size of the problem, in this case the number of atomic sentences in **p**, increases (Garey and Johnson, 1979). Thus there probably is not really any general *practical* mechanical method of determining whether propositions are tautologies.

PI's discovery techniques are mechanical in a weaker sense—they are implemented in a running computer program. Obviously, directed spreading activation and abduction are not guaranteed to find a potentially explanatory hypothesis. In PI, as in people, activation may spread to areas of memory that are irrelevant, while possibly explanatory rules remain dormant. Nevertheless, PI's spreading activation and abduction are techniques for making the finding of explanatory hypotheses more likely than chance. We have to agree with the critics of the idea of a logic of discovery that there is no algorithm *for* making discoveries that guarantees solutions to explanation problems. But we can maintain nevertheless that the process of discovery is algorithmic, employing many algorithms, such as those implemented in PI, which foster but do not guarantee the generation of solutions (see tutorial C for clarification of the nature of algorithms).

Just as initial thinking blends into plausibility assessment, so are both of these continuous with justification. We shall see in the next chapter how repeated abduction of a hypothesis that explains a whole set of facts can contribute to its justification. Alternative hypotheses may proliferate, but

PI does not attempt to weed out competing hypotheses immediately, since its simulated parallelism enables it to generate and entertain competing hypotheses at the same time. To go back to the example of the outrageously dressed man, if the rule that schizophrenics dress outrageously is active, PI will hypothesize that Micheal is schizophrenic, leading to comparative evaluation of this hypothesis and the rock-musician hypothesis using techniques described in chapter 5.

4.3. Theoretical Concept Formation

Peirce thought that abduction was a source of new ideas, but this is only true of ideas in the loose sense of hypotheses, not in the sense of concepts. We saw how the new hypotheses that Michael is a rock musician and that the arbitary instance of sound is a wave can be formed by abduction, but no new concepts were added in these inferences. PI already had to have concepts such as wave and rock musician.

The problem of how new concepts can arise is particularly great for theoretical concepts such as sound wave or electron. Much work in machine learning has concerned how concepts can be formed from descriptions of observations. But where do concepts that purport to refer to nonobservable entities come from? Positivist philosophers have wanted to deny that terms such as "electron" can be meaningful unless they are somehow defined via observations; vestiges of this are still found in many psychologists' talk of the need to "operationalize" ideas. In a similar vein, antirealist philosophers deny that "electron" is intended to refer to anything at all, but is only a useful device for making predictions. Chapter 8 discusses scientific realism. Here I want only to consider how a computational system could construct theoretical concepts.

PI has a crude mechanism for bottom-up concept formation that is described in section 4.4. To produce a new theoretical concept, however, we must combine existing concepts in ways that produce concepts whose instances are not directly observable. A strict notion of concepts, defining them in terms of necessary and sufficient observational conditions, would not permit sufficient flexibility to do this. For if there are strict observational conditions for the application of concepts A and B, there must also be observational conditions of a combined comcept A-B, which therefore is not a theoretical concept.

PI's mechanism of conceptual combination is much more flexible. Conceptual combination is triggered on the same occasions as generalization, when two active concepts have instances in common. Most possible conceptual combinations, however, are unproblematic and uninteresting. If you expect bananas to be yellow, there is nothing notable about the possible combination yellow-banana. PI only forms a permanent new combined concept when the original concepts produce differing expectations, as determined by the rules attached to them. For example, "striped apple" is a useful combination, since you expect apples to be mostly red or green rather than striped. Similarly, "feminist bank teller" is an interesting combination, since feminists are typically expected to have more professional occupations and be more politically active than bank tellers (for a discussion of the psychological issues behind these examples, see Holland et al., 1986, chapters 3, 4.)

When two concepts with common instantiations and conflicting expectations are noticed, PI produces a new combined concept with rules that reconcile the conflict in the direction of one of the donor concepts. Here is how it works in PI's simulation of the discovery of the wave theory of sound. The discussion of abduction described how PI constructs the message **(wave ($x) projected-true)** to explain why **(sound ($x) true)**. The simultaneous activation of these two messages leads to the construction of the concept of a sound wave. As Vitruvius' (1960, p. 138) discussion show, this combination requires the reconciliation of conflicting expectations. Water waves, the main source of the concept of a wave at the time, flow out in a single plane, along the surface of the water. Vitruvius contrasted this with the behavior of sound, which spreads spherically in many planes, as is obvious because people in the various rows of a theater can all hear the speakers. Sound waves have to carry over the known properties of sounds rather than the default properties of waves, so the newly constructed concept of a sound wave contains a rule that says that sound waves spread spherically. The theoretical concept of a sound wave, therefore, looks something like this:

Name: sound-wave
Data-type: concept
Superordinates: sound, wave
Subordinates:
Instances: x

Rules: R1   Condition: x is a sound-wave
                Action: x spreads-spherically

          R2   Condition: x is a sound-wave
                Action: x is sound

          R3   Condition: x is a sound-wave
                Action: x is a wave

Here R1 required the complex process of reconciling conflicting expectations to establish that sound waves spread spherically like sounds instead of in a single plane like waves. (Reconciliation in this case depends on the rule that sound spreads spherically being stronger than the rule that waves spread in a single plane.) It is unnecessary to carry over to the new concept of sound wave the various other rules about sounds and waves, since the automatically formed rules R2 and R3 will make possible the relevant inferences about sounds and waves.

Thus a theoretical concept can arise by putting together combinations of nontheoretical concepts. More complex kinds of combinations would account for theoretical concepts that have played an important role in science, such as force, electron, and black hole. The Newtonian idea of gravitational force would appear to be derived from the ordinary notion of a force familiar from our actions, but involves a nonvisible attraction. The combination might therefore be something like: force = nonvisible attraction from a distance. For the electron, the combination is something like: electron = tiny, nonvisible particle with negative charge. The concept of a black hole might be something like: object with such an intense gravitational field that no light can escape from it. The last combination, using the idea of gravity, shows how theoretical notions, once formed, can enter into further combinations. A similar example in cognitive psychology is the idea of an unconscious mental process, which combines the observable notion of a process with a theoretical one about the mind.

New theoretical concepts formed by conceptual combination can be powerful tools for ongoing scientific investigation. I argued in chapter 2 that PI's concepts are useful data structures because of their roles in organizing stored information and directing spreading activation to rules and problem solutions. The same applies to theoretical concepts in the philosophy of science: such concepts as "gene", "field", "electron", and "unconscious mental process" have aided scientists to explore difficult domains. In AI terminology, adding new representations such as sound-wave changes a problem space and can lead to new ways of solving problems.

By virtue of conceptual combination and the abductive mechanisms described earlier, PI is able to simulate acquisition of simple qualitative theories. Acquiring a theory such as the wave theory of sound consists of abductively forming explanatory rules and forming new theoretical concepts by combination. As chapter 3 insisted, however, acquiring a theory also encompasses learning applications, encoded in schemas for analogical problem solving. PI thus illustrates the acquisition of a theory conceived as a complex of rules, concepts, and problem solutions. Taking a computational approach to the philosophy of science has enabled a much more detailed description of theoretical structures and the processes of theory formation than would otherwise be possible. I shall now argue that it also makes possible a richer account of the meaing of theoretical concepts.

4.4. The Emergence of Meaning

How do words, ideas, sentences, and other representations become meaningful? Since Plato, this has been a central philosophical question, and it has become equally important for the cognitive sciences. The question is particularly acute for artificial intelligence: accomplishment of AI's ultimate goal of producing an intelligent computer presupposes that the symbols used in a computer can be as meaningful as those used by humans in their thinking. Searle (1980) argues unconvincingly that this goal is unattainable. Here I want to address a narrower question. In the philosophy of science, the central question about meaning has concerned theoretical terms: how can terms like "electron" that are so far removed from experience be meaningful?

From Hume to Carnap, positivist philosophers saw meaning as emerging from experience. The problem with their proposals, however, was that they allowed only a limited set of mechanisms by which emergence could take place. Hume (1888) contended that meaningful ideas could arise only through direct sense experience or simple definitions; Carnap (1928) tried to construct empirical definitions of scientific terms, but the project ultimately failed and was abandoned (Hempel, 1965). There is more to meaning than verification, because there is more to conceptual development than abstraction and definition.

As we have seen, AI provides a much richer set of techniques for investigating the development of knowledge than were available to the positivists. Different kinds of data structures besides sentences are available, and far more elaborate processes of inference can be modeled computationally than the positivists could employ. I shall propose that the meaning of a symbol can be understood in terms of the computational mechanisms that led to its construction and guide its use.

There are many disputes in the philosophy of language about the appropriate theory of meaning, and I shall not attempt to resolve them here. On one influential view, an account of the meaning of sentences can be given by a Tarskian account of the truth conditions of those sentences (Davidson, 1967; see tutorial B for a sketch of a Tarskian truth definition). But the Tarskian approach is no help at all with the current issue, which concerns the meaning of particular symbols corresponding to concepts. In a Tarskian truth definition, a predicate such as *blue* is associated with a set of objects, but there is a lot more to the meaning of that predicate than the set of blue objects. The *conceptual role semantics* defended by Harman (1987) provides a richer account (see also Block, 1986, and Johnson-Laird, 1983). On this view, the meanings of symbols are determined by their functional role in thinking, including perception and reasoning. The functional relations that determine a symbol's meaning concern both its relation to other symbols and its connection to the external world by perception and action.

Here is how meaning would emerge in PI if it were equipped by some robotic interface to detect simple features in the world. (PI currently has a simple simulated world that feeds observations into the system depending on location in a grid, but this falls far short of a real interface.) The cooccurrence of features triggers generalization, forming rules about how those features are related to each other. Detection of counterexamples to existing rules leads to the formation of more complex rules by specialization. Simultaneously activation of rules with the same complex of features in their conditions leads to the formation of new concepts more elaborate than the innate feature detectors represented by a kind of bottom-up concept formation. The simple mechanism now used by PI for this purpose looks for currently active rules with the same conditions and different actions; such pairs of rules indicate that some cluster of properties has general predictive value. For example, a new concept will be formed from the following two rules:

If x is a long-necked, spotted, four-legged thing, then x runs fast.
If x is a long-necked, spotted, four-legged thing, then x eats leaves.

The simultaneous activation of these rules shows that the complex of properties ⟨long-necked, spotted, four-legged⟩ is likely to be useful so PI forms the appropriate new conjunctive concept **long-necked_spotted_four-legged** analogous to our concept of a giraffe.

Concepts much farther removed from innate detectors can then be formed by combination of old concepts. As new concepts are formed, new generalizations and abductions employing those concepts become possible. The results are concepts and rules that are not related to the world in any direct way, but inherit meaning through the historical process of induction of new structures. This process is much more complex than positivists allowed, since it includes steps such as abduction and conceptual combination that permit daring leaps beyond what is observed, leading to theoretical concepts such as sound-wave. How are such concepts meaningful?

In the conceptual role semantics of Harman, the meaning of a symbol consists of its functional role, which in PI is determined by the rules, concepts, and messages in which it is used. In PI, the functional role of the symbol **long-necked_spotted_four-legged** is established by considering all the rules that have that predicate in their conditions or actions, as well as the other concepts that are related to it by subordinate or superordinate relations. These rules and relations need not provide a definition, but only expectations about what prototypical giraffes are like. Nor do they provide a guaranteed way of verifying perceptually that something is a giraffe, since some of the rules may well use predicates built up in ways that make them far removed from experience. But the rules are sufficient to give the term **long-necked_spotted_four-legged** a functional role that was not built in by an external programmer, having been developed internally by the program's own inductive mechanisms. In PI, then, the meaning of a term resides in its functional role, which is determined by the rules and concepts in which the term occurs. Meaning is not fixed by definitions, since there rarely are any. Rather, the role of a concept depends on what rules have been formulated using it and what other concepts it is related to by rules and subordinate/superordinate relations.

One advantage of a computational approach is that the notion of conceptual role can be understood much more precisely than by just saying that the role of a word is determined by the sentences in which it is used. In PI, the computational role of a concept such as **giraffe** is specified in terms of the processes that operate with it, which currently include

1. spreading activation to subordinate and superordinate concepts,
2. activating messages and rules that lead to the firing of rules and the activation thereby of additional concepts,
3. activation of past problem solutions analogous to the current one,
4. triggering of inductive inferences that can lead to new concepts, rules, or messages.

It should now be easy to see how theoretical concepts can have functional roles just as easily as concepts that are more directly tied to observation. When PI forms the concept **sound-wave**, it creates it as a structure already tied to other structures by virtue of the conceptual relations that sound-waves are a kind of sound and a kind of wave, as well as by rules such as that sound waves spread spherically. The concept is thus immediately ready to function in the inferences of the system, both in problem solving and in the triggering of new inductions.

Let me stress again how little this functioning has to do with definitions rather than inductively established connections. Richard Feynman (1985, p. 191) describes teaching physics in Brazil, where the students had all been trained to memorize definitions and formulas. He describes asking a question that the students could answer immediately, but then being surprised when they failed to answer the same question in a slightly different, more applied form. They had acquired definitions of concepts, but not enough knowledge to develop full conceptual roles for problem solving. In chapter 3, we saw that acquiring a scientific theory is a matter not only of learning rules, but also of how to apply those rules to various kinds of problems. Similarly, acquiring a concept in science or everyday life requires connecting it up in various inductive, hierarchical, nondefinitional ways with other concepts. That is how meaning emerges.

4.5. Innateness

To conclude my discussion of discovery, I want to consider the role that innateness might play in abduction and concept formation. Chomsky's (1972) approval of Peirce's ideas about abduction derives in part from some similar views they have about innateness. Chomsky argued that our abductions concerning rules of grammar were heavily guided by innate knowledge concerning language universals. More generally, Peirce maintained that abduction to scientific hypotheses would be impossible if nature had not endowed us with some special faculty for making good guesses. Undoubtedly each individual starts out with at least some innate concepts produced by evolution, for example, about spatial relations. Perhaps there are innate grammatical rules too. The extent of this innate repertoire is an empirical question.

But it may also be that the innate equipment we have for everyday problem solving and hypothesis formation is all that we need for language and science too. Perhaps something like PI's mechanisms for directing spreading activation and triggering inductions suffice to constrain learning. That there are preferences for certain kinds of hypotheses based on innate knowledge has some plausibility for basic things like moving around in our environment and maybe even for language. But it is not at all clear that we have any special faculty for guessing right when it comes, say, to theoretical physics. In science, we have bootstrapped ourselves sufficiently far enough away from the categories that evolution provided us that abduction and our accumulated knowledge are all we have to work with. Fortunately, constraining abduction within problem solving may be powerful enough without innate preferences for certain kinds of hypotheses. Peirce saw the need for constraints on hypothesis formation, but the computational mechanism of triggering abduction by the current state of activation during problem solving may be all that is needed. Indeed, an important part of the development of theoretical knowledge in science may be the transcendence of inadequate perceptual categories of space and time in favor of more powerful, nonintuitive, non-Euclidean ones. In current subatomic physics, many theorists are investigating the properties of spaces with ten or more dimensions, and it hard to see how their speculations might be at all constrained by biologically evolved preferences for certain kinds of hypotheses. Thus even if Chomsky is right in holding that we have innate preferences for certain kinds of grammars, there is no current reason to adopt Peirce's view that abduction to scientific hypotheses is innately constrained.

Only further empirical investigation will determine the extent to which we must postulate innate preferences for certain kinds of hypotheses. At least, however, we can be confident in not accepting the strong version of innatism proposed by Fodor (1975, p. 82). He argues that learning a concept is learning its truth definition: speakers understand a predicate "P" if and only if they have learned a definition that specifies the conditions under which "x is P" is true. It follows that the language of thought must be at least as rich as any natural language, or else it would not be possible to use it to learn the truth definition. The discussion of meaning in the last sections show that both steps in this argument are weak. First, there is no reason to associate understanding of a concept with its truth definition, since meaning accrues from conceptual roles arising from the place of a concept in various rules and concepts, not just definitions. And second, there are various inductive mechanisms in a system like PI for building up more and more complicated predicates without having to have them previously expressed. Fodor assumes that the language of thought is innately fixed, but we have seen that learning mechanisms that generate new rules and concepts can allow the language of thought to enhance itself.

4.6. Limitations of PI

I have freely used PI to show the possibility of a computational understanding of the discovery of hypotheses and concepts, but it is important to note that PI falls well short of providing a full account. PI has no means of interacting with the real world, so any inferences it makes depend on preselected symbolic information provided to it by the programmer. Its mechanisms for abduction are oversimplified in several respects. First, what gets explained by abductive inference may well be more mathematically complicated than the simple qualitative messages of PI. Second, abduction in PI does not sufficiently use background knowledge to rule out implausible hypotheses. I know, for example, that boomerangs fly out and come back, but I am not tempted to form a boomerang theory of sound, since knowledge about the kinds of things that boomerangs are and how they are used prevents me from identifying sounds with them.

Conceptual combination in PI is also limited by not taking background knowledge sufficiently into account. It forms the concept of a sound wave too mechanically, looking just at the rules for sound and waves, never asking the more theoretical question: How could a sound be a wave? PI's conceptual combination mechanism is also limited to dealing with intersecting concepts, where concepts A and B are such that any A-B is also A and B. But there are more complicated cases of conceptual combination: an electron microscope is not something that is both an electron and a microscope. More complicated mechanisms will be required for seeing how concepts such as electron and microscope can fit together.

Development of these additional mechanisms will worsen an already serious problem: Why suppose that PI is an accurate model of human thinking? There is at least loose experimental support for PI's mechanisms of spreading activation and generalization, but relatively little work has been done on psychological processes of abduction and conceptual combination. Moreover, even though it is consistent with the meagre historical record, PI's simulation of the wave theory of sound cannot be said to capture how the wave theory was discovered, only how it might have been. It would be desirable to run PI on historical cases where we have much more information about what the process of discovery really involved.

So there is lots to be done, not only in computational philosophy of science but also in cognitive psychology and the history of science, to further our understanding of the discovery of hypotheses and concepts. But PI provides a start in showing how processes such as abduction and conceptual combination can aid in theory formation.

4.7. Summary

A program such as PI can provide insight into how scientific theories can be discovered. Abduction—formation of explanatory hypotheses—is the primary means for introducing new theories. Active rules in a problem-solving system whose explananda are goals can suggest hypotheses that explain them. New theoretical concepts can be formed by conceptual combination. Meaning develops in a system by virtue of inductive mechanisms that establish conceptual roles, and there is no difficulty in attributing such roles to theoretical concepts as well as to those whose origins are closer to observation.

Chapter 5
Theory Evaluation

5.1. From Discovery to Evaluation

The last chapter described how mechanisms such as abduction and conceptual combination can lead to the formation of new theories that can explain general rules. But we clearly do not want to *accept* a theory merely on the basis that there is something that it explains. Recall the grisly joke about the scientist who cut off one of a frog's legs and said, "Jump", and the frog jumped. Then he cut off two more of its legs and said, "Jump", and the frog more or less jumped. Finally, he cut off the remaining leg and said, "Jump", but the frog did not jump. The scientist accordingly abduced that frogs with no legs are deaf. Clearly, we want to accept a theory only if it provides the *best* explanation of the relevant evidence.

Although the rubric "inference to the best explanation" is recent, originating with Harman (1965), the idea that hypotheses are to be accepted on the basis of what they explain has a long history, dating back at least to the Renaissance (Blake, 1960). The major weakness of the claim that inference to the best explanation is an important species of inductive inference is the lack of specification of how we determine what hypothesis or theory is the best explanation. By what criteria is one hypothesis judged to provide a better explanation than another hypothesis? Except for some very brief remarks about choosing a hypothesis that is simpler, is more plausible, explains more, and is less ad hoc, Gilbert Harman (1967) only addresses the problem as it concerns statistical inference. In later work, Harman (1973, 1986) talks vaguely of maximizing explanatory coherence while minimizing change. Keith Lehrer (1974, p. 165) has even remarked upon the "hopelessness" of obtaining a useful analysis of the notion of a better explanation.

I shall show, however, that actual cases of scientific reasoning exhibit a set of criteria for evaluating explanatory theories. The criteria—"consilience" (comprehensiveness), simplicity, and analogy—furnish a broad account of the justification of scientific theories, consonant with the earlier computational construal of theories. Once again, the system PI will provide a computational illustration of some of the key features of scientific reasoning, suggesting answers to such difficult questions as

1. How do we establish the set of competing theories to be evaluated?
2. How do we establish the evidence to be used in evaluating the theories?
3. How do we deal with situations where one theory does not explain everything that its competitors do, but we prefer it anyway because it explains the most important pieces of evidence?
4. What does it mean to say that one theory is simpler than another?

5.2. Case Studies of Theory Choice

To begin the investigation of scientific theory evaluation, I now present three important historical cases: Darwin on the theory of evolution, Lavoisier on the oxygen theory of combustion, and Fresnel on the wave theory of light. I shall only mention those aspects of the cases relevant to the current project of constructing criteria for theory choice. More thorough historical documentation was given in Thagard (1977b). The cases are ones where scientists have explicitly argued that their theories provide better explanations than do competing theories. Chapter 7 will discuss the relation between such studies of how science is done and the normative question of how it ought to be done.

Consider first Charles Darwin's long argument for his theory of the evolution of species by means of natural selection. In his book *On the Origin of Species*, he cites a large array of facts that are explained by the theory of evolution but are inexplicable on the then accepted view that species were independently created by God. Darwin gives explanations of facts concerning the geographical distribution of species, the existence of atrophied organs in animals, and many other phenomena. He states in the sixth edition of his book, "It can hardly be supposed that a false theory would explain, in so satisfactory a manner as does the theory of natural selection, the several large classes of facts above specified. It has recently been objected that this is an unsafe method of arguing; but it is a method used in judging of the common events of life, and has often been used by the greatest natural philosophers" (Darwin, 1962, p. 476). Many other quotations could be given to show that Darwin's argument in *On the Origin of Species* consists of showing that his theory provides the best explanation of a range of facts (see 8.1.2).

One of the greatest advances in the history of chemistry was the development by Antoine Lavoisier of the oxygen theory of combustion, which replaced the accepted theory based on the hypothetical substance phlogiston. Lavoisier offered explanations of combustion, calcination of metals, and other phenomena where there is absorption of air. He stated, "I have deduced all the explanations from a simple principle, that pure or vital air is composed of a principle particular to it, which forms its base, and which I have named the *oxygen principle*, combined with the matter of fire and heat. Once this principle was admitted, the main difficulties of chemistry appeared to dissipate and vanish, and all the phenomena were explained with an astonishing simplicity" (Lavoisier, 1862, vol. 2, p. 623, my translation). According to the accepted phlogiston theory, burning objects give off the substance phlogiston, whereas according to Lavoisier, burning objects combine with oxygen. The main point of Lavoisier's argument is that his theory can explain the fact that bodies undergoing combustion increase in weight rather than decrease. To explain the same fact, proponents of the phlogiston theory had to make such assumptions as that the phlogiston that was supposedly given off had "negative weight". Because the oxygen theory explains the evidence without making such assumptions, it can be inferred as the best explanation.

Other examples of arguments to the best explanation, this time in physics, are to be found in the history of the wave theory of light. In his *Treatise on Light*, Christiaan Huygens (1962) argued for his wave theory of light by showing how it explains the rectilinear propagation of light, reflection, refraction, and some of the phenomena of double refraction. The wave theory was eclipsed by Newton's particle theory, but Thomas Young attempted to revive the wave theory in three articles published between 1802 and 1804. The main improvement of Young's theory over Huygens' was the addition of the law of interference, which enabled the theory to explain numerous phenomena of colored light (Young, 1855, vol. 1, pp. 140–191). Finally, in a series of articles after 1815, Fresnel attacked the particle theory by arguing that the wave theory explained the facts of reflection and refraction at least as well as did the particle theory, and that there were other facts, involving diffraction and polarization, that only the wave theory could simply explain. He wrote to Arago, "Thus reflection, refraction, all the cases of diffraction, colored rings in oblique incidences as in perpendicular incidences, the remarkable agreement between the thicknesses of air and of water that produce the same rings; all these phenomena, which require so many particular hypotheses in Newton's system, are reunited and explained by the theory of vibrations and influences of rays on each other" (Fresnel, 1866, vol. 1, p. 36, my translation). Hence the wave theory should be inferred as the best explanation.

Many other examples of the defense of theories by arguments to the best explanation can be given. William Harvey (1962, p. 139) justified his theory of the circulation of the blood by its explaining so much. The general theory of relativity superseded Newtonian mechanics because it could explain more. The theory of continental drift was first thought to be a wild hypothesis, but when conjoined with plate tectonics it became too explanatorily successful to be denied. As we shall see in chapter 10, various theories about the extinction of the dinosaurs have been propounded on the basis of their explanatory power.

5.3. Consilience

The arguments of Darwin, Lavoisier, and Fresnel exemplify three important criteria for determining the best explanation. By "criteria", I do not mean necessary or sufficient conditions. We shall see that the complexity of scientific reasoning precludes the presentation of such conditions of the best explanation. A criterion is rather a standard of judgment that must be weighed against other criteria used in evaluating explanatory hypotheses. The tensions between the three main criteria will be described below. I call the three criteria *consilience*, *simplicity*, and *analogy*.

The notion of consilience is derived from the writings of William Whewell (1967). Consilience is intended to serve as a measure of how much a theory explains, so that we can use it to tell when one theory explains more of the evidence than another theory. Roughly, a theory is said to be consilient if it explains at least two classes of facts. Then one theory is more consilient than another if it explains more classes of facts than the other one does. Intuitively, we show one theory to be more consilient than another by pointing to a class or classes of facts that it explains but that other theory does not. That is just what Darwin, Lavoisier, and Fresnel were trying to do in the passages quoted above.

A closer look, however, shows that the matter is murkier than first appears. What, for example, is a class of facts? That is, what are the units to be used in assessing the best explanation? Also, what does it mean for one theory to explain more classes of facts than another? The simplest case would be when one theory explains everything that the other does and more, but we would also want to be able to consider cases where one theory explains a greater number of facts, even though what a competing theory explains is not a proper subset of what the first theory explains.

The most difficult feature of the notion of consilience is the notion of a class of facts. Whewell also sometimes wrote of "kinds" of facts, but this misleadingly suggests that the problem is ontological. Rather, the problem is merely pragmatic, concerning the way in which, in particular historical contexts, the scientific corpus is organized. The inductive logician must take this organization as given, just as do the scientists whose arguments are studied. Since in general the proponents of competing theories share the same historical-scientific context, they agree on the division of facts into classes. We, like Newton and Huygens, have no difficulty in deciding that reflection and refraction constitute more than one application of the wave theory of light. On the other hand, we would probably say that the distribution of species of finches and the distribution of tortoises on the Galápagos islands are not facts of different classes, and hence amount to only one application of the theory of evolution. They both concern geographical distribution in the given region. If Darwin had had any reasons to expect finches to be distributed in a very different way from tortoises, then perhaps the two species could have been counted as different applications. Notably, in the passage from the *Origin* quoted above, Darwin uses the "classes of facts" terminology.

Because applications are distinguished by means of background knowledge and historical precedents shared by competing theories, the theories in general agree about the individuation of applications. Sometimes, proponents of a theory will simply ignore one class of fact, as in many phlogiston theorists' refusal to consider the increase in weight of burning bodies. Unexplained facts are neglected by theorists who are more concerned with developing a theory than with criticizing it. But if a new theory comes on the scene and succeeds in explaining what the old one did, as well as facts previously unexplained, then, as a matter of logic, the old theory must attend to the newly explained facts. Additional complications may arise. Investigations by advocates of a new theory may show that the evidence explained by the old theory was faulty. For example, until Darwin, it was generally believed that there was a definite limit to the amount of variation a species could undergo, either under domestication or in nature; Darwin's study of artificial selection refuted this. Darwin's argument in the *Origin*, in the middle chapters on objections, also shows the possibility of debate concerning what the applications of a theory are. In most historical contexts, however, it is not hard to determine what classes of facts a theory should be expected to explain and what alternative theories are its competitors. Section 5.5.1 describes how evidence and competing theories are pragmatically assembled by the program PI.

I have not used the notion of law in defining consilience, because not all the facts adduced in favor of theories are laws in a completely general, unrestricted sense. Some are: Snell's law of refraction, Lavoisier's law that the increase in weight of a body burned is equal to the loss of weight of the air in which it is burned, and so on. But other facts make reference to particular objects: the perihelion of Mercury, the distribution of fossils in South America. Moreover, in Darwin's case and in current psychology, it would often be more accurate to say that the facts are tendencies or statistical effects rather than laws. All of these, however, are general enough to be represented as rules of the sort found in PI.

The historical relevance of the notion of consilience is manifest. Huygens pointed to classes of facts concerning the propagation, reflection, refraction, and double refraction of light. Young expanded the wave theory, and improved the argument for it by adding to the list of facts concerning color. Fresnel improved the argument still further by explaining various phenomena of diffraction and polarization. With his work, the wave theory of light became obviously more consilient than the Newtonian theory.

Similarly, Lavoisier presented a range of phenomena of combustion and calcination that his theory explained. By virtue of its explanation of the increase in weight of burning bodies, his theory was more consilient than the phlogiston theory. Darwin's theory of evolution was enormously more consilient than the creation hypothesis, as he showed by stating fact after fact explained by his theory but not by the creation hypothesis.

Many other important examples of consilience can be given. An outstanding one is Newtonian mechanics, which afforded explanations of the motions of the planets and of their satellites, of the motions of comets, of the tides, and so on. But the general theory of relativity proved to be more consilient by explaining the perihelion of Mercury, the bending of light in a gravitational field, and the red shifts of spectral lines in an intense gravitational field. Quantum mechanics far exceeds any competitor in that it provides explanations of the spectral frequencies of certain atoms, of the phenomena of magnetism, of the solid state of matter, and of various other perplexing phenomena, such as the photoelectric effect and the Compton effect.

A consilient theory unifies and systematizes. To say that a theory is consilient is to say more than that it "fits the facts" or "has broad scope": it is to say first that the theory explains the facts, and second that the facts that it explains are taken from more than one domain. These two features differentiate consilience from a number of other notions, which have been called "explanatory power", "systematic power", "systematicization", or "unification". For example, Carl Hempel (1965, pp. 280ff.) has given a definition of systematic power that is purely syntactic, and hence much more exact than the above definition of consilience. However, it is not applicable to the sort of historical examples I have been considering, since it concerns only the derivation of sentences formed by negation, disjunction, and conjunction from atomic sentences; it therefore does not represent the way in which Huygens, Lavoisier, and Darwin systematize by explaining a variety of facts, including ones expressed by laws. Another construction by Michael Friedman (1974) was an attempt to formalize how an explanation provides "unification" by reducing the total number of "independently acceptable" statements, but serious flaws have been found in it by Philip Kitcher (1976).

Behind such attempts is the assumption that explanatory power can somehow be assessed by considering the deductive consequences of a hypothesis. But deductions such as "A, therefore A", as well as more complicated examples that were discussed in section 3.5.2, show that not all deduction is explanation. Moreover, it is essential to the evaluation of the explanatory power of a hypothesis that what is explained be organized and classified. To take an example from Peirce (1931–1958, vol. 2, para. 462): We may infer that a man is a Catholic priest on the basis that the supposition explains such disparate facts as that he knows Latin, wears a black suit and white collar, is celibate, etc. We are not concerned with the explanation of a horde of trivial facts from the same class, such as that his left pant leg is black, his right pant leg is black, and so on. In inferring the best explanation, what matters is not the sheer number of facts explained, but their variety and relative importance. Assessment of variety presupposes that an inquirer have rich background knowledge about the kinds of things that the facts are about, requiring a detailed conceptual organization such as that found in PI.

Kitcher (1981) provides a valuable supplement to the notion of unification: a theory unifies not just by explaining different classes of facts, but by explaining them using similar problem-solving schemas. As we saw in chapter 3, the use of such schemas in problem solving fits very well with a qualitative, computational understanding of problem solving. Typically, a theory will achieve consilience by virtue of such schemas. I want to leave open the possibility, however, that not all the explanations furnished by a general theory are schema-based, so that unification by schemas should remain an associated feature of consilient theories, not a central property.

So far, I have been discussing a static notion of the consilience of theories, which presupposes that a totality of classes of facts—the total evidence—is given. This is generally how it appears when a scientist presents the results of his or her research. Arguments to the best explanation cite a range of facts that are explained. But a dynamic notion of consilience might also be taken into account in considering the acceptability of explanatory hypotheses.

Whewell's notion of consilience is essentially dynamic. He says, "The evidence in favour of our induction is of a much higher and more forcible character when it enables us to explain and determine cases of different kind from those which were contemplated in the formation of our hypotheses" (1967, vol. 2, p. 65). Dynamic consilience can be defined in terms of consilience: a theory is dynamically consilient if it is currently more consilient than it was when first proposed, that is, if there are new classes of facts that it has been shown to explain. It is difficult to state precisely a comparative notion of dynamic consilience. Roughly, one theory is more dynamically consilient than another if it has succeeded in adding more to its set of classes of facts explained than the other has.

Successful prediction can often be understood as an indication of dynamic consilience, provided that the prediction concerns matters that are new applications of the theory and provided that the prediction is also an explanation. Successful prediction in a familiar domain contributes relatively little to the explanatory value or acceptability of a theory: one more correct prediction of, say, the position of Mars would be of limited importance to Newtonian mechanics, although it would reinforce the belief that the theory explains facts of that class. In contrast, Halley's use of Newtonian theory to predict the return of the comet named after him was a mark of the explanatory power of the theory, which had not previously been applied to comets. Another example of this kind of dynamic consilience is Young's application of the law of interference to the phenomenon of dipolarization discovered by Arago and Biot.

Although dynamic consilience is often taken to be more impressive than ordinary consilience (cf. the notion of a progressive problem-shift in Lakatos, 1970), I see no reason to place special value on the temporal dimension. It is good for a theory to be dynamically consilient just because it is good for it to become more consilient in the usual sense, not because there is any special probative force to succeeding in new explanations or predictions after a theory has been formed. I shall argue in the next section that the criterion of simplicity accounts for cases where we are impressed by a theory that makes a prediction that is subsequently confirmed.

The maximally consilient hypothesis or theory is one that explains any fact whatsoever. This would be achieved by having such flexibility in the set of auxiliary hypotheses that any phenomenon could fall under the theory. Lavoisier accused the phlogiston theory of having this property, and psychoanalytic theory is also often subject to the charge of explaining too much. We might therefore want to put an upper bound on consilience, requiring that for a theory to be consilient, it must not only explain a range of facts, it must also specify facts that it could not explain. However, this requirement is unsatisfactory, because one way in which a theory could satisfy the upper bound condition is to specify facts in a totally different field; for example, psychoanalytic theory does not explain the speed of light. Moreover, scientists can legitimately contemplate adjustments to a theory or to its set of auxiliary hypotheses that would enable it to explain any anomaly within its field. After all, we want a theory to increase its consilience. The limit to these adjusments depends on the increase in consilience of the theory being offset by a decrease in satisfaction of other criteria. Simplicity is the most important constraint on consilience.

5.4. Simplicity

Simplicity is most clearly an important factor in the arguments of Fresnel and Lavoisier. The kind of simplicity involved in these cases has little to do with current philosophical notions of simplicity based on syntactic considerations. Rather, simplicity is pragmatic and intimately connected with explanation.

The explanation of facts F by a theory T requires also a set of auxiliary hypotheses A and a set of given conditions C. C is unproblematic, since it is assumed that all members of C are accepted independently of T or F. But A requires close scrutiny. An auxiliary hypothesis is a statement, not part of the original theory, which is assumed in order to explain one or a small fraction of the elements of F. This is not a precise definition, but examples should help to clarify its intent. In the case of Huygens, T would include such declarations as that light consists of waves in an ether, and that light waves are propagated according to Huygen's principle that around each particle in the medium there is made a wave at which that particle is the center. In order to explain the laws of refraction and reflection and other phenomena, Huygens assumes that waves are spherical. But in order to explain the irregular refraction in Iceland crystal, Huygens supposes that some waves are spheriodal. This last assumption, restricted in use to one class of fact, is an example of an auxiliary hypothesis. Similarly, Huygens assumed that the speed of light is slower in denser media, in order to explain Snell's law of refraction. (Newton's explanation of Snell's law assumed that the speed of light is faster in denser media.) The assumptions of spheroidal waves and the speed of light were not independently acceptable in the time of Huygens, so that they do not belong in C; and they were not used to explain any phenomena besides the ones mentioned, so that they must be placed in A rather than in T. One might want to reserve the term "theory" for the combination of T and A, but this would not reflect historical practice, and would blur the real distinction between statments that figure again and again in explanations and those whose use is much more limited.

Now we can say that simplicity is a function of the size and nature of the set A needed by a theory T to explain facts F. This is the main notion of simplicity used by Fresnel and Lavoisier. Fresnel accused the Newtonian theory of needing a new hypothesis, such as the doctrine of fits of easy transmission and easy reflection, for each phenomenon that it explained, whereas the wave theory uses one set of principles to explain the phenomena. Similarly, Lavoisier criticized the phlogiston theory for needing a number of inconsistent assumptions to explain facts easily explained by his theory: phlogiston was assumed to have negative weight when burned materials become lighter, but to have positive weight when calcined metals became heavier. These examples show how simplicity puts a constraint on consilience: a simple consilient theory must not only explain a range of facts, it must explain those facts without making a host of assumptions with narrow application.

An ad hoc hypothesis is one that serves to explain no more phenomena than the narrow range that it was introduced to explain. Hence a simple theory is one with few ad hoc hypotheses. But "ad hocness" is not a static notion. We cannot condemn a theory for introducing a hypothesis to explain a particular fact, since all theorists employ such hypotheses. The hypotheses can only be reprehended if ongoing investigation fails either to uncover new facts that they help to explain or to find more direct evidence for them, as in Fizeau's observation in the nineteenth century concerning the speed of light. Moreover, an auxiliary assumption will not be viewed as ad hoc if it is shared by competing theories.

This brings us to a comparative notion of simplicity. Let AT_i be the set of auxiliary hypotheses needed by T_i to explain a set of facts F. Then we adjudicate between T_1 and T_2 by comparing AT_1 and AT_2. But how is this done? The matter is not a neatly syntactic one, since any AT could be considered to have only one member, merely by replacing its elements by the conjunction of those elements. Nor can we use the subset relation as we did in comparing sets of classes of facts explained, because it is quite possible that AT_1 and AT_2 will have no members in common. The arguments of Fresnel and others suggests making a qualitative comparison, application by application. For example, on the issue of the speed of light in different media, there was a stalemate between the wave and corpuscular theories, because the assumptions they make are of a similar kind, and until the mid-nineteenth century there was no independent evidence in favor of either. On the other hand, Newton's theory has at least one auxiliary hypothesis, the "doctrine of fits of easy reflection and easy transmission", corresponding to which there is no auxiliary hypothesis in the wave theory. Young's principle of interference, which explains the colors of thin plates at least as well as the doctrine of fits, can be considered as part of the theory by virtue of its explanation of various phenomena concerning fringes. Thus the comparative simplicity of two theories can only be established by careful examination of the assumptions introduced in the various explanations they provide. As has often been remarked, simplicity is very complex. See 5.5.3 for a description of how PI assesses simplicity.

This analysis of simplicity sheds light on two issues discussed above: prediction and unification. Why are some philosophers more impressed when a theory predicts some new observed phenomena rather than one already known? From the point of view of consilience, there is no difference whether a theory explains a new or old class of facts; the comparative size of the set it explains is all that matters. I contend that the major reason why prediction of new phenomena appears so important is that such predictions are likely to be a sign of simple explanations. In making a prediction, one does not have the opportunity to adjust the theory to an already-known outcome by means of auxiliary hypotheses. Using only the theory and already familiar auxiliary assumptions, a future outcome is predicted with no opportunity for adjustments that are local to the prediction. In contrast, explanation after the fact can make many special assumptions to derive the outcome from the theory. Contrary to the views of Popper (1959), predictions are not to be valued because they can bring about falsifications; rejection of a theory requires showing that an alternative theory is a better explanation. Rather, successful predictions are to be valued as signs of the simplicity of a theory, showing that its explanations do not require post hoc additions. Simple explanations are also more likely to be ones that provide unifications, since the absence of added hypotheses means that the explanations are using the existing resources of the theory, including established explanation schemas, thus increasing the degree of unification found in the theory.

The above account of simplicity is superficially similar to one proposed by Elliott Sober (1975). Sober defines simplicity as informativeness, where a hypothesis H is more informative than H' with respect to a question Q if H requires less extra information than H' to answer Q. He applies this to explanation by saying that an explanation is simpler the fewer the initial conditions required in the deduction of the explanandum from the hypothesis. Thus if explanandum E is deducible from theory T_1 in conjuction only with initial condition C_1, whereas the deduction of E from T_2 requires conditions C_1 and C_2, then T_1 provides a simpler explanation. This has some plausibility, but Sober does not employ the notion of auxiliary hypotheses, which I have argued is crucial to simplicity. Lavoisier and Fresnel show no concern about syntactic complexity of the explanations given by their opponents: the number of initial conditions required is irrelevant. What matters is the special assumptions made in explaining particular classes of facts. Hence simplicity goes beyond the syntactic notion of informativeness discussed by Sober. We saw in discussing consilience that the individuation of classes of facts requires consideration of the history of inquiry and the cognitive structures of inquirers.

Besides comparing sets of auxiliary hypotheses AT_1 and AT_2, we might also consider judging simplicity by comparing T_1 and T_2. But I cannot see how in general this could be done. The number of postulates in a theory appears to have little bearing on its acceptability; all that matters is that each postulate be used in the explanation of different kinds of facts. Perhaps T_1 and T_2 could be compared as to number of parameters or predicates, but the relevance of this is doubtful. Nor does it make much sense to count number of rules. However, T_1 and T_2 can be compared at another level—ontological economy. Lavoisier suggests that the phlogiston theory is less simple than the oxygen theory, since it assumes the existence of another substance, phlogiston. Similarly, the creation hypothesis is ontologically more complex than the theory of evolution. One might suppose that the wave theory was actually less ontologically economical than the corpuscular theory, since it assumed the existence of the ether, although Newton's theory had its own major ontological assumption—the existence of light particles.

T_1 is more ontologically economical than T_2 if T_2 assumes the existence of entities that T_1 does not. This criterion of ontological economy is subsidiary to those of consilience and simplicity because Occam's razor counsels us only not to multiply entities beyond necessity. Necessity is a function of the range of facts to be explained without the use of a lot of auxiliary assumptions. Ontological complexity does not detract from the explanatory value or acceptability of a theory, so long as the complexity contributes toward consilience and simplicity. Lavoisier can be construed as arguing, not that his theory is better because it is more ontologically economical, but that his theory is more consilient and simple than the phlogiston theory, so phlogiston need not be assumed to exist. Hence ontological economy is not an important criterion of the best explanation.

But simplicity, illustrated by the arguments of Lavoisier and Fresnel, is important. Theories must not achieve consilience at the expense of simplicity through the use of auxiliary hypotheses. The desire for global unification represented by the criterion of consilience must be tempered by the desire to avoid ad hoc explanations. If a global theory's consilience depends on lack of simplicity, we may be wise to settle for a number of separate and more local theories to explain a range of facts. Inference to the best explanation is inference to a theory that best satisfies the criteria of consilience and simplicity, as well as a third, analogy. Before discussing analogy, however, I want to develop further the notions of consilience and simplicity by describing how the program PI takes them into account in assessing the best explanation.

5.5. Inference to the Best Explanation in PI

Consilience and simplicity have been shown to be important criteria for determining the best explanation, but the account of their application has so far been qualitative and imprecise. Many philosophers of science have looked to probability theory for more exact analytical tools, but I shall argue in section 5.8 that probability theory is of little help. Appropriate formalisms for developing a more thorough model of theory evaluation can come, however, from artificial intelligence. Earlier chapters showed how computational models can help in our understanding of the discovery and application of theories, and I shall now make a similar case for theory evaluation, describing how it is implemented in PI. The pragmatic character of the classes of evidence explained should become clearer, as well as how sets of competing theories and evidence can be assembled.

5.5.1. Competing Theories and Evidence
Following Hempel (1965) I refer to a fact or generalization that is to be explained as an *explanandum* (plural *explananda*). When PI finds an explanation, it records the success by adding what was explained to the list of explananda of the explanatory hypothesis, and adding the hypothesis to the list of explainers of the explanandum. For example, when the wave theory of sound succeeds in explaining why sound reflects, the rule that sound reflects is added to the list of explananda of the wave theory, and the wave theory is added to the list of explainers of sound reflection. After each explanatory success of a theory T_1, PI asks if T_1 is the best explanation. Answering this question requires comparing T_1 against alternative explaining theories with respect to the total available evidence.

But what makes a theory an alternative to T_1, and what is the total evidence that must be taken into account? To try to consider all possible explanations and all possibly relevant evidence would be too computationally expensive. Instead, PI uses a simple algorithm to compile lists of alternative theories and relevant evidence on the basis of explanations already performed. It looks at the list of explananda explained by T_1, then checks to see what other theories have been used to explain these. Any T_2 that explains some of the explananda of T_1 is a competitor of T_1. But that is not the whole story, since we want to find a full set of competitors. For example, we would easily find that the particle theory of sound is a competitor of the wave theory, if it is also on record as having offered an explanation of why sound reflects. But suppose that the particle theory explains something that the wave theory does not, and moreover there is some additional theory that also explains the additional explanandum. Then the additional theory also gets counted as an alternative to the wave theory of sound. Accordingly, PI looks at the explananda of this new set of alternative theories, and then considers their explananda in turn. When a continuing search turns up no new competitors or explananda, PI concludes it has a full set of competitors and evidence.

PI triggers a search for the best explanation whenever a theory that has already been found to explain something is found to explain something new. PI asks whether the theory is the best explanation of the available evidence, taking into account the sets of competitors and relevant evidence. Finding these sets is fully tractable because explanation is not just a deductive relation between theories and explananda. If that were so, there would always be an unlimited number of potentially explanatory theories and evidence whose assembly would be unfeasible. Instead, PI looks at what has been found to explain what. As we saw in chapter 3, explanation from a computational perspective can be viewed as a historical process whose results are stored in the processing system, not as an abstract

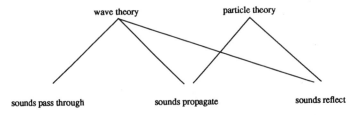

Figure 5.1
Consilience of the wave theory of sound.

relation between theories and explananda. Crucially, the explanatory successes of hypotheses are noted during the performance of the system.

Similarly, real scientists do not consider all possible theories and explananda when they evaluate theories. If they have been responsible in reading the literature, they are aware of likely competing theories and can use a procedure similar to what PI does to compile sets of such theories and pieces of evidence. In science, however, there is also an important social dimension, involving interaction among scientists and social regulatory forces such as peer review. Discussion of such issues will have to wait until chapter 10, as will the important question of what prompts the explanatory acts of which theory evaluation takes note.

5.5.2. Consilience in PI

After compiling lists of competitors and relevant evidence, PI selects the best explanation out of the set of competitors, including the original explainer, by comparing the sets of explananda of the theories. Pairwise comparisons are simplest when the set of explananda of one theory T_1 is a proper subset of the set of explananda of another theory T_2. In this case, T_2 is clearly a better explanation of the relevant evidence than T_1. In chapter 4, we saw how PI uses abduction and conceptual combination to discover, not only the wave theory of sound, but also the particle theory of sound. PI's mechanism for theory evaluation leads it to prefer the wave theory to the particle theory for the same reason that the Greeks did: both theories explain why sound reflects and propagates, but the wave theory can explain why sounds can pass through each other without obstruction. Figure 5.1 depicts the greater consilience of the wave theory. Similarly, in the above quotations from Darwin, Lavoisier, and Fresnel, each scientist is clearly arguing that his theory explains more than its main competitor.

What gets explained? Chapter 4's discussion of abduction showed that there are two kinds of structures that can be thought of as providing explanations. In the simplest case, we abduce a fact to explain another fact given a rule, as when we abduce that John was caught in traffic in order to explain why he was late. In the more complex case, abductive rule formation produces a rule that is used to provide explanations of other rules. The wave theory of sound is such a case, since the rule that all sounds are waves is used to explain such rules as that sounds reflects. PI uses essentially the same algorithms for both cases, compiling lists of competing theories and relevant evidence and then seeing what hypothesis explains the most explananda.

In the simulation of the choice of the wave theory of sound over the particle theory of sound, the evaluation is relatively easy because what the particle theory explains is a proper subset of what the wave theory explains. Often, however, the decision concerning the best explanation will not be so clear-cut. We usually want a theory not only to explain the most phenomena, but also to explain the most *important* phenomena. It would be ridiculous, for example, if the wave theory of sound increased the size of its set of explananda by explaining why sound propagates on Mondays, why it propagates on Tuesdays, and so on. Such trivialities make no difference if the explananda of one theory form a proper subset of the explananda of another. But if no subset relation holds between the explananda of two theories, we have to ask: Which theory explains the most important phenomena? In such cases, PI calculates the total importance of the explananda of each competing theory, and concludes that the best explanation is the theory whose explananda have the highest total importance.

But where does importance come from? In the most interesting case where it is a set of rules that are being explained, PI judges the importance of a rule to be its *strength*. The strength of a rule, in PI as in the classifier systems of Holland (Holland et al., 1986), is a function of the past usefulness of a rule, not just its probability or certainty. We are at least as certain that sound propagates on Mondays as we are that it propagates in general, but the weaker rule will receive far less use. Important rules, then, are those that most often contribute to useful problem solutions. The strength of a rule is not independent of its probability: true rules are more likely to be useful. But strength is a far better indicator of importance than probability, and enables PI to ignore trivial explananda. For this quantitative calculation of consilience, PI considers the sum of all the importances (ranging from 0 to 1) of the facts that it explains. If all facts are equally important, then degree of consilience can be taken to be just the number of facts explained.

5.5.3. Simplicity in PI

We saw that consilience is not the only criterion relevant to evaluating the best explanation. A theory should not only explain a lot of facts, but should also explain without making many special assumptions.

PI implements a simplicity criterion using the sets of cohypotheses established when a hypothesis in formed by abduction. We saw in section 4.2.2 that H_1 and H_2 are cohypotheses if both must be formed together in order to accomplish an explanation. The simplest case is where abduction is based on a rule with multiple conditions:

If A & B & C & D then E.
E is to be explained.
_____

Therefore, maybe A & B & C & D.

Abduction here requires hypothesizing A, B, C, and D all together, so they constitute cohypotheses. For example, suppose I am trying to explain why the Princeton football team was beaten by Yale in 1986. A very simple explanation is furnished by the rule: If one football team is much better than another, it beats it. This requires no assumptions except that Yale's football team is better than Princeton's. A more complex rule that might provide a competing explanation is: If one football team is worse than another but the stronger team has players who have bet heavily against themselves, then the stronger team loses. Here abducing that Princeton's football team is really better than Yale's would require making the additional, unwarranted assumption that Princeton players had bet against themselves. The simplicity of a hypothesis, then, is a function of how many additional cohypotheses it required in accomplishing its explanations, and one hypothesis is simpler than another if it has a lower ratio of cohypothese to facts explained. It is important to consider the ratio because we do not want to value a hypothesis whose simplicity derives from not explaining anything at all over another hypothesis that uses auxiliary hypotheses while accomplishing explanations.

This general idea has been implemented in PI as follows. If a hypothesis has more cohypotheses than facts explained, its simplicity is judged to be 0, since it needs a special assumption for everything it explains (compare the complaint of Lavoisier against the phlogiston theory). Otherwise, its simplicity is calculated by the formula

$$\text{simplicity (H)} = \frac{\text{facts explained by H} - \text{cohypotheses of H}}{\text{facts explained by H}}.$$

PI calculates the simplicity of a hypothesis by dividing the difference between the number of facts it explains and the number of cohypotheses it uses by the number of facts it explains. This yields values from 0, for a hypothesis that has to assume as much as it explains, to 1, for a hypothesis that has no cohypotheses at all. We do not have to worry about dividing by 0, since if a hypothesis does not explain anything, its simplicity will never be evaluated.

To give a global assessment of which hypothesis is the best explanation, PI considers both consilience and simplicity. The easy cases are where one hypothesis is superior to all others on one dimension and at least as good on the other. If one hypothesis is both more consilient than another and at least as simple, it is obviously the best. But when the two dimensions conflict, with H_1 more consilient than H_2 but H_2 more simple, PI constructs numerical values for consilience (see the last section) and simplicity. Then the explanatory power of a hypothesis is calculated by

$$\text{value (H)} = \text{simplicity (H)} \times \text{consilience (H)}.$$

This metric makes it clear how using an ad hoc assumption to explain just one additional fact does not make for a better explanation. For example, if H explains 6 facts without special assumptions and needs 1 cohypothesis just to explain 1 additional fact, its value becomes $(7-1)/7 \times 7$, which is still 6, its original value. Individuating facts is obviously crucial here, but that has already been taken care of by the mechanisms for problem solving and abduction that notice and store what explains what. (Note that this formula only works if the facts explained are of equal importance; otherwise, one might be able to increase the total value of a hypothesis by using a cohypothesis to explain a particularly important fact. Hence for explananda of varying importance, the definitions of simplicity and consilience must be complicated to take into account the relative importance of all of these: the facts explained by the hypothesis, the facts explained using cohypotheses, and the total evidence explained. This has not yet been implemented.)

Note that PI is quite capable of picking as the best explanation a theory that does not explain everything explained by its competitors. Contrary to the views of philosophers such as Popper, we cannot reject a theory merely because it occasionally fails (see section 9.2). If it is simpler and explains more important facts than its competitors, a theory can be accepted as the best explanation. After a theory has been so designated, PI makes parameter adjustments to ensure that it gets used in problem solving and explanation rather than its competitors. If the theory is a rule, its strength is increased and those of its competitors are decreased; if the theory is a hypothetical message, its confidence value is increased and those of its competitors are decreased.

This account of inference to the best explanation in PI can be viewed from both descriptive and normative viewpoints. It shows how the descriptive account of theory evaluation in the first part of the chapter can be made much more precise and integrated with a computational account of theories. Speculatively, it can be taken as an approximation to what scientists actually do when they evaluate theories. Clearly, however, there are respects in which PI comes closer to how scientists ought to think than to how they usually do think. For example, PI is exhaustive in considering all retrievable evidence and competing hypotheses, whereas scientists often are biased toward their own theories. I return to these normative issues in later chapters.

5.5.4. Limitations

Although PI is able to capture some of the key elements in the historical cases of theory choice described above, it has numerous deficiencies. I have not yet simulated any historical case that would seriously test PI's calculation of simplicity and overall explanatory value. (In the simulation in appendix 3, the criterion of consilience suffices to show the superiority of the wave theory of sound over the particle theory. Note also that the simulation simplifies by starting with the laws about the properties of sound to be explained already decomposed into arbitrary instances, although only slight modifications are required to do it the more round-about way in which the explananda are rules.) It would be desirable to reconstruct cases such as the oxygen-phlogiston dispute in sufficient detail to note sets of cohypotheses and to evaluate the applicability of PI's mechanisms and metrics. It will probably turn out that the simple multiplicative value got from values for simplicity and consilience is too crude to capture the complexities of historical arguments. Moreover, actual historical cases may well require a more complicated notion of cohypothesis than PI's current one based on multiple clauses in the conditions of rules. And more holistic algorithms can be developed (Thagard, 1987).

One aspect undoubtedly not captured in PI's current implementation is scientists' use of highly general arguments for and against particular theories. A theory can be defended not just on the basis of its consilience and simplicity, but also because, on scientific or even metaphysical principles, it is the right *kind* of theory. Such reasoning involves a third criterion for the best explanation, analogy.

5.6. Analogy

Analogy plays an important part in the arguments of Darwin and the proponents of the wave theory of light. Darwin used the analogy between artificial and natural selection for heuristic purposes, but he also claimed the analogy as one of the grounds for belief in his theory (Darwin, 1962, chapter 1; 1969, vol. 3, p. 25). Huygens, Young, and Fresnel each used the analogies between the phenomena of sound and those of light to support the wave theory of light. However, at first sight analogy appears to have little to do with explanation. Darwin's analogy between artificial and natural selection and Huygens' analogy between sound and light are intended to support the respective theories, but it is not clear how this is accomplished. I shall argue that the analogies support the theories by improving the explanations that the theories are used to give.

Logic books commonly represent arguments from analogy as follows:

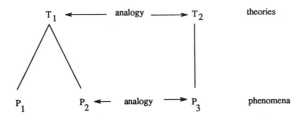

Figure 5.2
The criterion of analogy.

A is P, Q, R, S.
B is P, Q, R.
_____

So: B is S.

We conclude that an object or class B has a property S, on the grounds that it shares a number of other properties with A, which has S. Thus Darwin might argue that since natural selection is like artificial selection in a number of respects, it too leads to the development of new forms. Huygens might argue that since light is like sound in a number of respects, it also consists of waves. Now, perhaps arguments like this capture part of the use to which Huygens and Darwin put analogy, but severe problems are caused by the presence of disanalogies. Huygens takes pains to point out numerous ways in which sound and light do not resemble each other. Most crucially, sound is not propagated in straight lines. In Darwin's case, there is also a patent disanalogy: the absence in natural selection of an intelligent being that performs the selection. Yet in neither case does the presence of disanalogies daunt the arguer. But if there are properties T and U that A and B do not share, surely it is not legitimate to conclude that because A and B share P, Q, and R, they also share S. Hence the above schema does not adequately represent the use of analogy in scientific arguments.

A better characterization of analogical inference can be given by using the concept of explanation. Suppose A and B are similar in respect to P, Q, and R, and suppose we know that A's having S explains why it has P, Q, and R. Then we may conclude that B has S is a promising explanation of why B has P, Q, and R. We are not actually able to conclude that B has S; the evidence is not sufficient and the disanalogies are too threatening. But the analogies between A and B increase the value of the explanation of P, Q, and R in A by S.

The explanatory value of analogies should be clear from the discussion of the role of analogies in problem solving and abduction in chapters 2 and 4. Figure 5.2 provides a picture of the relation between an established theory T_1, which explains phenomena P_1 and P_2, and T_2, which explains P_3 and is supported by having analogies with T_1. By virtue of the mappings between T_1 and T_2, a richer understanding of the objects posited by T_2 is made possible, since some of the information and procedural knowledge of T_1 can be carried over. Some of the techniques that T_1 employs to solve problems about P_1 and P_2 can be carried over to help T_2 solve problems about P_3. In PI's model of analogical problem solving, a stored solution to one problem can help by suggesting new subgoals or hypotheses to aid in solving a new problem. Moreover, just as T_1's consilience with respect to P_1 and P_2 establishes a lower level analogy between those two phenomena, showing them to be similar at least in the respects in which they can both be explained by the same theory, so the correspondence between T_1 and T_2 might make possible the conception of P_3 as an analog of P_1 and P_2. For example, when the wave theory of light is supported by analogies with the wave theory of sound, reflection of light waves can be conceived as analogous to the similar behavior of sound and water waves.

We saw in chapter 4's discussion of analogical abduction that analogy plays an important role in discovery, directing inquiry toward certain kinds of hypotheses. But the additional point here is that analogy can also be used to support hypotheses already discovered. Support may thus be gained for hypotheses that are, for example, uniformitarian rather than catastrophist, mechanical rather than teleological, or determinist rather than statistical, as well as to support hypotheses invoking particular mechanisms such as selection and wave propagation. Analogy is a legitimate criterion for inference to the best explanation because analogies play an important role in improving explanations. We get increased understanding of one set of phenomena if the kind of explanation used is similar to ones already used. This is because the rules and problem solutions used by a new theory to deal with a phenomenon are enhanced by connections with well-established rules and solutions. We have seen analogy used in this way by Huygens and Darwin. The explanatory value of the wave hypothesis is enhanced by the model taken over from the explanation of certain phenomena of sound. Similarly, the explanatory value of the hypothesis of evolution by means of natural selection is enhanced by the familiarity of the process of artificial selection. Explanations in terms of the kinetic theory of gases benefit from the mechanical model of billiard balls. Moreover, having a rich analogy with an established field is likely to lead to dynamic consilience, since explanations of new classes of facts may be achievable using further analogies.

I am not claiming that explanation is reduction to the familiar: scientific explanations often employ unfamiliar notions and introduce entities as peculiar as positrons and black holes. However, other things being equal, the explanations afforded by a theory are better explanations if the theory is familiar, that is, introduces mechanisms, entities, or concepts that are used in established explanations. The use of familiar models is not essential to explanation, but it helps. Many philosophers of science would argue that analogy is at best relevant to the discovery of theories and has no bearing on their justification, but the historical record of examples such as Darwin's defense of natural selection and the cognitive importance of analogies shows the need to include analogy as one of the criteria of the best explanation.

How could PI's assessment of the best explanation add a criterion of analogy? PI could easily detect whether the explanations achieved by a theory employ analogies with problem solutions achieved by well-established theories, giving some preference to theories that have such analogies. We should not ignore consilience and simplicity for the sake of analogy, but, especially in the early stages of a research program, it might be legitimate to use analogy as one of the reasons for pursuing a theory that was still inferior. How to incorporate such reasoning into assessments of the best explanation remains an open question.

5.7. Meaning and Commensurability

My discussion of inference to the best explanation presupposes that it is possible to compare the explanatory worth of competing theories. On the radical views of Kuhn (1970b) and Feyerabend (1965), however, objective evaluation is highly problematic. Kuhn suggests that a paradigm is so all-encompassing that it is not possible to stand outside it in order to compare it against other paradigms. In particular, the meanings of different terms will vary from theory to theory, so that theories will turn out to be "incommensurable", not evaluable by any objective external criteria. Many historical philosophers of science follow Hanson (1958) in maintaining that all observation is "theory-laden", making it hard to see how observational evidence can be used to evaluate theories.

In chapter 3, I described many affinities between a rich, computational account of the structure of scientific knowledge and Kuhn's account based on paradigms. We saw the importance of patterns of problem solving and explanation based on exemplars, and the role of conceptual organization in guiding ways of thinking about phenomena. Kuhn correctly argued that this degree of organization would make theory evaluation potentially more problematic than positivists had allowed. A more detailed computational analysis of the structure of scientific knowledge shows, however, that Kuhn's apparently relativistic conclusions are not warranted.

Consider first the vexing question of meaning. Kuhn points out that mass in relativity theory is significantly different from mass in Newtonian mechanics, since the former but not the latter is convertible to energy. One therefore might be tempted to talk of the two theories employing different concepts, which would indeed make them hard to compare. This conclusion, however, presupposes a rigid view of the nature of concepts. Granted, if a concept is defined by a set of necessary and sufficient conditions, to change those conditions is to change the concept. But we saw in chapters 2 and 4 that this traditional notion of a concept is insupportable. Concepts in a system such as PI are much more fluid, using default rules to express prototypes, with no recourse to strict necessary and sufficient conditions. Adding a new rule about convertibility to energy to a concept such as mass does not produce nearly as dramatic a shift in meaning as would replacement of a definition on the traditional account of concepts: the computational role of the revised concept will for many purposes remain the same as that of the old concept. We can note that the Einsteinian concept of mass is different in important ways from the Newtonian one, without seeing an insurmountable gap between the two theories. For the concepts still possess in common many rules that involve default expectations about the behavior of objects under normal Newtonian conditions. Similarly, Nersessian (1987) argues that the traditional representation of concepts in terms of necessary and sufficient conditions blocks understanding of the development of the concept of a field in physics.

Kuhn asserts that a change of paradigm dramatically affects how we look at the world, and even remarks that proponents of different paradigms live in different worlds. I do not want to underestimate how substantially a theory can affect our thinking. A theory, construed not just as a set of sentences but as an interrelated network of concepts, rules, and problem solutions is a powerful but sometimes inflexible intellectual tool. But theories are not self-contained. Unless one adopts the rigid view of meaning rejected above, the evidence for theories can be seen to consist of statements that employ concepts whose meaning is not significantly determined by the theories. The functional role of concepts is established, not just by the theory, but also by rules that are relatively theory-independent. For example, evaluating the wave and particle theories of light involves comparing how they explain such properties of light as reflection, refraction, and diffraction. Rules describing such properties can be expressed using concepts whose functional roles are only minutely affected by the competing theories. We can admit that observation is theory-laden in a weak sense without adopting the relativist conclusion that it is theory-dependent. If one looks in detail at the historical record in episodes such as the transition from the phlogiston to the oxygen theory, one often finds a gradual process of adjustment to and adoption of a new theory (Perrin, 1986). Hence there is no reason to believe that in general theories are incommensurable or that theory evaluation is impossible. It is another question whether we can say that a theory accepted as the best explanation is *true*; see chapter 8 for an attempt to justify the use of inference to the best explanation and an argument that scientific theories can tell us about the world.

5.8. Probability

Philosophers such as Salmon (1966) and Horwich (1982) have recommended using Bayesian probability theory to illuminate theory evaluation. Recent work in AI has also considered probabilities as highly relevant to medical diagnosis and other kinds of abduction. Charniak and McDermott (1985, chapter 8; cf. Pople, 1977) advocate the use of Bayesian methods of assessing evidence. Sometimes it is indeed desirable to use Bayes' theorem, one simple form of which is

$$p(h/e) = \frac{p(h) \times p(e/h)}{p(e)}$$

Interpreted in terms of hypotheses, this says that the probability of a hypothesis h given evidence e is equal to the prior probability of h times the probability of e given h, divided by the probability of e.

There are various cases, including many of medical diagnosis, where Bayes' theorem is useful, but theory evaluation does not seem to be one of them, since the relevant probabilities are difficult if not impossible to find. Consider the case of the wave theory of sound, where we are evaluating the conjecture that sound consists of waves on the basis of how well it explains the various phenomena of sound. To use Bayes' theorem, we would need to know three things: the prior probability of the wave theory of sound; the probability of sound reflecting, propagating, and passing through given its being a wave; and the probability that sound reflects, propagates, and passes through. Moreover, for the sake of calculation of p(e), we would need to know the extent to which the properties of sound are statistically independent of each other. How could such knowledge be acquired? I see no reasonable way of estimating such probabilities in cases such as the wave theory of sound, Darwin's theory of evolution, and other qualitative theories. In medical diagnosis, you often can get reasonable estimates of probabilities, knowing, for example, what percentage of people with a particular symptom actually have a particular disease. But qualitative theory formation and evaluation of the sort performed by PI is not amenable to such techniques. Nor will the set-covering methods of Reggia, Nau, and Wang (1983) apply, since these depend on sets of related causes and symptoms that do not correspond to any kinds of knowledge available in the scientific contexts discussed above.

As Harman (1986) points out, the general use of probabilities in belief revision is computationally intractable. To evaluate a theory T we would have to be able to assign probabilities to various conjunctions of T together with the possible evidence propositions, but the number of such conjunctions grows exponentially. There are, however, heuristic ways of avoiding the combinatorial explosion (Peng and Reggia, 1986), for example, by using qualitative means such as those in PI to select a relevant subset of theories and evidence, and then applying probability calculations to only small sets in which exponential growth is not a problem. I see little point, however, in adopting this strategy, since we lack a useful answer to the question: Where do the probabilities come from in the first place? Only in the case of overtly statistical theories—ones that concern observed statistical distributions—are probabilities in the sense of frequencies available. Proponents of the subjective interpretation of probability advocate thinking of probabilities as degrees of belief that can be determined by means such as betting behavior, but I am unable to attach much sense to the question of how to bet, for example, on the theory of evolution. The study of theory evaluation would only gain an illusory precision by abandoning qualitative considerations for probabilistic ones.

5.9. Conclusion

Criteria for theory choice—consilience, simplicity, and analogy—turn out to be intimately connected with explanation rather than probabilities. Unlike hypothetico-deductive and Bayesian models of theory evaluation, the best explanation view gives an integrated account of the nature and importance of explanatory breadth, simplicity, and analogy. Because it accounts for many different aspects of scientific reasoning and applies to examples from different sciences, we can say recursively that the theory of inference to the best explanation outlined above is a highly consilient one.

Application of the criteria of consilience, simplicity, and analogy is a very complicated matter. Proponents of the hypothetico-deductive method often assume that one measure, such as degree of confirmation, suffices for theory evaluation. But as Gerd Buchdahl (1970) has urged, there are often tensions among the various components of the support for a theory. Consilience and simplicity militate against each other, since making a theory more consilient can render the theory less simple, if extra hypotheses are needed to explain the additional facts. The criterion of analogy may be at odds with both consilience and simplicity, if a radically new kind of theory is needed for simple explanatia of all the phenomena. Capturing the multi-dimensional character of scientific theory evalution is yet another virtue of the view that scientific inference is inference to the best explanation.

I mention as a final merit of the above account that it makes possible a reunification of scientific and philosophical method, since inference to the best explanation has many applications in philosophy, especially in meta-physics. Arguments concerning the best explanation are relevant to problems concerning scientific realism (see chapter 8), other minds, the external world, and the existence of God. Metaphysical theories can be evaluated as to whether they provide the best explanation of philosophical and scientific facts, according to the criteria of consilience, simplicity, and analogy.

5.10. Summary

Theory evaluation consists of picking the best explanation from a set of competing theories. The best explanation is determined by the criteria of consilience, simplicity, and analogy. Consilience is a measure of how much a theory explains. As in the program PI, consilience should be measured by looking at the past explanatory successes of the theory. PI is capable of evaluating not only which theory explains the most facts, but also of considering which theory explains the most important facts. Simplicity is a criterion that constrains consilience by ensuring that a theory does not achieve consilience by means of ad hoc auxiliary hypotheses. Analogy contributes to a theory's explanatory value because its problem solutions are likely to be facilitated using existing problem solutions in another, more well-established, domain. Given a flexible view of the meaning of concepts, incommensurability is not a problem. Probabilities are largely irrelevant to theory evaluation.

Chapter 6
Against Evolutionary Epistemology

The last two chapters presented a computational account of how scientific theories can be discovered and evaluated, using mechanisms such as conceptual combination, abduction, and inference to the best explanation. This chapter criticizes another approach to describing the growth of scientific knowledge, *evolutionary epistemology*. By "evolutionary epistemology" I mean Darwinian models of the growth of scientific knowledge. Such models rely on analogies between the development of biological species and the development of scientific theories. Recent proponents of evolutionary epistemology include the psychologist Donald Campbell (1974), the sociobiologist Richard Dawkins (1976), and philosophers of science Karl Popper (1972), Stephen Toulmin (1972), and Robert Ackerman (1970). I shall argue that the analogy between the evolution of species and the growth of scientific knowledge is seriously defective: clear examination of the practice and history of science shows the need for a non-Darwinian approach to historical epistemology.

6.1. *What Makes a Good Analogy?*

We saw in chapters 4 and 5 that analogy plays a powerful role not only in the discovery but even in the justification of theories. Hence in general the use of biological analogies by evolutionary epistemologists is unobjectionable. Yet clearly some analogies are much better than others: what distinguishes the good ones? The discussion of analogy in the last chapter showed that there is much more to evaluating an analogy between a base and a target than just counting their similarities and differences.

On the view defended in Holland et al. (1986, chapter 10), analogies are to be understood pragmatically, in terms of their role in problem solving. We saw in chapter 3 the power of analogical problem solving, in which useful features of one kind of problem solution are carried over to furnish a solution of a new problem. It does not matter much if there are features of the old solution that differ markedly from the new problem, as long as there are some useful features that carry over. Hence we should conclude that a good analogy is simply one that contributes to the solution of a given set of problems.

The problem addressed by both computational philosophy of science and evolutionary epistemology is how to characterize the development of scientific knowledge. A critique of evolutionary epistemology must do more than just point out differences between biological evolution and the growth of knowledge, since a few differences might be irrelevant to the problem-solving effectiveness of biologically inspired models. I shall argue that the differences between the development of science and the evolution of species are so severe that use of the analogy can only lead to seriously defective answers to the problem of describing how knowledge grows.

6.2. The Evolutionary Approach

The neo-Darwinian model of species evolution consists of Darwin's theory of natural selection synthesized with twentieth-century genetic theory. The central ingredients of the neo-Darwinian model are variation, selection, and transmission. Genetic variations occur within a population as the result of mutations and mixed combinations of genetic material. Individuals are engaged in a struggle for survival based on scarcity of food, territory, and mating partners. Hence individuals in whom variation produces traits that provide some ecological or sexual advantage will be more likely to survive and reproduce. Their valuable traits will be genetically transmitted to their offspring.

Evolutionary epistemology notices that variation, selection, and transmission are also features of the growth of scientific knowledge. Scientists generate theories, hypotheses, and concepts; only a few of these variations are judged to be advances over existing views, and these are selected; the selected theories and concepts are transmitted to other scientists through journals, textbooks, and other pedagogic measures. The correspondences between the development of species and the development of knowledge are indeed striking, but only at this superficial level. We shall see that variation, selection, and transmission of scientific theories differ decisively from their counterparts in the evolution of species. Evolutionary epistemology does, however, have some salutary features. Like computational philosophy of science, it is naturalistic and historical, and it admits the possibility that the units of knowledge are more complex than sets of sentences. Nevertheless, evolutionary epistemology can be shown to give highly misleading accounts of the variation, selection, and transmission of ideas.

6.3. Variation

First consider variation. The units of variation in species are genes, with variation produced by errors in the process by which genes are replicated.

Since the changes in genes are generally independent of the individual's environmental pressures, genetic variation is often said to be random. A better characterization is that of Campbell, who discusses *blind* variation (Campbell, 1974, p. 422). He outlines three important features of blindness. First, variations emitted are independent of the environmental conditions of the occasion of their utterance; that is, the variations that occur are not prompted by the environment, but occur through autonomous mechanisms. (This is not strictly true of biological variation, because of the effects of environmental mutagens, but for now we can ignore these as special cases.) Second, the occurrence of trials (genetic changes) individually is not correlated with what would be a solution to the environmental problem that the individual faces. And third, variations to incorrect trials are not corrections of previous unsuccessful variations. Biological variation clearly is blind. For example, birds whose habitat changes dramatically do not become more likely to undergo mutations that will make them better adapted to the new environment.

Obviously, however, the development of new theories in science is not blind in any of these respects. When scientists arrive at new ideas they usually do so as the result of concern with specific problems. Hence, unlike biological variation, conceptual variation is dependent on environmental conditions. Whereas genetic variation in organisms is not induced by the environmental conditions in which the individual is struggling to survive, scientific innovations are designed by their creators to solve recognized problems; they therefore are correlated with solutions to problems, in precisely the way in which Campbell says blind variations are not. Scientists also commonly seek new hypotheses that will correct errors in their previous trials, as in Kepler's famous efforts to discover a formula to describe the orbit of Mars (Hanson, 1958). Thus the generation of the units of scientific variation does not have any of the three features of blindness that Campbell describes as characteristic of evolutionary variation.

For Campbell (1974, 1977), the claim that new knowledge is arrived at by a blind process is virtually definitional. He states (1974, p. 422), "In going beyond what is already known, one cannot go but blindly. If one can go wisely, this indicates already achieved wisdom of some general sort." He says (1977, p. 504) that "blind" is meant to contrast with "prescient" or "clairvoyant". He thinks that if variations are constrained at all, they are constrained by existing knowledge that was itself obtained by blind variation and selective retention. Campbell presents us with a choice: either knowledge arises through blind variations, or, as in Plato's *Meno*, knowledge is something we had all along or at least knew directly how to get.

The discussion of inductive mechanisms in chapter 4 shows that Campbell has presented a false dichotomy. Theoretical development need be neither blind nor prescient. In the program PI, all learning occurs in the context of problem solving. Truly blind variation never occurs, since all induction is triggered during the attempt to solve some problem. We saw that this kind of focusing was crucial to avoid an explosive generation of useless and irrelevant concepts and rules. For example, blind use of the mechanism of conceptual combination would generate all sorts of new concepts that would never have practical application, producing an unlimited number of new constructs like "striped sound" or "green bank teller" that would severely impede the performance of the system. Instead, the triggering conditions ensure that inductive operations will only be performed on messages, rules, and concepts that have been activated by current problem-solving attempts. There is no prescience here, since nothing guarantees that the structures activated will lead to a solution to the current or future problems. But variation is clearly not blind either, since formation of concepts and rules that may be useful in solving a problem is more likely to occur during the attempt to solve that problem.

Superficially, conceptual combination bears some resemblance to the biological operation of *crossover*, which recombines genetic information through the exchange of segments between pairs of chromosomes. But combination of concepts in PI is far more directed than that sort of exchange, since deciding what rules to form for a new concept based on the rules attached to the two donor concepts requires complex heuristics. Forming a concept such as sound wave or feminist bank teller is not simply mixing together sound and wave or feminist and bank teller, but involves determining what rules potentially conflict and how to reconcile them.

The links between problem solutions and inductive variations are even closer for the different varieties of abduction. In simple abduction, we form a particular hypothesis to explain some puzzling fact. Suppose my problem is to solve a murder, and I activate the information that Fred was seen fleeing from the scene of the crime along with the rule

> If x murdered y, and x does not want to be caught, then x flees the scene.

I may then naturally form the weak hypothesis that Fred was the murderer. This hypothesis could well be false, but it was not formed blindly, since it was constrained by the current problem-solving situation, by the mechanism of abduction, and by the availability of rules concerning murder. Blind variation would be as likely to generate such hypotheses as that Attila the Hun was the murderer, or, with complete irrelevance, that Attila the Hun wore argyle socks. A computational approach makes it clear that some guidance is crucial to narrow down the possible set of hypotheses. (For discussion of how a related lesson was learned in research on automatic programming, see Lenat, 1983.)

In existential, analogical, and rule-forming abduction, the ties between problem solutions and knowledge generation are not as tight as in simple abduction, but still suffice to show that these mechanisms are a far cry from blind variation. In abductive rule formation an explanatory rule would never have been formed if not for some simple abduction performed previously: recall that the rule that all sound consists of waves depended on the prior abduction that an arbitrary example of sound consists of waves. Once again there is no attempt to generate rules blindly; doing so would only create chaos. Similarly, analogical abduction proposes new hypotheses using past problem solutions, but only those problem solutions that have been found by directed spreading activation to have some relation to the desired problem solution are candidates for analogizing, guaranteeing that there is some connection between the problem situation and what hypotheses are formed. Analogical abduction is therefore neither prescient nor blind, but constrained in potentially useful ways by the problem situation. In the vocabulary of AI, rules of inference such as the varieties of abduction can be understood as heuristics—useful rules of thumb—for guiding the search for problem solutions.

Campbell's consistent reply to this kind of objection is to maintain that the knowledge about kinds of domains and the methods of heuristic search must themselves have evolved by blind variation and selective retention. His question-begging response is based on the lament: How else could they have evolved? He claims (Campbell, 1960, p. 394) that there is no essential disagreement between his viewpoint and the theory of heuristic search, since any machine that developed its own heuristics would have to do so by trial and error of heuristic principles. This is not quite so: Lenat (1983) has developed a program that has heuristics for generating heuristics. Still, we have to reach bottom somewhere. Where do the initial heuristics come from if not by blind variation? In an organism, the heuristic search devices with which it is born are presumably there as the result of eons of biological evolution: the species has evolved with those innate heuristics because of their survival value. Just as a computer has to be preprogrammed with some mechanism for solving problems and performing inductions, so an organism has to have some built-in hardware and software for learning.

This retreat to the biological level does not save evolutionary epistemology as a model for the growth of science, although it does point to another more plausible view that has been discussed under the heading of "evolutionary epistemology": some aspects of human knowledge may be better understood as the result of seeing the knower in a biological context, taking into account the evolution of the species. But the biological roots of the human information processing system are not directly relevant to the task of developing a model for the growth of scientific knowledge. Even though, at some primordial biological level, heuristics for developing hypotheses may have arisen by blind mutation, we cannot ignore the fact that our descriptions of inductive procedures must make reference to mechanisms that at that level are far from blind. The biological details distract us from the issue at hand, describing the growth of scientific knowledge. Taking evolutionary epistemology seriously as a model of scientific knowledge development would shift our attention away from mechanisms for problem solving and learning, such as those in PI, that can help to focus and constrain the generation of new hypotheses and concepts.

We can distinguish between two kinds of evolutionary epistemology, which I call "biological" and "individual". The biological kind says, in a naturalistic spirit, that considerations of the nature of human knowledge should take seriously the biological origins of our capacity to know. This is fine. The individual kind, however, tries to base an understanding of how knowledge develops in individual thinkers on an analogy with the development of species, but the severe problems with the analogy cannot be avoided by retreating to the biological kind of evolutionary epistemology.

We saw in PI that the generation and evaluation of hypotheses are linked because of the intimate connection of abduction and inference to the best explanation. Similarly, Toulmin notes (1972, pp. 337ff.) that in the history of science variation and selection are "coupled": the factors responsible for selection are related to those responsible for the original generation of variants. Scientists strive to come up with variants that will survive the selection process. Abduction generates only hypotheses with some initial plausibility, ones that have been found to explain at least something. Similarly, the role of analogy in looking for a new theory corresponds roughly to a criterion of analogy used in arguments that a theory be accepted. In contrast, species variation and selection are "uncoupled": the factors that produce genetic change are unrelated to the environmental struggle for survival, except in special cases where the environmental threat is unusually mutagenic. The coupling of variation and selection for scientific theories makes theory choice a much more efficient procedure. If variation were blind, we would be faced with the necessity of choosing among an unmanageably large number of theories, many of them irrelevant. Instead, the intentional, quasi-logical process by which hypotheses are generated narrows the range of candidates that must be considered for selection. Evolutionary epistemology would lead us to overlook the ways in which processes like abduction and analogy tie together generation and selection, the context of discovery and the context of justification.

Another difference between biological and scientific development is that the rate of theoretical variation seems to be partly dependent on the degree of threat to existing theories. In Kuhnian terminology, there is more likely to be a proliferation of new concepts and paradigms when a field is in a state of crisis due to the mounting failures of the dominant paradigm. The rate of biological variation is not similarly sensitive to degree of environmental pressure on organisms. An interesting project for computational philosophy of science would be to make inductive mechanisms even more sensitive to the problem-solving context, varying in application depending on such factors as the availability of established theories. Abduction, for example, might be made less likely to generate new hypotheses when there are already established explanations for facts to be explained.

This completes my argument that the differences between biological variation and theoretical variation are so severe that attempts to apply the the former to the latter will likely lead to poor solutions to problems about the generation of theories. The main differences have concerned blindness, direction and rate of variation, and coupledness of variation and selection. It is ironic that the great merit of Darwin's theory—removing intentional design from the account of natural development—is precisely the great flaw in evolutionary epistemology. The relevant difference between genes and theories is that theories have people trying to make them better. Abstraction from the aim of scientists to arrive at progressively better explanations of phenomena unavoidably distorts our picture of the growth of science. This is as true of the selection of theories as it is of the origin of theories.

6.4. Selection

The differences between epistemological and biological selection arise from the fact that theory selection is performed by intentional agents working with a set of criteria, whereas natural selection is the result of different survival rates of the organisms bearing adaptive genes. Nature selects, but not in accord with any general standards. Nature is thoroughly practical, favoring any mutation that works in a given environment. Since there is such an enormous range of environments to which organisms have adapted, we have no global notion of what it is for an organism to be fit. Fitness is not inherently a property of an organism, but is a function of the extent to which an organism is adapted to a specific environment. (I here ignore, as not relevant to the question of evolutionary epistemology, important controversies in biology and philosophy concerning the units of selection.)

In contrast, selection of theories and concepts occurs in the context of a community of scientists with definite aims. These aims include finding solutions to problems, explaining facts, achieving simplicity, making accurate predictions, and so on. Perhaps at different times different aims are paramount, so that there may be inconstancy and even subjectivity in the application of criteria for theory choice. The application of such criteria may well be much more complex than PI's current algorithm for theory evaluation. Nevertheless, when scientists are advocating the adoption of a new theory, they appeal to some of a basic set of criteria according to which their theory is superior to alternatives. Since the rise of modern science in the seventeenth century, there has been much agreement at the general level about what theories should accomplish in explanation, problem solving, and prediction, even if the application of these general aims in particular cases has been controversial. The controversy derives from the complexity of the set of criteria, not from any fundamental disagreement about the whole range of desiderata. Everyone wants simple theories that explain a lot. Hence selection of theories is strikingly different from the selection of genes. Survival of theories is the result of satisfaction of global criteria, criteria that apply over the whole range of science. But survival of genes is the result of satisfaction of local criteria, generated by a particular environment. Scientific communities are unlike natural environments in their ability to apply general standards.

Progress is the result of application of a relatively stable set of criteria. Progress is only progress with respect to some general set of aims, and results from continuous attempts to satisfy the members of the set in question. Since scientists do strive to develop and adopt theories that satisfy the aims of explanation and problem solving, we can speak of scientific progress. In contrast, there is no progress in biological evolution, since survival value is relative to a particular environment, and we have no general standards for progress among environments. We could perhaps says that evolution of Homo sapiens is progressive given our environment and our extraordinary ability to adapt to it, but our species may well someday inhabit an environment to which so-called lower animals are much better adapted. A postnuclear war environment saturated with radioactivity would render us less fit than many less vulnerable organisms. Biological progress might be identified with increase in complexity, control over the environment, or capacity for acquiring knowledge, but none of these is a universal trend in evolution. As G. G. Simpson summarizes (1967, p. 260), "Evolution is not invariably accompanied by progress as an essential feature." Hence the Darwinian model of development employed in evolutionary epistemology lacks a concept of progress essential in historical epistemology.

What is progress according to the computational account of theories? The answer is directly tied to the methodology of inference to the best explanation. Scientific progress consists in finding new theories that provide greater and greater satisfaction of the criteria of consilience, simplicity, and analogy. Consilience is clearly the most important: we want explanation of more and more classes of facts. Section 5.7 argued that we do not have to worry about incommensurability of theories. No theory of light could fail to include among its classes of facts explained the phenomena of reflection, refraction, and diffraction. No gravitational theory, no matter how much it deviated conceptually from general relativity, would be accepted if it did not have application to the class of facts about the motion of the planets in our solar system, a class crucial to both Newtonian and Einsteinian theories. I am not saying that scientific progress requires incorporation of all previous classes of facts explained. But there are structures in our cognitive systems sufficiently close to ordinary experience that facts can be classed independently of the general theoretical framework that incorporates them. Successive theories can be expected to include explanations of the acknowledged important classes of facts. Otherwise, inference to the best explanation would never lead to the abandonment of the old theory in favor of the new. In this partial accumulation lies scientific progress.

Thus the selection of theories shows further the weakness of evolutionary epistemology, which would shift attention away from the conscious application of general criteria and the achievement of progress, both of which are important for understanding the growth of science. Let us now consider biological and epistemological transmission.

6.5. Transmission

Modern genetic theory provides us with an account of how genes that increase the fitness of an organism are preserved and transmitted to the organism's offspring. Preservation and transmission of conceptual survivors is quite different. A beneficial gene is replicated in specific members of a population, but a successful theory is immediately distributed to most members of a scientific community. Preservation is by publication and pedagogy, not by any process resembling inheritance. Dissemination of successful theories is much more rapid than dissemination of beneficial gens. This is one reason why conceptual development seems to be so much more rapid than biological development. (The others include the intentional aspect of theoretical variation and the progressive aspect of theory selection, already discussed.) Thus at the level of transmission of units of variation, as well as at the levels of variation and selection, the growth of knowledge is different from the evolution of species.

It is sometimes claimed that the growth of knowledge is Lamarckian rather than Darwinian, since pieces of knowledge gained by one inquirer can be immediately passed on to others, like Lamarck's acquired characteristics. But as Hull (1982) trenchantly points out, sociocultural evolution is neither Darwinian nor Lamarckian, since it is not genetic. Genes serve as templates for new genes, which produce organisms. In contrast, theories and their components do not produce new theories. To use Hull's simile, a theory is like a parasite inhabiting those who hold it and capable of spreading to others. We saw in chapter 3 that scientific theories are communicated through standard problems studied by those new to a field. By learning how to solve the problems, budding scientists acquire the rules, concepts, and problem solutions that constitute the relevant theory for the domain being studied. The nongenetic character of theory transmission is yet another reason not to import biological concepts into historical epistemology.

Even the units of variation and transmission have very different properties. Dawkins (1976) postulates "memes" as the conceptual replicating entities analogous to genes. But this postulation is gratuitous since we already have notions that describe the entities that develop in scientific and cultural change. These entities include rules, theories, laws, data, concepts, and so on. Talk of memes does nothing to overcome the substantial problems of explicating the nature of theories, concepts, and world-views. Earlier chapters offered a computationally and psychologically plausible account of what constitutes scientific knowledge. Historical epistemology needs to build on some such framework, without postulating entities like memes whose only function is to foster misleading biological analogies.

Discussion of transmission of ideas in scientific communities might suggest a third, *social* kind of evolutionary epistemology in addition to the biological and individual kinds distinguished earlier. One might advocate thinking of scientists as individuals in whom ideas arise, with transmission of ideas being like the spread of a biological trait in accord with the principles of population genetics. Once again the biological analogy conceals more than it reveals. More careful sociology of scientific knowledge investigates the influence of scientific elites, communication networks, and other social organizations that have properties not found in populations of species other than humans (Crane, 1972). To get a theoretical metaphor that is better able to deal with such complexities than does population genetics, we should look instead to the idea of parallel computation (see chapter 10).

6.6. Conclusion

Because the variation, selection, and transmission of scientific ideas differ in such fundamental ways from their biological analogs, Darwinian natural selection provides a poor model for understanding the growth of science. It misleadingly suggests that variation in scientific ideas is blind, that their selection is by local criteria, and that their transmission is genetic. It ignores the pragmatic, problem-solving context of induction. Thus employment of the evolutionary analogy leads away from solutions to important problems about the growth of knowledge, not toward them. Hence evolutionary epistemology, conceived as the application of the Darwinian model to scientific development, should be abandoned. The Darwinian model is powerful and seductive, but its use must be restricted to domains to which it has legitimate application. Like many sociobiological accounts of aspects of human culture, evolutionary epistemology takes the mechanism of natural selection beyond the realm of plausible applicability.

I hope that the discussions of the growth of science found in this work convince the reader that it is possible to have a naturalistic and historical epistemology without Darwinizing. Computational accounts of theory discovery and selection can go far beyond the vague Darwinian metaphor of variation and selection. Of course, an intrepid evolutionary epistemologist might claim my accounts as specifications of the Darwinian process and even maintain their compatibility. I am reminded of the children's fable of Stone Soup, in which a visitor convinces villagers that he can make soup using only his magic stone, although he does get them to enhance the stone soup using some chicken, vegetables, and so on. No doubt we can use the Darwinian model to start epistemological soup, but why bother with the stone?

6.7. Summary

Evolutionary epistemology describes the growth of scientific knowledge using analogies with biological evolution. Although it is possible to generate superficially plausible conceptual analogs of biological variation, selection, and transmission, closer analysis shows that the analogy between biological and epistemological evolution impedes rather than fosters understanding of scientific development. In particular, the account of discovery in chapter 4 shows that scientific theories are not generated by blind variation, and the discussion of theory choice in chapter 5 demonstrates important differences between it and biological selection. Hence evolutionary epistemology is much inferior to computational philosophy of science as a framework for understanding scientific knowledge.

Chapter 7
From the Descriptive to the Normative

The previous chapters gave descriptions of how scientific knowledge grows through processes of problem solving, discovery, and theory evaluation. These descriptions were naturally tied to the fields of cognitive psychology, artificial intelligence, and history of science. But philosophy has always been concerned, not merely with what *is*, but also with what *ought* to be, with the *normative* as well as the descriptive. Logic, philosophy of science, and epistemology in general are essentially normative fields, providing evaluations as well as descriptions of methods for achieving knowledge. Whereas psychology is supposed to describe how people do think, logic and epistemology are concerned with how people ought to reason. Similarly, whereas history of science describes what scientists have done, philosophy of science is concerned with how science ought to be conducted. Thus even computational philosophy of science has to have a normative side, but on what basis are we to make normative judgments? How can we objectively establish canons of logic and scientific method? Can we justify the use of forms of reasoning such as abduction and inference to the best explanation?

Traditionally, philosophers have seen two ways of justifying ways of reasoning. The rationalist approach attempts to discover principles of reasoning through *a priori* reflections on the necessary properties of the rational mind. But the proliferation of formal logics and the empirical study of kinds of human reasoning have destroyed the plausibility of the claim that there is an essential way in which rational beings do and must think. Moreover, the rise of scientific reasoning is a relatively recent cultural phenomenon, owed to renaissance Europe; so it is even less plausible to suppose that principles of scientific reasoning can be derived by a pure rationalist method. Empiricist philosophers have attempted to justify logic by saying that logical principles are *analytic*, true by definition, a view that is equally incompatible with the proliferation of alternative logics.

Today it is more fashionable to say that normative canons of logic and philosophy of science are not to be had at all. Paul Feyerabend (1975) summarizes his epistemological anarchism in the dictum: Anything goes. Richard Rorty (1979) exhorts philosophers to abandon foundational epistemology for hermeneutic "edification". The pessimism of Feyerabend and Rorty stems from failures of analytic philosophy and positivist philosophy of science to carry out their programs of using the techniques of logical analysis to establish a clear foundation for knowledge, including scientific knowledge. Is there an alternative to postpositivist depression?

Yes: we can arrive at normative principles of reasoning by reflection on descriptions of how everyday and scientific reasoning actually works. Such reflection does not derive the normative from the descriptive; there is no immediate deduction of ought from is. Nevertheless, descriptive studies contribute substantially to establishment of normative principles. This chapter outlines a methodology for this contribution. Chapter 8 then applies the methodology, most importantly to the justification of inference to the best explanation. Readers more interested in computational issues than in normative ones can skip to chapter 10.

To show how normative conclusions can be drawn from descriptive matters, I shall consider several areas in which philosophers have found the descriptive to be relevant to the normative. After a brief critique of Nelson Goodman's well known discussion of the justification of induction, I examine three richer cases of descriptively based development of normative principles. The two base cases are historical philosophy of science and wide reflective equilibrium in ethics, which are used to suggest a model for the more complex case of deriving logical principles from psychological practice. Finally, I generalize from all three cases to a general model of how to go from the descriptive to the normative in a manner consistent with the computational approach of earlier chapters.

7.2. Goodman: Normative Conclusions through Reflective Equilibrium

Hume (1888) raised the skeptical question of whether inductive reasoning from evidence to more general conclusions could ever be justified. Nelson Goodman (1965) proposed an influential dissolution of Hume's problem of induction. Goodman suggested that principles of inductive inference, like principles of deductive inference, are justified merely by conformity with accepted inferential practice. Goodman writes, "The point is that rules and particular inferences alike are justified by being brought into agreement with each other. A rule is amended if it yields an inference we are unwilling to accept; an inference is rejected if it violates a rule we are unwilling to amend. The process of justification is the delicate one of making mutual adjustments between rules and accepted inferences; and in the agreement achieved lies the only justification needed for either" (Goodman, 1965, p. 64—emphasis omitted). Subsequently, John Rawls (1971) proposed that ethical principles could be established by a similar method, through the achievement of what he called "reflective equilibrium" between moral principles and individual moral judgments. Applying this term to Goodman's method, we can say that, according to Goodman, justification of principles of reasoning is the result of achieving reflective equilibrium between inferential principles and practice. Thus the normative emerges from the descriptive.

Stich and Nisbett (1980) showed that Goodman's proposal is much too liberal. They cited psychological studies suggesting that it is all too easy for people to achieve reflective equilibrium despite poor practices such as the gambler's fallacy or the making of regression errors. (An example of the gambler's fallacy is supposing that the flip of a coin will be heads just because there has been a run of tails. An example of a regression error is assuming that a child of tall parents will be even taller. See Nisbett and Ross, 1980.) Goodman's proposal leaves no grounds for criticizing someone who arrives at a mutually adjusted set of bad principles and correspondingly bad practices. Stich and Nisbett propose that questions of justification can be answered by considering the reflective equilibria of inferential experts. However, concern with the principles and practices of experts only pushes Goodman's problem farther back, for we can still ask whether the experts are justified in reflective equilibrium. Talk of reflective equilibrium begins to look only like a smokescreen for a relatively sophisticated form of logical and methodological relativism. I shall argue that reflective equilibrium is at best incidental to the process of developing normative principles. Moreover, when the dispensability of equilibrium considerations becomes evident, Stich and Nisbett's emphasis on the social component of justification becomes avoidable, along with its potentially relativistic implications.

7.3. Historical Philosophy of Science

In recent years, many philosophers of science have shifted from the methods of logical reconstruction pioneered by the Vienna Circle to methods involving detailed study of historical or contemporary examples of scientific practice (Laudan, 1979; see also tutorial A). Instead of approaching science with the view that it needs to be cleaned up in order to reach standards commensurate with empiricist epistemology and the rigor of symbolic logic, the historical approach treats the philosophy of science as an empirical discipline (Hausman, 1981). Close attention must be paid to what scientists actually do, and prescriptions about what scientific method ought to amount to should be founded in actual practice. The implicit manifesto of this approach was Kuhn's *Structure of Scientific Revolutions*, originally published in 1962. From his and other historical studies, many

philosophers of science concluded that the elegant work of logical positivists on axiomatics, reduction, deductive explanation, and formal confirmation theory was often irrelevant to science, and so did not provide
adequate normative standards. A few philosophers of science have followed
Feyerabend (1975) in anarchistically concluding that no normative standards
of scientific method are appropriate. But this is not a direct consequence of
the deemphasis of logical reconstruction and the embrace of historical
methods, for we can use historical studies to generate methodological
principles whose sway can be extended normatively to cover the general
practice of science. But how does this work?

Consider first the nature of theory evaluation, which can provide the
first rough approximation to the selection of logical principles. The discussion of theory evaluation in chapter 5 suggests that theory choice is based
on methods that are comparative, coarse-grained, and dynamic. Theory
choice is comparative in that it involves the assessment of a number of
competing theories with respect to the empirical evidence, not just the
adequacy of a particular theory. Theory choice is coarse-grained in that the
units for comparing the relative explanatory strength of competing theories
are not individual statements deducible from the theories but large classes
of facts explained by theories, or, in the terminology of Laudan (1977),
problems solved by the theories. Finally, theory choice is dynamic in that
assessment of theories must take into account increases in the availability
of competing theories and evidence to be explained. We can expect that
the assessment of normative standards in philosophy of science, ethics, and
logic will also be comparative, coarse-grained, and dynamic, in ways that
will shortly be described.

But doing historical philosophy of science is in many respects different
from doing empirical science. In the first place, the selection of case studies
is very important. We do not typically study what Henry Snerd was doing
at the Miscellaneous Technology Corporation research lab in 1934; rather,
most studies concentrate on cases recognized as exemplary accomplishments of science. Galileo's physics, Newton's mechanics, Lavoisier's chemistry, and Darwin's theory of evolution have for obvious reasons been
favored objects of study: they have been licensed by the subsequent
history of science as genuine achievements. The progressive development
of science enables us to pick out examples of scientific method that can be
assumed, at least provisionally, to be typical not only of how science is
done but of how it should be done. In doing empirical science, we might
study a particular phenomenon because we think it to be typical of a wide
range of phenomena, but there is no normative association. In historical
philosophy of science, on the other hand, case studies acquire normative
significance because of the background belief that such scientists as Galileo,
Newton, and Darwin generally knew what they were doing.

Admittedly there are many pitfalls. Although we intensively examine Newton's work on mechanics and optics, we are leery of his studies of alchemy and astrology, since that work has not been vindicated by later scientific developments. Studies abound on Darwin's theory of natural selection, but historians as well as philosophers have spent much less time on his discredited theory of pangenesis. Hence we do not assume that the actual practice of even an esteemed scientist is always to be taken as normatively significant. Moreover, the philosophical historiography of science is a highly theory-laden activity, since the methodological findings of philosophers in the papers and diaries of the scientists studied are undoubtedly influenced by the philosophers' antecedent philosophical expectations. As Hausman (1981) stressed, empirical philosophers of science cannot help but begin with the philosophical tools familiar to them. Retrospective philosophical evaluations of pieces of scientific work may change over time as philosophical theories and scientific views develop. Thus historical philosophy of science is unavoidably based on philosophical history of science. Philosophical history of science is not, however, an arbitrary enterprise, since even the philosophical historian must feel constrained by the actual statements of the subjects of investigation.

My characterization of historical philosophy of science applies best to mature sciences such as physics or biology. Philosophers of social sciences face more severe problems, since there is much less general agreement in those fields, both about current theories and about what constitute the great historical achievements. Thus the empirical philosopher of economics or psychology will be working with much noisier data than will the philosopher of natural science, and hence will have to be much more careful in the leap from is to ought. There is much less general agreement about the accomplishments of Marx or Keynes or Freud or Piaget than there is about Galileo, Newton, and Darwin.

Historical philosophy of science is comparative in that we ought to consider which of different methodologies best describes and explains what is going on in a concrete case. It is coarse-grained in that we are not trying to account deductively for a general array of scientific practices, but aim to explain a restricted number of practices deemed historically significant. And it is dynamic, in that one criterion we should use in evaluating a philosophical account of methodology concerns how well the account leads to subsequent illuminating historical work. We may, of course, decide that a particular instance of scientific work is not of philosophical significance because the scientist in question was not employing the correct methodology. But this does not invalidate our general historical procedure, since a judgment would have to be based on reflection on other cases.

Historical philosophy of science can also gain from reflection on bad science. My discussion in chapter 9 is intended to illuminate the difference between science and pseudoscience by considering some cases of pseudo-sciences, particularly astrology and creationism. It can also be instructive to consider examples where eminent scientists produced flawed theories, to see whether the flaws are the result of methods different from those that produced their successes. Typically, however, historical philosophy of science concentrates on the positive cases of scientific achievement.

I have only scratched the surface in discussing how descriptive case studies in the history of science can be relevant to normative issues in the philosophy of science, but will return to the topic in section 7.7. I want now to summarize the elements of descriptive/normative relation in historical philosophy of science that may prove applicable to the general question of the relevance of the descriptive to the normative. The result is a crude schema that is labeled "HPS", for historical philosophy of science:

HPS

1. We select cases of actual scientific practice. Selection is made on the basis of subsequent events in the history of science that have marked the cases as significant contributions to the growth of scientific knowledge.
2. We develop case studies that describe scientific practice.
3. We assume—or this can be argued for—that scientists have generally been successful in achieving the epistemic goals of science.
4. Then the actual methods of the scientists in our case studies are at least an approximation to what the methods ought to be. Within the limitations of the historical record, we describe the scientists' methods.
5. We reflect philosophically on the methods found in the case studies, developing more complex normative models, which can then be applied to other case studies.

This description of HPS is schematic, and its linearity is highly misleading. It seems to suggest that we proceed first by doing history and then by deriving methodological principles. But of course our historiography is unavoidably influenced by expected methodological conclusions. History and philosophy of science should be viewed as part of a dynamic system of recurring influences, best represented not by a sequence of steps, but by a feedback process as in figure 7.1. Methodological conclusions are reached after the historical/methodological loop has been repeatedly run.

The model HPS is only a crude approximation to what actually goes on in historical philosophy of science, but at this point a more faithful model would obscure the relations between descriptive and normative matters that I am trying to illuminate. A more accurate characterization of historical

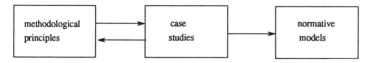

Figure 7.1
HPS: historical philosophy of science.

philosophy of science is found in section 7.7. Let us now compare the simple process just described with what happens in ethical theory.

7.4. Wide Reflective Equilibrium

John Rawls (1971) recommended an ethical method aimed at achieving "reflective equilibrium" of particular moral judgments and general moral principles. This method has been developed further by Norman Daniels (1979) on which most of the following discussion draws. The method of wide reflective equilibrium is described by Daniels as follows (1979, pp. 258ff.):

> The method of wide reflective equilibrium is an attempt to produce coherence in an ordered triple set of beliefs held by a particular person, namely, (a) a set of considered moral judgments, (b) a set of moral principles, and (c) a set of relevant background theories. We begin by collecting the person's initial moral judgments and filter them to include only those of which he is relatively confident and which have been made under conditions conducive to avoiding errors of judgment.... We then propose alternatives sets of moral principles that have varying degrees of "fit" with the moral judgments. We do *not* simply settle for the best fit of principles with judgments, however, which would give us only a *narrow* equilibrium. Instead we advance philosophical arguments intended to bring out the relative strengths and weaknesses of the alternative sets of principles (or competing moral conceptions). These arguments can be constructed as inferences from some set of relevant background theories (I use the term loosely). Assume that some particular set of arguments wins and that the moral agent is persuaded that some set of principles is more acceptable than the others.... We can imagine the agent working back and forth, making adjustments to his considered judgments, his moral principles, and his background theories. In this way he arrives at an equilibrium point that consists of the ordered triple (a), (b), (c).

As with scientific theory choice and historical philosophy of science, we have here a method that is comparative, coarse-grained, and dynamic. The particular moral judgments are not at all like incorrigible intuitions to which moral principles must conform: the judgments can be revised in the light of the principles just as the principles can be revised in the light of the judgments. The revisability of particular moral judgments does not show a complete difference in kind from the empirical evidence used to evaluate scientific theories. For in the first place even observation statements in science are not incorrigible, and in the second place assessment of theories is not usually according to how they explain particular observations, but according to how they explain general classes of facts expressed in empirical generalizations that may well turn out to be false (see chapter 5).

But there is at least a difference in degree between the status of moral judgments and the observational evidence used in assessing scientific theories: moral judgments are, or ought to be, more corrigible. Moral judgments are not constrained by causal interaction with an external environment in the way in which observations are. Although it is not unusual for scientists to throw out pieces of data that they have some reason to believe are defective, most data are taken very seriously. Historical philosophy of science provides an intermediate case of corrigibility. We must be prepared to admit that our interpretation of a particular case study is wrong, or even that for general reasons the case study was not an appropriate one, perhaps because the scientist's description of his or her procedure had been corrupted by unfortunate attention to some misguided philosopher. (Darwin, for example, whose letters and notebooks often show great methodological sophistication, talks at one point in his *Autobiography* of working on true Baconian principles.) Nevertheless, corrigibility is limited by our antecedent conviction that work by the distinguished scientist we have chosen typifies the best scientific research.

A most important aspect of Daniels' characterization of wide reflective equilibrium is the role of (c) a set of background theories. Coherence is to be achieved not only between moral judgments and principles, but also with theories concerning such matters as the nature of human beings and of society. Psychological theories about the actual or possible moral behavior of individuals will play a role in the interplay of particular moral judgments and general principles. But this is only one respect in which the method of wide reflective equilibrium takes us from the descriptive to the normative. The general moral principles that are developed in the move to equilibrium are clearly normative in content, but the status of the particular judgment is ambiguous. True, a moral judgment that a particular sort of action is wrong has normative content, but it functions in the method of wide reflective equilibrium partly as a descriptive report of the attitude of a person toward the sort of action. Through a process of reflection, descriptions of how a person feels about a certain sort of action are supplanted by a judgment of how a person ought to feel about an action.

Empirical background theories can play a particularly important role in the assessment of moral principles when they concern the physical or psychological limitations of human agents. Most ethical theorists accept the principle that "ought" implies "can", so that, conversely, if it is physically impossible for an agent to perform a certain action, then the moral principle that says that the agent ought to perform the action must be rejected. For example, the (false) psychological theory that people are capable of acting only in their own self-interest would require the rejection of an ethical theory that maintained that people have a general obligation to be altruistic. In less extreme cases, we might only have the psychological result that there are certain things that are very hard, but not impossible, for people to do. Then the "ought" implies "can" principle does not have a direct bearing, but the psychological difficulty and resultant costs of carrying out certain actions should figure in our estimation of the coherence of our judgments, principles, and background theories. This is especially clear in the context of explicitly consequentialist ethical theory, where part of the set of consequences to be taken in account in assessing the rightness of an action concerns the psychological effects on the agent.

Let us now attempt to schematize the model for reaching normative conclusions found in Daniels' description of wide reflective equilibrium. The order of steps does not represent any fixed temporal order, but is only meant to suggest a possible way of proceeding. Call the model "WRE", for wide reflective equilibrium:

WRE

1. We have a set of particular moral judgments about what is right or wrong, selected for expected freedom from error.
2. We postulate a number of general moral principles that explain and justify the particular judgments.
3. We attempt to come up with a maximally coherent set of beliefs, consisting not only of the moral judgments and principles, but also taking into account our background theories, especially concerning psychological limitations.
4. We reach a state of reflective equilibrium, and conclude that the acceptance of the moral principles in the final set of beliefs is justified.

As with HPS, this description is misleadingly linear: the process of reaching reflective equilibrium is better represented by the flow chart in figure 7.2. Ethical principles can just as easily provide a starting point as moral judgments. Normative principles are outputs from the system only after repeated adjustments of moral judgments and principles in the light of background theories have been made.

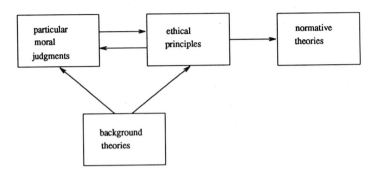

Figure 7.2
WRE: wide reflective equilibrium in ethics.

7.5. HPS, WRE, and the Relevance of Psychology to Logic

We are gradually winding our way toward a general picture of the relation between the descriptive and the normative. HPS (historical philosophy of science) and WRE (wide reflective equilibrium) are important preliminary models for relating the descriptive and the normative in their own spheres, but neither is adequate for answering general questions about the relation of the descriptive and the normative. HPS and WRE neglect essential aspects of another case of going from the descriptive to the normative, involving the relation of psychology and logic. A richer model of the descriptive/normative relation in psychology and logic will be developed in the next section. This richer model for psychology and logic will in turn provide the basis for a general descriptive/normative model.

First, more must be said about the problem of the relevance of psychology to logic. I use the term "logic" broadly, encompassing the study of deductive, inductive, and practical inference. (Practical inference concerns what to do—how to make rational decisions.) These three branches of logic are clearly related to philosophy of science and ethics in some respects. One of the main problems of philosophy of science is the inductive logic of assessing scientific theories, and another concerns the foundations of statistical inference, so my discussion of HPS is not distinct from discussions of inductive inference; and ethics is often concerned with what ethical decisions to make, so it is closely related to practical inference. Hence, HPS and WRE should not be thought of as models taken from some field alien to logic, but merely as examples of explicit characterizations of how descriptive matters can have logical relevance.

Recent empirical work in psychology shows numerous systematic discrepancies between popular inferential practice and accepted logical norms (Tversky and Kahneman, 1974; Kahneman and Tversky, 1979; Nisbett and

Ross, 1980). Such discrepancies elicit three possible responses, which can be crudely characterized as follows:

1. People are dumb. They simply fail to follow the normatively appropriate inferential rules.

2. Psychologists are dumb. They have failed to take into account all the variables affecting human inferences, and once all the factors are taken into account it should be possible to show that people are in fact following the appropriate rules.

3. Logicians are dumb. They are assessing the inferential behavior of human thinkers against the wrong set of normative standards.

In this discussion, I assume the egalitarian position that everybody gets to be dumb some of the time. The problem is to establish a methodology for mediating among people's inductive behavior, psychologists' descriptions of that behavior, and the logicians' normative principles used to judge the appropriateness of inferential behavior.

7.5.1. Limitations of HPS

HPS will not furnish the required methodology. The crucial difference between doing historical philosophy of science and using psychological findings to revise logical principles is the special status of the case studies in HPS. When we select Darwin or Newton for special scrutiny in HPS, we do so with the understanding that the scientific thinking of the subject is exemplary. Subsequent developments in the history of science have warranted our belief that our stellar scientists knew what they were doing, at least tacitly. When the psychologists tell us that people frequently do not take into account regression phenomena (Tversky and Kahneman, 1974), we do not assume that the subjects know what they are doing: instruction in statistics can be expected to change their inferential behavior in desirable ways.

But neither can we find experts in general inferential behavior who are analogous to our exemplary scientists. We need to distinguish between two sorts of experts: those who are expert at performing a task and those who are expert at explicitly saying how a task should be done. The two kinds of expertise need not coincide, as we see in athletics in the contrast between the inarticulate star performer and the pedagogically helpful but athletically inept coach. In HPS, we ought to pay more attention to what the subjects of our case studies do than to what they say they do, since scientists' explicit methodological pronouncements are as likely to be reflections of what they think they are expected to say as they are to be reflections of their methodological practice. In logic, we do not have as clear a set of people certified as experts in their practice, independent of their pronouncements.

We might suppose that for deductive inference we could take mathematicians as our practicing experts, for inductive inference we could take statisticians, and for practical inference we could take high level managers. But in all these cases, practice is severely infected by philosophical views. Intuitionistic mathematicians eschew the use of some classical logical principles; statisticians have grave disputes about the foundations of their work; while practicing statisticians generally use a grab bag of whatever methods—Bayesian, Neyman-Pearson, or Fisher—seem useful in a particular context. With practical logic, the decision-making behavior of high level managers may be uninformative; since to the extent they use formal principles, they probably use ones taught to them in business school by people who are more certified as experts in the logic of decision making than as practicing expert managers. Developing principles in logic, then, is like doing historical philosophy of *social* science. Whereas in natural science there is enough consensus in the scientific community that selection of cases for study is quite uncontentious, the schisms in the various social sciences preclude doing case studies whose validity would be universally accepted. For example, a study of explanation in economics would get different results if the investigator concentrated on Marx's capital theory rather than neoclassical theories. In psychology, one would derive a very different methodological picture from attention to gestalt psychologists' practice rather than behaviorists'. Similarly, logical practice among the alleged experts in deductive, inductive, and practical inference is not sufficiently uniform and historically validated to allow the use of the case study methodology of HPS. Chapter 6 contended that there has been progress in natural science, but its accomplishment is much more problematic in the social sciences and especially in everyday inferential practice. Without a background argument for the sort of progress that underlies our confidence in scientific case studies, we cannot use an HPS methodology in going from psychology to logic.

Psychological studies might nevertheless be useful in determining how people do or perhaps should reason; but as is not the case in HPS, we shall not be able to move to normative judgments primarily on the basis of the studies. Of course, in historical philosophy of science, we do not immediately leap from "is" to "ought" either. But there the leap is at least indirectly possible through assumptions about the nature of the growth of scientific knowledge.

7.5.2. Relevance of WRE for Psychology and Logic

Unlike HPS, the model based on wide reflective equilibrium resembles the psychology/logic problem in the absence of case studies or particular moral judgments with assumed prior validity. Hence the justification of ethical principles is much shakier than the justification of methodological principles in the philosophy of science. Like particular moral judgments, common inferential practice is revisable in the light of overriding normative principles. Just as in WRE we have a dynamic of particular judgments and general moral principles, so in the psychology/logic case we can look for a process of development of inferential practice and normative logical principles as the result of critical assessment of both. In the logical case as in the ethical, we are seeking a wide rather than a narrow reflective equilibrium. This means that we want coherence not only of inferential practice and normative principles but also of both of these with background theories and beliefs.

The relevant background information is of two kinds. First, we need an account of the inferential capacities of human beings. As Goldman (1978) has suggested, the principle of "ought" implies "can" is relevant to epistemology and logic as well as ethics. We should not demand of a reasoner inferential performance that exceeds the general psychological abilities of human beings. For example, we cannot prescribe that cognizers believe all the logical consequences of their beliefs, since none of us has infinite storage or inferential capacity. In the same spirit, we do not want to prescribe normative logical principles that are too horribly difficult for humans to follow. What does "too difficult" mean here? To answer that, we need a second kind of background information, concerning the goals of the inferential behavior. With deductive and inductive inference, we have the minimal goals of achieving true beliefs and avoiding false ones, but that is a much too simple view of the matter. Other epistemic goals include achieving explanations and holistically coherent belief systems. Much of scientific knowledge, as well as most of everyday knowledge, has instrumental import, so that what deductive and inductive strategies we adopt will depend in part on our practical aims. Deductive or inductive principles that are inordinately costly in psychological terms may be supplanted by principles that prima facie are intellectually inferior. Especially in the logic of decision making we see the relevance of the psychological and social limitations on human cognition to the question of what standards are normatively correct. As March (1978) points out, the application of apparently optimal decision strategies may not be optimal given restraints on human abilities.

The application of WRE to the psychology/logic case thus suggests that we should strive to reach reflective equilibrium among the following four factors:

a. common inferential practice,
b. normative logical principles,

c. background theories about the cognitive capacities and limitations of human beings, and

d. background views about the goals of inferential behavior.

However, this is still a too simple account of the matter, for in disputes about logical principles we often find other, more philosophical concerns brought to bear. For example, debates about the foundations of statistical inference often concern in part what philosophical interpretation of the probability calculus should be adopted: proponents and critics of Bayesianism debate the merits of subjective probabilities versus objective logical or frequentist views. Dummett (1978) argues for intuitionistic logic and mathematics largely on the basis of verificationist theories of meaning. Thus we have to add to the matrix of elements taken into account in achieving reflective equilibrium

e. background philosophical theories.

7.5.3. Narrow Reflective Equilibrium?

Cohen (1981a) asserts without argument that the psychology/logic case involves a narrow reflective equilibrium. He compares the case of fitting logical principles with logical practice to devising a grammar that fits a population's linguistic practice. The latter is indeed a case of narrow reflective equilibrium (Daniels, 1980): we are only concerned with a fit between principles and practice, and background theories do not play a role. But in constructing a set of logical principles we are doing much more than simply matching up with actual practice. Practice can improved. Logical practice has improved enormously with the developments in deductive, inductive, and practical logic of the past several hundred years. In contrast, linguists do not aim to improve the overall grammar of a linguistic population, since their task is descriptive. The logician, on the other hand, is concerned to develop a set of principles that is inferentially optimal given the cognitive limitations of reasoners. This requires reference to background psychological and philosophical theories and to the goals of inferential behavior. Hence logical principles could only be arrived at by a process of wide reflective equilibrium.

In his replies to commentators, Cohen (1981b) gives two reasons for considering narrow rather than wide reflective equilibrium. He says that the background issues about philosophical problems are too controversial and too fine-grained to be brought to bear on experimental studies of human rationality. All that follows from this is that establishing logical principles using wide reflective equilibrium will be difficult, since it requires at least provisional answers to hard philosophical questions that lurk in the background of disputes about logical principles. But we already know from the longevity and complexity of disputes about inductive and deductive principles that the establishment of such principles is never easy. We cannot evade philosophical issues about meaning, ontology, and inferential goals. Consideration of these issues, as well as background psychological theories, requires wide reflective equilibrium, rather than narrow.

In a situation where narrow reflective equilibrium is sought, the descriptive inputs are relatively incorrigible. The linguist is concerned to report grammatical practice, not to reform it. Similarly, in historical philosophy of science, our concern is not usually to say what the exemplary scientists should have done. Another case of relative incorrigibility is scientific theory choice, where, despite being theory-laden, observations are not typically overridden. In contrast, in ethics, where we seek wide reflective equilibrium, we expect background knowledge and the improvment of principles to lead to revision and improvement in intuitive ethical judgments. Similarly in logic and psychology, the descriptive input is subject to change as education brings about improvement in inferential practice. Cohen's assumption that basic inferential practice must be rational is as insupportable as intuitionism in ethics.

7.6. From Psychology to Logic: Criteria for Inferential Systems

7.6.1. First Approximation: FPL

We can now give a rough characterization of what the above discussion suggests is the appropriate methodology for assessing the relevance of psychological studies to normative principles. The following model, called "FPL" for "from psychology to logic", suggests a possible procedure for attempting to resolve disputes about normative principles. As with HPS and WRE, the steps have no rigid temporal significance.

FPL

1. We do empirical studies to describe inferential behavior.
2. We generate sets of logical principles that explain and justify that inferential behavior.
3. When inferential behavior deviates from logical norms, we consider whether new norms are needed or whether we can just revise inferential behavior to bring it in line with existing norms.
4. This consideration depends on somehow developing a maximally coherent set of beliefs about people's actual behavior, their optimal behavior given their cognitive limitations and the goals of inferential behavior, and background philosophical issues.
5. The logical principles among the maximally coherent set of beliefs are then deemed to be justified.

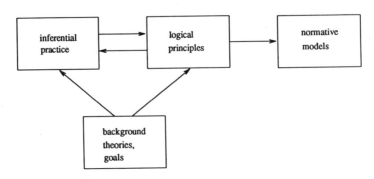

Figure 7.3
FPL: from psychology to logic.

Once again, we have a process whose dynamic features are best represented in a flow chart, as in figure 7.3.

By analogy with WRE, we repeatedly adjust logical practice and principles in the light of background theories until reflective equilibrium is
reached; then the principles arrived at in the equilibrium state are "out-
putted" as normatively correct. But we cannot escape asking: What is it
that determines that we have reached a state of reflective equilibrium? In
the linear description of FPL, we must ask what it is to reach step 4 and
achieve a "maximally coherent" set of beliefs. Without an account of how
to evaluate coherence among practice, principles, goals, and background
theories, FPL has little content. I shall now describe a list of criteria
for assessing the coherence of such a set of beliefs, then argue that the
existence of such a set renders any discussion of reflective equilibrium
redundant.

7.6.2. Criteria for Coherence
An inferential system is a matrix of four elements: normative principles,
descriptions of inferential practice, inferential goals, and background psychological and philosophical theories. How do we assess the coherence of
such a system? Most important, how can we say that one system is more
coherent than another? I propose three main criteria: *robustness, accommodation,* and *efficacy.* A system is robust if its normative principles account for
inferential practice in a wide range of situations. Robustness in inferential
systems is analogous to consilience in theory choice, where a theory is
consilient if it explains a wide range of facts (see chapter 5). In a robust
system, our normative principles justify and explain a variety of inferential
behavior. However, we do not expect the principles to account for all
inferential behavior, since we need to leave open the possibility that even
after considerable reflection, people's behavior still deviates from logical

norms. We can accommodate such behavior by using background psychological theory to explain why people sometimes deviate from the
system's logical norms. Thus accommodation provides a criterion supplemental to robustness: to the extent that principles do not robustly account
for inferential practice, we expect to be able to explain that practice by
reference to psychological factors that interfere with the application of
logical principles; the deviant practice is thereby accommodated. This criterion is nontrivial, for our current psychological theories may lack the
resources to explain deviations from inferential principles.

By efficacy of a system, I mean the extent to which the principles and
practices of a system lead to satisfaction of the relevant inferential goals.
This is in part an empirical matter. We must observe how well principles
enable us to satisfy such goals as preserving truth in deduction, achieving
explanatory theories in induction, and meeting human needs in practical
inference. Efficacy also should take into account how easily principles will
be applicable given human information processing mechanisms; for this
information, we depend on background psychological theories.

Schematically, we can summarize these three criteria by the following
questions:

1. Robustness: to what extent do the normative principles account for
inductive practice?
2. Accommodation: to what extent do available background theories
account for deviations of inductive practice from the normative
principles?
3. Efficacy: given background theories, to what extent does following
the normative principles promote the satisfaction of the inferential
goals?

These criteria can be used to assess the comparative coherence of competing systems. In a given domain, we can assume that background theories
and goals will be common to competing systems, and this gives us some
hope of reaching an objective conclusion that one system is more coherent
than the other. In particular, comparison of the efficacy of the two systems
may enable us to make choice of systems more than a matter of purely
internal coherence. Choice will obviously be highly complex, with difficult
trade-offs between pairs of criteria, but nevertheless may be determinate
and objective. The core, then, of the method FPL is development of an
inferential system that is highly coherent according to the above criteria.

7.6.3. Beyond Reflective Equilibrium

But now we can abandon the presumption that the achievement of reflective equilibrium is somehow essential to the justification of logical norms.
The notion of reflective equilibrium has been useful in getting us to our

current model FPL, since it has enabled us to elucidate the Goodmanian process of mutually adjusting principles and practice, while also taking into account background theories. But we can quickly see that the notion of equilibrium is of no help in justifying principles.

The problem, as Stich and Nisbett (1980) pointed out, is just that equilibrium may be too easily reached. An individual may reach reflective equilibrium while possessing an inferential system that is resoundingly nonefficacious: people can rest contentedly with the gambler's and other fallacies. Stich and Nisbett's move to discussion of expert reflective equilibrium is of no help, since they recognize that the experts can achieve specious equilibria too. At the end of their paper, they seem reduced to the relativist conclusion that rational resolution of debates between conservative experts and "cognitive rebels" may be impossible.

This conclusion is avoided by seeing that the justification of a set of normative principles is based, not on the reflective equilibrium of any individual or group, but on the place of the principles in a defensible inferential system. Defense is based on arguments that the system is coherent according to the criteria discussed above. General and expert inferential behaviors are relevant, since their description is part of inferential practice that is one component of the system S. But other factors besides inferential practice play a role in determining which S and set of normative principles will be optimal. The criteria of accommodation allow that we may well expect to have general or expert inferential behavior that does not conform to the normative principles.

If one takes the notion of reflective equilibrium too seriously, one is pushed to unsatisfactory answers to the question: *Whose* reflective equilibrium? There are two possible answers, one populist and one elitist. The populist strategy, favored by Cohen (1981a), is to emphasize the reflective equilibrium of the average person. This founders, because education in sophisticated inferential techniques can be expected to provide the individual with a much more efficacious system. The elitist strategy, favored by Stich and Nisbett (1980), is to emphasize the reflective equilibrium of experts. This, too, is inadequate, for it leaves us no way of saying why the experts should be in equilibrium, or of mediating disputes among experts. On my account, the experts—or for that matter ordinary persons—ought to have their principles and practices in equilibrium if they have a highly coherent inferential system. Coherence is to be evaluated according to criteria to which the achievement of reflective equilibrium is irrelevant. What we are really after is not equilibrium, but progress: the development of better and better inferential systems. Improvement of inductive systems may well come about through an oscillating process of richer and more efficacious principles, practices, theories, and goals even if during the process we never achieve equilibrium.

Compare scientific theory choice. Someone might claim that a theory becomes acceptable when one is able to reach a "reflective equilibrium" between the theory and the observations it is supposed to explain. But that would clearly obscure the nature of the justificatory process. As we saw in chapter 5, what makes the theory acceptable is that it provides a better explanation of the evidence than competing theories, according to criteria such as explanatory breadth, simplicity, and analogy. Reflective equilibrium would then be a mere epiphenomenon of the justified acceptance of the theory. Similarly, once we can provide criteria for assessing logical norms vis-à-vis competing inferential systems, reflective equilibrium is seen not to be an essential feature of the justification of those norms. At best, the notion of reflective equilibrium provides a metaphor for describing the complex process, better represented in figure 7.3, of how the development of a justified system of logical norms involves the interaction of numerous components including descriptions of inductive practice.

I have argued that reflective equilibrium—Goodman's fit between inferential practice and normative principles—is not in itself a source of justification of the principles. It may, however, provide an indirect way of telling what principles are justified at a particular time. The point here is social, not epistemological: the experts or others being in reflective equilibrium does not justify anything; for this, we need arguments that the inferential system in question is optimal with respect to the criteria discussed. However, when we face the practical problem of deciding what are most likely to be the best logical principles to use, we would be wise to follow the advice of Stich and Nisbett and consult the inferential experts. Since they are more familiar with alternative inferential practices, background theories, and inferential goals than are ordinary people, experts are more likely to have highly coherent inference systems. To the extent that the experts can be identified by the robustness, accommodation, and efficacy of their inference principles, my proposal converges with that of Stich and Nisbett.

The metamethodological question naturally arises: What legitimates the three proposed criteria for inferential coherence? Here we have a development from the descriptive to the normative at a higher level: I have advocated these criteria because they seem to be the ones actually used when we set out to evaluate inferential practices, and because they seem to promote the establishment of the sorts of inferential principles we want. In short, the criteria are, in an extended sense, robust and efficacious. There is no circularity here of the sort that is found in inductive justifications of induction. We have long since abandoned the search for a full foundationalist justification of inferential practice (cf. Rescher, 1977).

It might be argued that efficacy is all we really need: if we know that a method accomplished inferential goals, why worry about who uses it and why? Goldman (1986) recommends the evaluation of methodological rules according to such performance criteria as reliability, power, and speed, preferring, for example, rules that produce a high ratio of true beliefs to false ones. The problem with this proposal is that such criteria of efficacy are often very hard to apply: how could we ever know what kind of truth ratio we get from inference to the best explanation? Section 8.1 illustrates an approach to justifying this kind of inference that emphasizes robustness.

7.6.4. On Deductive Logic

Resnik (1985) has lucidly criticized attempts such as the above to show the relevance of psychology to deductive logic. He argues that the major concern of logicians is to characterize what arguments we should accept, a task independent of the social project of improving people's reasoning. Logicians are concerned with whether a particular kind of inference is valid, leading only from true premises to true conclusions, not with how many people employ it or how hard it is for them to do so.

Formal logic since Frege and Russell has been an impressive research program, yielding techniques for formalizing many different kinds of deductive arguments and a set of powerful mathematical tools for analyzing logical systems. As such, it is immune from the psychological considerations that I have claimed are relevant to selection of logical principles. But that immunity comes at the price of narrow applicability. The study of reasoning has always been a centerpiece of philosophy, but formal deductive logic captures so little of what is interesting about reasoning that it would be a grave mistake to take it as paradigmatic. At best, logic only tells you what you may infer from a given set of premises, not which of the infinite set of consequences you should infer. To answer such questions even deductive logic has to become more pragmatic, looking at the goals of the reasoning process. These goals encompass much more than just preserving truth: we want to reach interesting and helpful conclusions. Unlike their nineteen-century counterparts, twentieth-century logicians say that such pragmatic matters are no concern of theirs. The result of the mathematicization of logic has been loss of contact with the great epistemological concern about how knowledge can be made to grow. As Harman (1986) and Goldman (1986) argue, current studies in deductive logic have little to do with reasoning. For the purposes of epistemology and the philosophy of science, reasoning, not formal logic, is what needs to be studied. Logic fails as an epistemological ideal not just because it is difficult for people to do right—in that case they might just be urged to try harder—but because it is a different sort of enterprise from most of what is involved in the growth of knowledge.

7.7. From the Descriptive to the Normative: A General Model

I have now discussed three domains in which descriptive findings have been found relevant to normative issues, and developed for the third case of psychology and logic an elaborate new model of the descriptive/normative relation. I now want to propose a fully general model that subsumes all the elements of going from the descriptive to the normative so far discussed. I call the model "FDN", for "from the descriptive to the normative." To avoid misleading linearity, I shall not state it as a series of steps. I do not want to suggest that reaching normative conclusions from descriptive information is always a "bottom-up" procedure, starting with descriptive matters and proceeding to normative principles. Rather, we often proceed "top-down" as well, with our normative principles guiding what empirical information is gathered.

The dynamics of FDN are better represented in figure 7.4, which illustrates how one can start simultaneously with normative principles and descriptive practices. As in the psychology/logic case of FPL, these principles and practices, as well as background theories, constitute a system that must be evaluated according to plausible criteria. Robustness, accommodation, and efficacy are our best current candidates for such criteria, since they played such an important role in the most elaborate model so far developed, FPL. The result of application of such criteria can be not only improved principles but also improved practices, as people strive to live up to normative principles. As the system repeats, new principles and practices are considered again. Practices and principles can be improved in parallel,

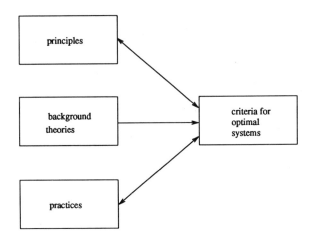

Figure 7.4
FDN: from the descriptive to the normative.

and such improvement can go on without there ever being any output from the system as there is in figures 7.1–7.3.

The application of the general model FDN will be illustrated in chapter 8 with the justification of inference to the best explanation. Since that application primarily concerns the philosophy of science, I shall now provide a fuller account of the method of historical philosophy of science.

Section 7.3 contained a rough account of how historical case studies can play a role in developing normative methodological principles in philosophy of science. The richer models FPL and FDN suggest several additions. Of the criteria for evaluating inferential systems in FPL, only robustness is implicitly used in the earlier model HPS, when we ask what methodological principles best characterize the actual practice of scientists described in case studies. But in more sophisticated studies in historical philsophy of science, accommodation and efficacy also play important roles. These roles may not be evident in the published studies, but they underlie selection of historical materials in the first place.

We saw above that historical philosophy of science is historically selective, both for which scientists are studied and for what aspects of their work are considered. Landmark scientific investigations are chosen because these are thought to have contributed greatly to the goals of inquiry. Even if no explicit statement of these goals is made, the historical philosopher of science naturally chooses for study works that have had the greatest impact on subsequent science. It is therefore presumed that the methodological principles to be discovered in the selected case studies promote the satisfaction of the goals of scientific inquiry. Thus, in the terminology of FPL, there are grounds for presuming the methodological principles to be efficacious. Moreover, by selecting only the exemplary aspects of scientific practice for study, we have dodged problems of accommodation, since other cases of deviation from derived methodological principles are largely ignored. We assume that a full account could satisfy the criterion of accommodation by accounting for deviant practices using background theories. For example, we might seek a historical, psychological, or sociological explanation for Newton's work in alchemy, accounting for its deviation from methodological principles we might derive from his more respected work in mechanics and optics. Historical philosophy of science is thus much more complicated than simply deriving methodological principles from robust scientific practice. Implicit judgments of efficacy and accommodation must also be made.

The establishment of logical or methodological principles is not a one-shot derivation from existing practices, principles, theories, and goals. Settlement of issues in logic and philosophy of science requires assessment of competing systems, dynamically developed through a dialectic of principles and practices against a backdrop of goals and theories. We seek mutually reinforcing improvement in all the components of the logical or methodological system, revising not only principles and practices, but also background theories and goals. Epistemological progress depends on advances on all fronts.

7.8. The Role of Computational Studies

Assuming that FDN is a valid model for developing normative conclusions on the basis of descriptive studies, how should one proceed? Historical case studies are of great value, but there are severe problems in using them systematically to test philosophical ideas. A recent attempt has been made to systematize philosophical theories about the growth of scientific knowledge so that they can be tested more rigorously against the historical record (Laudan et al., 1986). But it does not appear to be possible to do more than look for a qualitative fit between theories and historical practices.

As chapter 10 discusses further, computational studies offer a more intensive way of testing the consequences of views about the nature of science. Encoding a methodology in an artificial intelligence program makes possible computational tests of the efficacy of various ideas about how knowledge grows. It would be wonderful to have specifications of the methodological ideas of Kuhn, Popper, and other theorists that were complete and specific enough to be implemented computationally. Comparative runs on sample problems and observations in selected domains could then establish which sets of ideas are most efficacious over time in adding to the stock of scientific knowledge.

More modestly, PI's computer simulations have already proved valuable for testing ideas about knowledge generation. For example, early work on conceptual combination showed the need for tightly constraining when new combined concepts are formed. Otherwise, the system quickly began to fill up with redundant concepts. Writing LISP code for combining the concepts of sound and wave into sound-wave was not difficult, but trivial problems occurred, such as the tendency of the program to produce such idiocies as sound-sound-wave, a completely uninteresting conceptual combination. Without further constraints, any run of PI would have been inundated with clutter. Fortunately, a principled constraint was found: PI now forms a new combined concept only when some conflict has to be reconciled between the existing concepts. There is no reason to keep around such combined concepts as "brown cow" or "red apple", since the combinations do not violate any of our initial expectations. In contrast, "striped apple", "femininist bank teller", and "sound wave" require reconciliation of prior default expectations so PI keeps them around as useful combinations. (As section 4.3 described, the conflict in the latter case arises because sound flows out spherically, whereas familiar waves such as those in water flow in a single plane; this conflict was pointed out by Vitruvius.)

Another case where computational studies were invaluable in determining the efficacy of kinds of induction was described in section 4.2.4. In an earlier version, PI did a kind of abduction to rules to explain particular instances. This worked fine for a few examples that were used to test the particular inference, but later runs on a larger knowledge base quickly showed that rule abduction from instances was much too profligate, and it was replaced by the much more constrained kind of rule formation from abduced instances. Thus a computational approach to the philosophy of science can be very useful in developing normative accounts of knowledge generation.

7.9. Irrationality

To be rational is to follow established normative principles; to be irrational is to violate them. If the above methodology is successful in establishing principles of reasoning, we can castigate as irrational behavior that violates them. In contrast, Quine (1960) and others have urged a "principle of charity", according to which we should reinterpret people's utterances and other behaviors in such a way as to understand them as acting rationally. Thagard and Nisbett (1983) argued that most such principles of charity are too strong, preventing us from recognizing as irrational forms of deductive, inductive, and practical reasoning that clearly are in violation of norms. We defended the following modest principle of charity:

> Do not judge people to be irrational unless you have an empirically justified account of what they are doing when they violate normative standards.

This principle prevents us from judging people to be in violation of logical principles when they may simply be following principles other than those we have in mind. For example, a deductive logician might illegitimately accuse someone of committing the fallacy of affirming the consequent by arguing **"If p then q, q, therefore p."** when the kind of reasoning actually being employed is abduction. In order to judge someone as irrational, we should be able to say why they are doing what they are doing in violation of logical principles. We will see in chapter 9, for example, how proponents of astrology and other pseudosciences can be understood as irrationally using natural but nonefficacious kinds of thinking.

7.10. Summary

Logic and philosophy of science are normative disciplines concerned with how people ought to reason. But normative principles can be based in part on descriptions of how people do reason and science is done. However, Goodman's proposal to base justification of normative principles on a process of reaching reflective equilibrium between principles and practice presumes too direct a link between the descriptive and the normative. Assessment of inferential principles requires evaluation of whole inferential systems, including principles, description of practices, and background theories and goals. This evaluation employs such criteria as robustness, accommodation, and efficacy. Similar criteria are also employed implicitly in historical philosophy of science. Application of criteria for evaluating inferential or methodological systems provides an objective method for applying descriptive studies in the establishment of normative principles. This method is general enough for use in computational philosophy of science, and computational techniques are potentially very valuable for judging efficacy. Once normative principles are established, we have grounds for judging violators of those principles to be irrational.

Chapter 8
Justification and Truth

The discussion of abduction and inference to the best explanation in chapters 4 and 5 was largely descriptive. But the descriptive/normative methodology developed in the last section now makes it possible to consider the justification of these kinds of inference. The first section of this chapter argues that their use by scientists and people in general is indeed justified. Then the separate question of whether inference to the best explanation leads to truth is taken up in the context of a defense of scientific realism, the view that science in general leads to truth. Finally, I argue that a degree of methodological conservatism is a consequence of the earlier computational account of the nature of scientific knowledge.

8.1. The Justification of Inference to the Best Explanation

8.1.1. How Not to Justify Inference to the Best Explanation
Chapter 5 described criteria used by scientists to assess the best explanation, and showed the compatibility of the historically derived account of theory choice with the descriptive computational view that scientists' theories are processing systems. But how might we reach the normative conclusion that scientists ought or ought not to use inference to the best explanation? Before presenting an account of how inference to the best explanation can be justified in accord with the methodology of chapter 7, I shall criticize the account given by Fumerton (1980) of what it would take to justify inference to the best explanation, and at the same time refute his argument that reasoning to the best explanation is subordinate to induction by simple enumeration. (This is a version of the form of inference called "generalization" in chapter 4, reaching a general conclusion from examples.)

Philosophical logicians tend to search for one fundamental sort of inductive rule. Harman (1965, 1973) has argued that inference to the best explanation is fundamental, and induction by simple enumeration is derivative. We saw in section 4.2.4 that not all inductive inference is concerned with explanation. More recently, Fumerton (1980) has argued that there is no process of reasoning to the best explanation distinct from straight-forward induction by simple enumeration and deduction.

Some terminological clarification must precede further discussion. Fumerton discusses "inductive reasoning" as an alternative to reasoning to the best explanation, meaning by the term what is more usually called induction by simple enumeration or what earlier chapters called generalization. I follow another common usage in speaking of both inference to generalizations by enumeration of instances and inference to the best explanation as kinds of inductive reasoning. Statistical inference provides examples of other kinds.

Fumerton starts (1980, p. 591) by schematizing inference to the best explanation as

Q is the case.
If P were the case, then Q would be the case.
Therefore, P is the case.

He has no difficulty in showing that this sort of abductive schema will license many bad arguments, unless it is buttressed with additional evidence that converts the inference into a combination of induction (by enumeration) and deduction. However, his arguments are not so effective against the more sophisticated formulation of inference to the best explanation we saw in chapter 5.

Fumerton recognizes that we need to provide criteria for assessing the best explanation. He considers the criteria of consilience, simplicity, and analogy, offered in Thagard (1978a) and in chapter 5, and claims, "The relevant epistemological question is whether the more consilient, simpler, more analogous theory is, ceteris paribus [other things being equal], more likely to be true" (Fumerton, 1980, p. 596). He then goes on to argue that the need to justify such criteria shows that inference to the best explanation is dependent on enumerative induction. He continues (p. 596), "If ... we are justified in trusting more consilient theories, ceteris paribus, only because for the most part more consilient theories have turned out to be more successful, then inferring that the correct explanation is, ceteris paribus, the most consilient explanation would amount to a straightforward instance of reasoning by enumerative induction."

This attempt to reduce inference to the best explanation to enumerative induction is defective at several levels. Reductions of inference rules do not generally show that there is anything dependent about the rules reduced. We can easily do deductive logic without *modus ponens*, so long as we have rules such as *modus tollens*, contraposition, and double negation, but this in no way shows that modus tolens is parasitical. Fumerton's argument against the simple pattern of reasoning displayed above is effective because he shows that enumerative inductive and deductive reasoning is needed if the schema is to represent valid inferences. His argument about inference to the best explanation based on my criteria, on the other hand, does not show a similar dependence. There must be criteria for the best explanation, but it is not part of the premises of an argument to the best explanation that the criteria lead to truth, just as it is not part of the premises of enumerative induction or of deduction that these forms of reasoning lead to truth.

Inference to the best explanation cannot be justified by enumerative induction since there are many counterexamples. We can easily find cases where scientists were led from true premises and a legitimate selection of the best explanation to a theory we now know to be false. Newtonian mechanics, the wave and particle theories of light, the phlogiston theory of combustion, and numerous other historically important theories were inferable from true premises at one time, so the legitimacy of inference to the best explanation would be suspect indeed if it rested on simple enumeration. Whewell thought that consilience was a virtual guarantee of truth, but history has seen his favorite examples of consilience superseded by still better explanations. This is not cause for despair about either the efficacy of inference to the best explanation or the ability of science to achieve truth; but it is enough to refute Fumerton's claim that inference to the best explanation must be based on enumerative induction from cases where truth has been achieved. Like theory choice in science, justification of a form of inference is comparative, requiring showing that it is better than alternatives.

If inference to the best explanation were parasitical on enumerative induction, we ought to be able to recast the Darwin, Lavoisier, and other examples in chapter 5 in terms of a simpler form of reasoning. But it is totally mysterious how we could infer the claims that evolution has occurred by natural selection and that light consists of nonobservable waves by an enumerative induction. In contrast, inference to the best explanation allows the postulation of nonobservable events and processes.

A final problem with Fumerton's proposal to make the validity of inference to the best explanation dependent on the validity of enumerative induction is that it leaves unanswered the question of how enumerative induction is justified. On pain of circularity, we cannot justify enumerative induction by describing instances of its past success, so why should we have to justify inference to the best explanation in such terms? A more sophisticated justification of each type of inference is needed.

8.1.2. Alternative Justification
The descriptive/normative methodology of chapter 7 evaluates inferential systems, consisting of principles, practices, and background theories and goals, according to the criteria of robustness, accommodation, and efficacy.

Abduction and inference to the best explanation fare well on the criterion of robustness, according to which we want inferential principles to capture much of inferential practice. We saw in chapter 4 that abduction is pervasive in ordinary and scientific reasoning. Ordinary people appear to be less adept at evaluating explanations in order to infer the best. But the scientific case studies in chapter 5 were only a small sample of a vast population of cases either where scientists explicitly give arguments to the best explanation or where their arguments can easily be reconstrued as such.

For instance, it is common for a theory to be supported by some novel prediction that has been confirmed by observation. But what makes a confirmed prediction interesting is that it signals the extension of the explanatory apparatus of a theory to some new class of facts, increasing its consilience. Prediction of observations is not in itself the mark of a good theory. We want prediction of important observations, that is, ones that signal the application of the theory to new classes of facts. Moreover, mere prediction should not be enough to convince us of the empirical applicability of a theory, since we need to know how the theory generates the predictions it does. A theory is more than a black box for generating predictions; it also serves to characterize the causal mechanisms that are the basis of the predictions. Prediction without explanation is theoretically vapid, whereas, with examples such as Darwin's theory of evolution, there are important cases of explanation without much prediction. Hence the frequency with which scientists cite predictions rather than explanations in support of their theories does not undermine the robustness of inference to the best explanation. Inference to the best explanation is something that people can actually do, unlike more abstract and mathematical forms of reasoning. In contrast, Bayesian accounts of theory choice, which assume elaborate probabilistic mechanisms for which there is no psychological evidence, lack this descriptive robustness.

Van Fraassen (1980) argues that we cannot tell whether scientists are using inference to the best explanation or merely defending their theories as more empirically adequate than alternatives. Similarly, Lloyd (1983) contends that for Darwin explanation was not a central concern, and his apparently Whewellian talk of explaining classes of facts was just a matter of the theory being empirically adequate for different sets of phenomena. But Darwin's own statements belie this interpretation, as he frequently cites the explanatory merits of the theory of evolution by natural selection as evidence of its truth (Darwin, 1962, pp. 92, 476; 1903, vol. 1, p. 455). Darwin's writings mark him as a scientific realist. Recker (1987) contends that Darwin's argument in the *Origin* was intended to defend the "causal efficacy" of natural selection and that pointing out its explanatory power was only one part of this argument. Separate, according to Recker, was Darwin's use of analogy to show independently that natural selection was a true cause. Darwin's own statements, however, suggest that that he was a follower of Whewell on this methodological issue, holding that the explanatory power of natural selection is all that is needed to show that it is a true cause (Thagard, 1977a).

People, including scientists, do not always use inference to the best explanation to provide a more thorough evaluation of their abductions. According to the accommodation criterion of my descriptive/normative methodology, we should be able to give psychological explanations for such deviations, to rule out the hypothesis that people are not using some alternative form of inference. Recent research of Kunda (1987) provides such explanations. She shows how theory formation and evaluation is systematically affected by motivation: people make inferences on less evidence when they are motivated to reach a conclusion. For example, coffee drinkers are less prone to accept the hypothesis that coffee causes cancer. People will not always arrive at the best explanation according to criteria such as consilience, since their desire to reach a conclusion favorable to them may lead them to consider only part of the relevant evidence and only some of the alternative theories. As chapter 10 discusses, scientists are also not immune from motivationally biasing their inferences to the best explanation. A full application of the criterion of accommodation would require looking at specific cases when scientists have failed to infer the best explanation and explaining their failure by their use of motivated inference or some other psychologically plausible process.

The most difficult criterion to apply to the justification of abduction and inference to the best explanation is efficacy, according to which our inferential principles should promote the satisfaction of our inferential goals. But what are the goals of scientific theory choice, and, even more generally, what are the aims of scientific inquiry?

Efficacy of abduction must be judged differently from efficacy of inference to the best explanation, since their functions are different. Abduction only generates hypotheses, whereas inference to the best explanation evaluates them. All we should expect of abduction, therefore, is that it tend to produce hypotheses that have some chance of turning out to be the best explanation. Abduction of the sorts discussed in chapter 4 will always be to hypotheses that explain at least something and therefore have at least a bit of initial plausibility. In this respect abduction is clearly more efficacious than blind generation of hypotheses, which seems to be the main alternative.

With inference to the best explanation, the stakes are much higher. The three most often cited goals we hope to achieve in selecting a scientific theory are prediction, explanation, and truth. I have already argued that the goal of prediction can be subsumed under that of explanation, so I shall not discuss it further. Of the trio of possible goals, by far the most problematic is truth. On the correspondence theory of truth, which dates back to Aristotle, a statement is true if it corresponds to a real state of the world. Philosophers have not made much progress in characterizing what states of the world are, or what correspondence means. Even if we could say more fully what truth is, it seems impossible to construct a convincing direct argument that inference to the best explanation, including criteria such as consilience and simplicity, leads to the acceptance of true theories. For we do not have any immediate way of determining that our theories are true, aside from saying that they are best explanations. Fortunately, any other theory of theory choice will have the same problem, so inference to the best explanation is at least not less efficacious with respect to truth than other methodologies. Goldman (1986) has argued that justification is based on reliability: methods are justified if they result in a satisfactory ratio of true beliefs to false beliefs. This seems appropriate for simple processes such as perceptual ones, but has no apparent application to theoretical knowledge. Because of its robustness and other properties, however, inference to the best explanation can be justifiable in a way that is independent of the question of whether it leads to truth. This will be important for the argument in the next section about scientific realism. (Some philosophers take it as part of the definition of "explanation" that only a true theory can explain. My usage, compatible with how scientists such as Darwin write when defending their theories, allows explanation to provide evidence for truth without presupposing it.)

An argument that inference to the best explanation leads to truth can be constructed much more indirectly. If we can show that scientific inquiry in general leads to truth, and that inference to the best explanation is a central part of that inquiry, then we can conclude that inference to the best explanation leads to truth. The doctrine that scientific inquiry leads to truth is called *scientific realism*, and will be defended in the next section.

We are left with the aim of explanation. It is not as trivial as it sounds to claim that inference to the best explanation promotes, better than other inferential strategies, the scientific aim of developing explanatory theories. The account of inference to the best explanation given in chapter 5 sets out more explicitly than other accounts how to evaluate the explanatory successes of theories, showing how the individual criteria of consilience, simplicity, and analogy are each intimately linked with explanation. Since inference to the best explanation is structured to maximize the goal of explanation, including prediction, we can expect it to be highly efficacious with respect to those goals, and the historical record suggests that it has been. Thus use of inference to the best explanation is justified in accord with the methodology of chapter 7.

8.2. Scientific Realism

Many scientists, particularly social scientists, assume a look of embarassment when a philosopher or kindred soul mentions the word "truth". But it remains a central question in the philosophy of science whether science aims at more than the explanation and prediction of phenomena and intends to describe the world as it "really" is. Controversy has raged between scientific realists, who maintain that science aims for and achieves at least approximate truths, and others who maintain that science is only concerned with instrumental success or with showing that a given theory is empirically adequate with respect to observable phenomena. Recent critics of scientific realism include van Fraassen (1980) and Laudan (1981). Its defenders include, for example, Boyd (1981), Putnam (1975), Hausman (1982), and various authors in the work edited by Churchland and Hooker (1985). A novel, hybrid position, supporting realism about theoretical entities but not about theoretical laws, has been defended by Cartwright (1983) and Hacking (1983).

Realists typically justify their position by an inference to the best explanation, saying that the view according to which science aims for and sometimes achieves approximately true accounts of the world makes much better sense of the daily practice and historical progress of science than do antirealist positions. I shall construct and defend an elaborated version of that argument. First, however, I shall show that my computational account of theories is compatible with both realist and nonrealist views.

8.2.1. Realism and Computation

Any account of the nature of scientific theories should be amenable to both realist and nonrealist construals. Consider, for example, the syntactic view of theories discussed in chapter 3, which takes a theory to be a set of sentences in a deductive formal system. This view can be construed realistically by supposing that theoretical sentences, even those containing theoretical terms like "electron", can be accepted as true or false. Or it can be construed instrumentally, treating a theory as merely a tool for deductively making predictions. Similarly, the set-theoretic view can be applied realistically, saying that the models (in the set-theoretic sense) that the theory specifies include models of real things, including theoretical entities. Or, nonrealist proponents of the set-theoretic view, such as van Fraassen (1980), can maintain that theories are only concerned with a subset of models, namely, those that concern observable entities. A theory that accounts for observable phenomena is said to be "empirically adequate"; van Fraassen maintains that we should always take the conservative route of merely accepting a theory as empirically adequate rather than accepting it as true.

At first glance, the emphasis in chapter 3 on the procedural functions of theories as computational entities suggests that the construal favors an instrumentalist interpretation of theories, emphasizing their cognitive uses rather than their truth. Indeed, instrumentalism is easily accommodated by the computational system account. Toulmin (1953) and Hanson (1970) have compared theories to maps, providing inference patterns to guide us around the phenomena. My account fleshes out this metaphor: guidance comes through the internal interconnections within the system of concepts and rules that directs us from concept to concept. As Gruber (1974, p. 255) states in his discussion of Darwin, "A theory is not only a way of organizing existing knowledge and of generalizing specific predictions that can be tested empirically ... [it is] also a way of handling the personal flow of information."

But the pragmatic, computational account of theories is not committed to instrumentalism, since truth and falsity can be taken as properties of the rules attached to concepts. The concept of dog is neither true nor false, but the rules attached to it can have truth values. But now we face a major philosophical problem: we saw in chapter 2 than rules attached to concepts are mostly default rules, ones that state what is typically or usually true, not what is universally true. Construed as universal generalizations, they are strictly speaking false. For example, the concept of dog might include the rule

If x is a dog, then x has four legs.

This is a very useful rule, even though we all know that there are three-legged dogs. The discussion of idealization in chapter 3 showed that scientific laws should similarly be construed as default expectations. The rule

If x is water, then x boils at 212 degrees Fahrenheit.

does not hold at elevations well above sea level. Many principles of physics are true only *ceteris paribus*, other things being equal. How can we construe them as true when we know that often other things are not equal? Philosophers following Popper (1959) have tried to give formal accounts of *verisimilitude*, degree of closeness to the truth, in terms of sets of true consequences of a theory. But these attempts have foundered on the problem that all theories have an infinite set of true consequences. Moreover, as we saw earlier, the problem of calculating the set of consequences of a theory is computationally intractable.

What might it mean to say that one rule is closer to the truth than another? PI's mechanism of specialization suggests an answer. When PI has a strong general rule "if A then B" that encounters a counterexample, it does not simply throw that rule away, for the value of the rule as a default expectation has already been established. Rather, it produces a specialized rule of the form "if A and S then not-B", where S is some unusual circumstance intended to provide an account of why a particular A is not B. In the water case, we would construct the rule

> If x is water and above sea level, then x does not boil at 212 degrees Fahrenheit.

We would not want, however, to say that the new rules is closer to the truth than the original one, which provides an approximation in a wide variety of cases. What is important here is what we have a whole set of rules that among them can describe many cases, not that any one rule gets it exactly right. Cartwright (1983) discusses "how the laws of physics lie", but makes too much of the inadequacy of individual laws of physics. What matters is that the laws can function together to provide reliable expectations about various cases. We want therefore to be able to say that the rules in a conceptual system together provide a set of true descriptions, without their being true in isolation. To take one of Cartwright's examples, consider the law of gravitation, that two bodies exert a force between them that varies inversely as the square of the distance between them and directly as the product of their masses. Strictly speaking, this is false for charged bodies subject to electromagnetic forces, but in that case we would be able to apply a more complex rule. No rule will be true for all situations, but different complexes of rules will truly describe a wide variety of situations.

This holistic view of the truth of rules and theories makes it possible to understand theories, construed computationally, as being true. An argument, however, is needed to justify such an understanding.

8.2.2. An Argument for Realism

According to the account in chapter 5, an attempt to use inference to the best explanation to justify scientific realism should proceed as follows. First, we should assemble the evidence that realism is supposed to explain. Then, we should consider alternative explanations of that evidence. Finally, we should judge whether realism is in fact the best explanation. My argument will only be concerned with realism in the established natural sciences of physics, chemistry, and biology; a later section discusses realism in the much younger cognitive sciences.

Science differs from other human endeavors in several respects. The first and most salient is technological application. Scientific theories have spawned many practical successes, from recombinant DNA work in biology to the development of atomic energy in physics ("success" here is not an ethical term; for good or bad, we can do more with the theory of nuclear fission than without it). A second noteworthy feature of science is its degree of accumulation of knowledge. We saw in chapter 5 that science is not strictly cumulative, sometimes simply leaving old views behind, but in key aspects, such as the replacement of Newtonian mechanics by relativity theory, there is a degree of continuity that is remarkable, especially in contrast to other human developments, such as those in political or artistic spheres. A third feature, related to but distinct from technological application and cumulativity, is the surprising degree of agreement one finds among scientific practitioners. At the frontiers of science, controversy about theoretical interpretations is usually lively, but arguments are waged against a background of common theory. In physics, for example, there is little dispute about the general theory of relativity, and in biology some form of theory of evolution is accepted, even though there are disagreements about particular versions. On a world scale, the degree of agreement about the natural sciences is extraordinary compared with other human practices such as politics and fashion.

Realism provides at least a rough explanation of these salient facts of technological application, cumulativity, and agreement. The reason that scientific theories have technological application is that they are at least approximately true: science works because it tells you more or less how the world is. Similarly, scientific knowledge can accumulate because there is just one way that the world is, and we can find out more and more about how it is, correcting old mistaken views. Finally, we can explain the degree of agreement among scientists by noting that they are all interacting with the same world whose causal influence is responsible for the degree to which their observations agree. By virtue of these explanations, realism can be judged to be a consilient theory. Is there any more consilient? If not, and no other criteria are relevant, then realism should be accepted as the best explanation.

Antirealists can criticize this argument on various fronts. The most general is to deny that inference to the best explanation is a valid form of argument, in this metaphysical context any more than in science. I respond to this objection in the next section. Once inference to the best explanation is admitted as a legitimate mode of inference, response to the argument must consist of offering alternative explanations.

Van Fraassen (1980, p. 40) offers a Darwinian alternative to saying that relation to a material world explains the otherwise miraculous success of science: "I claim that the success of current scientific theories is no miracle. It is not even surprising to the scientific (Darwinist) mind. For any scientific theory is born into a life of fierce competition, a jungle red in tooth and claw. Only the successful theories survive—only the ones which *in fact* latched on to actual regularities in nature." (By actual regularities here he means observable ones only.) The plausibility of this alternative explanation depends on the adequacy of a Darwinian account of scientific inquiry. We have already seen in chapter 6 that the Darwinian model of science offered by evolutionary epistemologists is seriously defective, revealing little about scientific method. Hence, the Darwinian explanation of the success of science does not provide much of an alternative to realism.

A metaphysical alternative to realism is *objective idealism*, the doctrine that there is an objective world but that it is a mental construct sharable by all thinkers. That science is merely tapping into this objective mental reality might indeed explain why science has technological applications and scientists often agree, but it seems to explain too much. If objective idealism were true, why should science be difficult at all? Knowledge ought to be gainable without the labors of experiment and theory that scientists exert.

Crucial to the above argument is its generality: realism is a general hypothesis that explains why science overall is successful. I am not offering explanations of the success of particular theories of the sort criticized by Laudan (1981). He shows that it is problematic to explain the success of particular theories by the assumption that they refer to the real world, for there have been successful theories, such as the wave theory of light with its luminiferous ether, that failed to refer; and there have been theories, such as atomic theory, that for a long time were not successful, even though a realist would now take them to refer. The explanations that realism affords may be weak at this particular level, but still strong at explaining the general technological application, cumulativity, and agreement found in science but not in other human enterprises. Hence, we can infer realism by inference to the best explanation.

My argument supports a full-fledged realism about theories and theoretical entities. Hacking (1983) advocates realism only about entities which we can believe in for practical reasons. There are many experiments in which researchers *use* electrons, for example spraying them. He says, "If you can spray them, then they are real" (1983, p. 22). Without an arguably true theory, however, there are no grounds for maintaining that you are spraying anything. Phlogiston, for example, had various "uses": experimenters used it to turn calxes into metals and to kill sparrows. Only from the vantage point of the superior oxygen theory can we see that experimenters were really working with oxygen, not phlogiston.

8.2.3. Inference to the Best Explanation Is Not Circular

Fine (1984, p. 85) has charged that arguments of the sort just given are circular: "Suppose ... that the usual explanation-inferring devices in scientific practice do not lead to principles that are reliably true (or nearly so), nor to entities whose existence (or near-existence) is reliable. In that case, the usual abductive methods that lead us to good explanations (even to 'the best explanation') cannot be counted on to yield results even approximately true. But the strategy that leads to realism, as I have indicated, is just such an ordinary sort of abductive inference. Hence, if the nonrealist were correct in his doubts, then such an inference to realism as the best explanation (or the like), while possible, would be of no significance—exactly as in the case of a consistency proof using the methods of an inconsistent system." In short, antirealists can say that since they do not accept the use of inference to the best explanation in science, they certainly are not going to accept it in defense of the metaphysical position of realism.

But recall that my justification of inference to the best explanation earlier in this chapter said nothing at all about the truth of the conclusion. Inference to the best explanation is justified because it is robust, accommodating, and efficacious with respect to goals other than truth. The justification implies, therefore, only that we should accept theories on the basis of inference to the best explanation, not that we should accept them as true. But notice what happens when the argument gets applied to scientific realism. If realism is the best explanation, we should accept it, still without supposing it to be true. But to accept realism is to suppose that scientific theories can be said to be true, and once truth is seen as a property of scientific theories, there is no reason not to see it also as property of metaphysical theories such as realism.

This chain of argument is complex, so a schematic presentation may help to make it clear that inference to the best explanation does not encounter circularity in defending realism. Here is the chain of reasoning over this and the previous chapter:

1. I argued for a methodology for going from the descriptive to the normative.
2. I used this methodology to justify the use of inference to the best explanation in the acceptance of theories.
3. I applied inference to the best explanation to defend realism.
4. Thus realism is acceptable and antirealism is not: we should accept the view that scientific theories can be accepted as true.

This argument does not, unfortunately, warrant the conclusion that realism is *true*, only that it is acceptable in some weaker sense. But that is enough to rout the antirealist, who would have to admit that realism is the superior position. Most important, there is no circularity in this use of inference to the best explanation to argue for scientific realism.

8.2.4. *Computation and Observation*
Crucial to the position of the antirealist is the view that there is an epistemologically important distinction concerning what is observable. Empiricists such as van Fraassen urge us to restrict our conclusions cautiously to empirical adequacy, avoiding the formation of beliefs about what we cannot observe. But as critics such as Churchland (1985) have noted, it is parochial to give such primacy to human observation. What is so special

about *our* senses of sight, sound, smell, and touch? We can easily imagine aliens with sense modalities very different from ours who might nevertheless reach the same theoretical conclusions as us about such phenomena as gravitation.

Less fancifully, consider some future computer that might have a television camera for observing the world, robot arms for interacting with it, and the software needed for forming rules and concepts about the world. The computer would start with primitive detectors for edges and shadows, but would have to form complex concepts out of these. Given the inductive steps required, it would seem that for the computer virtually all concepts would be theoretical concepts. But the computer's inductive mechanisms would lead it to conclude that there are tables and chairs and give it a conceptual role semantics for the symbols that it uses for these kinds of things.

If current theories of perception are correct (Rock, 1983; Gregory, 1970; Marr, 1982), human vision involves no less complex a kind of information processing than machine vision. On Rock's view, perception is a kind of problem solving, in which the mind's "executive agency" prefers a solution that accounts for stimulus variations. He says, "The executive agency seeks to explain seemingly unrelated co-occurring stimulus variations on the basis of a common cause and ... in the case of stationary configurations, it seeks solutions that explain seeming coincidences and unexplained regularities that otherwise are implicit in the nonpreferred solution" (Rock, 1983, p. 133). If such theorists are correct, the antirealist espousal of the virtues of observation over leaps of inference to the best explanation is misleading, for even simple kinds of perception involve inference to the best explanation. There is no direct perception, no observation uncorrupted by inference; hence there is no epistemological primacy to observations. Observations are pragmatically important in that they are a good source of intersubjective agreement (because the world causes them, says the realist). But their inferential component precludes contrasting them sharply with conclusions reached by inference to the best explanation.

The inferential nature of observation does not, however, support a full-blown doctrine of the "theory-ladenness" of observation (Hanson, 1958). Kuhn and others have concluded that observations are theory-relative, which has the severe consequence of incommensurability discussed in section 5.7. Observation is inferential, so that any given observation might be influenced by theory, but the inferential processes in observation are not so loose as to allow us to make any observation we want. Rock points out that although perception is thoughtlike, it is largely autonomous, as is evident in extreme cases where we know we are witnessing a perceptual illusion but still see it. Such illusions are systematic and largely unalterable even when we know better. Similarly, there are few cases of disagreement about scientific observations, because all humans operate with the same sort of stimulus-driven inference mechanisms.

8.2.5. Realism in the Cognitive Sciences

The argument that realism is the best explanation of technological application, cumulativity, and agreement does not, unfortunately, apply very well to the social sciences. Take psychology, for example. The past twenty years of cognitive theorizing have as yet made only limited contributions to our ability to learn and understand. We have no grand theory of cognition on the scale of Newtonian mechanics or Darwin's theory of evolution. Fundamental disagreements still exist about the ingredients of a computational account of mind, and there remain doubters whether a computational route is the best one at all. A typical dispute concerns whether the mind's representations include mental images. The existence of schemas corresponding to PI's concepts is an equally controversial issue. We lack enough evidence to warrant the claim that the processing system embodied in PI is more than a very rough approximation to the structures and processes of the human mind. Clearly, cognitive psychology is still at a stage more given to abductions than to convincing inferences to the best explanation.

Some psychologists follow their behavioristic predecessors in forswearing the speculations rampant in computational psychology. They prefer to stick close to the data, aiming only for empirical adequacy rather than for the flights of theory that the proponents of cognitive science enjoy. However, psychology's lack of success so far in achieving a wealth of theoretical truths is no grounds for not attempting to achieve them. Scientific realism is a doctrine about the aims of science as well as the successes. Cognitive science should have the same aim as its elders—physics, chemistry, and biology—to produce general theories that account for a wide variety of empirical phenomena. The view that thinking is analogous, or even identical, to computation has ample theoretical and empirical life remaining, and currently provides the best available route for helping psychology to emulate the theoretical successes of the natural sciences.

8.3. Methodological Conservatism

According to the arguments in this chapter, a scientific theory can rationally be accepted, and accepted as true, if it can be justified by an inference to the best explanation. Correlatively, we should reject a theory if a competitor can be shown to be a better explanation of the evidence according to the relevant criteria. However, just as acceptance of a theory is much more complex than merely adopting an attitude toward a set or propositions, so rejecting a theory is not simply a matter of erasing a proposition from the blackboard of the mind. If a theory is an elaborate conceptual system with great utility for processing information, its abandonment will be a very difficult undertaking.

This difficulty has a clear consequence for the question of conservatism in science. Consider the Kuhn-Popper debate over the attitudes of scientists toward their theories or paradigms (Kuhn, 1970a,b; Popper, 1970). Popper maintains that it is a mark of scientific rationality that a scientist be readily prepared to abandon one's conjectures when they encounter experimental disconfirmation. Kuhn presents an image of a scientist as tenaciously retaining a familiar paradigm in the face of difficulties that are treated as mere puzzles to be solved using the paradigm. A paradigm is abandoned only when a more powerful paradigm becomes available. As a description of the history of science, Kuhn's account can easily be shown to be superior to Popper's, but what of the normative issue: should scientists be as conservative as Kuhn describes?

If a theory is a complex conceptual system, then it would seem that we have little choice in the matter. Unlike a propositional conjecture, a conceptual system is not easily abandoned. If learning a theory requires adoption of a whole network of concepts and rules for solving problems and handling the flow of information, then there is great utility attached to its retention, over which, in any case, we do not have voluntary control. (See the psychological literature on perseverance of beliefs reviewed by Nisbett and Ross, 1980.) It becomes fully understandable why a scientist would not abandon a fertile way of thinking in the face of a few anomalies, and why it is a prerequisite for abandonment that a new paradigm (conceptual system) becomes available. Prescription about what revisions a person ought to make in his or her belief system therefore must take into account the difference between accepting or rejecting a proposition, on the one hand, and acquiring or supplanting a conceptual system on the other.

In PI, to accept a proposition is to add a message or rule to a concept, and rejection is a corresponding deletion. But adding an entire concept is not the same as accepting a set of propositions. A new concept must be integrated with existing knowledge by establishing its place in the processing system: new information is useless until procedural connections with existing concepts are in place, allowing for spreading activation of relevant concepts and problem solutions. Once a complex conceptual system such as that needed for solving physics problems is functioning as a whole, piecemeal revision becomes problematic.

Sklar (1975, p. 378) has discussed the following principle of methodological conservatism: "If you believe some proposition, on the basis of whatever positive warrant may accrue to it from the evidence, a priori plausibility, and so forth, it is unreasonable to cease to believe the proposition to be true merely because of the existence of, or knowledge of, alternative incompatible hypotheses whose positive warrant is no greater than that of the proposition already believed." An analogous principle for conceptual systems might be something like

> If you have a conceptual system for a domain, it is unreasonable to give it up merely because there is available a plausible alternative conceptual system.

This principle derives its support from two considerations. First, because ought implies can, we cannot be enjoined to abandon a conceptual system if it is not possible for us to do so. We cannot reprogram ourselves: the construction and alteration of conceptual systems is not within our conscious control. We have no direct access to the structures and processes that guide our thinking. Hence it is not reasonable to expect someone to suspend use of a processing system just because an alternative exists. Second, even if it were possible, it appears that there are empirical grounds for viewing the abandonment of a functioning conceptual system as undesirable. For by and large it is better to have some elaborate system for processing information than none at all. To abandon a conceptual system for a domain is to be left with no categories for approaching problems in the domain, so that thought grinds to a halt. The rational strategy to adopt when one learns of the existence of a plausible alternative conceptual system to one's own is to attempt to learn the system in much the same as its proponents have done, acquiring complexes of rules that will compete with old ones in solving problems. Learning a new system is difficult, because of interference from the concepts and problem solutions already in place. However, if one does successfully develop the alternative conceptual system in parallel with one's original one, then rational choice of the second over the first becomes possible. As we saw in chapter 5, criteria unimpeded by incommensurability can establish one conceptual system as a better explanation of the facts. A new, whole conceptual system can then assume the procedural role of the previous system. But it is neither possible nor desirable to abandon an old way of understanding a domain until an alternative is in place.

The conservatism and holism that follow from the conceptual theoretic approach can be compared to similar views of Quine (1960, 1963), who suggests several powerful metaphors for the structure of knowledge. Science is a web of belief, a connected fabric of sentences that face the tribunal of sense experience collectively, all susceptible to revision and adjustment like the planks of a boat at sea. Part of the power of these metaphors is that they help lead us away from the standard view that knowledge consists in discrete sentences, confirmed and contentful in isolation. Rather, knowledge forms an interconnected whole. But Quine's metaphors do not take us far enough. How is a set of sentences connected by more than deductive relations? How do we juggle an interconnected set of sentences to come up with the best total account? Computational systems such as PI offer much richer descriptions of the interconnections of what we know. These descriptions follow the basic insight of Quine's holism that we do not infer sentences in isolation, but in addition organize our knowledge topically and dynamically in a psychologically realistic way. Richness comes through adoption of a procedural viewpoint and abandonment of the fabric of sentences in favor of more complex cognitive structures and operations. The web of belief does not consist of beliefs, but of rules, concepts, problem solutions, and procedures for using them. Methodological conservatism is an unavoidable result. Neither conservatism nor holism, however, undermines the possibility of objective evaluation of theories.

8.4. Summary

Inference to the best explanation is neither justifiable by nor reducible to enumerative induction. Rather, it must be justified by the descriptive/normative methodology discussed in chapter 7. The criteria for inferential systems discussed there display the advantages of inference to the best explanation over other inferential principles. It is robust in that it captures much of inductive practice in the realm of theory choice, and it is efficacious in promoting the aims of explanation and prediction. The computational view of theories is compatible with both realist and nonrealist construals of theories, but the realist view that scientific theories can achieve truth is defensible by an argument to the best explanation. Because theories are complex systems, their rejection is very difficult, and methodological conservatism is unavoidable.

Chapter 9
Pseudoscience

One of the most important normative problems in the philosophy of science is the demarcation of science from pseudoscience. What distinguishes sciences such as physics, chemistry, and biology from pseudosciences such as astrology and creationism? Logical criteria for demarcating science were proposed by the logical positivists and by Karl Popper, but these have proved to have serious flaws. Many philosophers have become skeptical about whether any defensible principles of demarcation can be found. Some relativist philosophers of science such as Feyerabend (1975) would argue that the demarcationist program failed and ought to be abandoned. Similarly, Rorty (1979) gives science no special epistemological status, treating it as just another form of discourse. Less radically, Laudan (1983) says that the science/nonscience distinction adds nothing beyond the distinction between reliable and unreliable knowledge. In contrast, this chapter argues that we can distinguish pseudoscience from science by systematically noting features of pseudosciences, contrasting them with features of science. The result is a conceptual profile of pseudoscience that does not provide a set of necessary and sufficient conditions but nevertheless suffices for branding some fields as pseudoscientific.

9.1. The Problem of Demarcation

Several questions must be addressed before discussing various criteria for distinguishing science from pseudoscience.

1. Why is it important to demarcate science and from what should it be distinguished?
2. What is the logical form of a demarcation criterion?
3. What are the units that are marked as scientific or pseudoscientific?

My motivation for attempting to distinguish science from pseudoscience is different from that of the logical positivists or Popper. The logical positivists intended to demarcate science from metaphysics, the branch of philosophy concerned with the fundamental nature of reality. In the tradition of Hume (1888), they claimed that a proposition could only be meaningful if it is analytic (true by definition) or empirically verifiable. Ayer's *Language, Truth and Logic* (1946) was the English language manifesto of the positivist movement and Ayer devoted much energy in both the first and second editions to stating a principle of verification with logical precision. With evangelical vigor, Ayer condemned most philosophical discussion as metaphysical nonsense, meaningless because it employs propositions that are neither true by definition nor verifiable by experience. Questions such as the existence of God and the relation of the mental and the physical were to be abandoned as nonsensical.

For reasons summarized below, the verifiability principle failed, so nowadays few are inclined to demarcate science from metaphysics. For philosophers such as Peirce (1931–1958) and Quine (1963), science and philosophy (including metaphysics) are continuous enterprises, shading into each other, just as do the descriptive and the normative issues of chapter 7. By rejecting the positivists' distinction between analytic and empirical propositions, Quine opened the possibility that metaphysics could be neither strictly empirical nor analytic, just as science is not.

Attacking metaphysics is not, however, the only reason to attempt to demarcate science. Karl Popper's (1959, 1965) principle of demarcation differed from the verifiability principle in that his target was not metaphysics in general but current theories that purported to be scientific, particularly Freudian psychoanalysis and Marxian economics. Moreover, he did not claim to be saying anything about meaning: nonscience could be demarcated from science without saying that it was meaningless. For Popper, the key mark of science is not verifiability but falsifiability: a theory must be capable of being shown to be false by empirical test. The problems with Popper's falsifiability principle will be reviewed in the next section. As a demarcation criterion, it fares no better than the verifiability principle; either excluding too much or too little, it leaves his targets unscathed.

I think that the distinction between science and pseudoscience is important because of a set of more vulnerable targets, whose presence and substantial impact can be seen by a glance through magazines on the supermarket shelves. According to Martin Gardner (1981), there are ten times more practicing astrologers in the United States than astronomers. Social and intellectual arguments against pseudosciences such as astrology and palmistry have an essential philosophical component that presupposes some sort of demarcation criterion. The social importance of distinguishing science from pseudoscience is especially evident in recent controversies in the United States over the teaching of so-called "creation science". Proponents of creationism attempt to evade constitutional requirements of separation of church and state by claiming that creation science is at least as scientific as evolutionary theory. Again, criteria of what constitutes science are presupposed. In the recent court case concerning whether creation science should be taught in Arkansas public schools, the nature of science was a key issue and philosophers and scientists gave testimony on the issue (Overton, 1983).

Hence for social reasons we must take seriously the demarcationist aim of the logical positivists and Popper, but our aim should be to distinguish science from egregious examples of pseudoscience such as astrology and creationism. We need three categories instead of the logical positivists' two. They had science, which was Good, and metaphysics, which was Bad, but I want to have science, which is Good, pseudoscience, which is Bad, and many other intellectual activities that are just nonscientific. Literary criticism and gourmet cooking, for example, are not scientific but do not purport to be, and therefore should not be branded as pseudoscientific.

The second question above concerns the form of a demarcation principle. Ideally, we would like a definition of the form

X is scientific if and only if C,

where X is an idea or proposition or field and C are necessary and sufficient conditions of X being scientific. Laudan (1983, p. 119) asserts, "Without conditions that are both necessary and sufficient, we are never in a position to say '*this* is scientific; but *that* is unscientific.'" This insistence reflects the traditional view that the meaning of concepts is captured by attempting to give necessary and sufficient conditions for their application. But the discussion of concepts and meaning in chapters 2 and 4 showed the dispensability of such quixotic efforts. Concepts such as those in PI do not provide necessary and sufficient conditions for application of concepts, but only default rules that apply to most instances. They state, for example, what can be expected to hold typically of birds, not what is true of all and only birds. If ordinary concepts do not have sets of necessary and sufficient conditions, we can hardly expect to find such conditions for complex philosophical concepts such as "science". Rather, we should aim for a list of features that are typical of science and a contrasting list of features that are typical of pseudoscience. The lists will furnish contrasting conceptual profiles, so that to determine whether a field is a science or a pseudoscience, we must ask whether the characteristics of the field match better with the features of typical sciences or with those of typical pseudosciences. Demarcation betweeen science and pseudoscience is thus based on their contrasting profiles. The features in these profiles are criteria in a loose sense: they are not necessary and sufficient conditions, but, like the criteria for theory choice in chapter 5 and the criteria for normative logical systems in chapter 7, they provide ways of telling good from bad.

The third question remains: what sorts of things are subject to demarcation? For the positivists and Popper, sentences or propositions were labeled as scientific or nonscientific, since it is these that are subject to verification or falsification. The alternative view of the structure of scientific knowledge presented in chapters 2 and 3 casts doubt on the feasibility of such atomic units of demarcation. For reasons that will become clear following the discussion of psychological and historical criteria below, a much larger and more complex unit of demarcation is needed. The objects demarcated as scientific or nonscientific are not ideas or propositions or even theories, but fields. A field should be understood as a historical entity embracing theories, their applications, and the practitioners of the field. It is thus a social as well as an epistemic notion. Having a richer unit of demarcation makes possible the unusually complex demarcation criteria discussed below.

9.2. Verifiability and Falsifiability

The logical positivists and Popper shared the assumption that science can be distinguished from nonscience on logical grounds. For the positivists, the distinctive feature of a scientific statement was that it is capable of verification by experience; for Popper the distinctive feature is being capable of falsification by experience. Verifiability and falsifiability are preeminently matters of logic: to verify a statement is to use deduction to predict observations that confirm it; to falsify a statement is to use deduction to predict an observation statement whose falsity implies the falsity of the theoretical statement that implies it.

Two major criticisms have been levied against the verifiability principle: first, it cannot be stated in a way that excludes metaphysics without excluding science as well; and second, the principle is itself unverifiable and therefore metaphysical. Ayer's final attempt in the second edition of *Language, Truth and Logic* to give a logically precise definition of "verifiable" in terms of the derivability of observation statements was demolished by Church (1949). A strong criterion of verifiability would rule out scientific generalizations and theories, while a weak criterion, merely requiring of a proposition that it have some logical connection with possible observations, did not rule out the statements that the positivists wanted to damn as metaphysical. As Passmore (1968, p. 390) summarizes, "This indeed is the dilemma in which the logical positivists, like Hume before them, constantly found themselves—throw metaphysics into the fire, and science goes with it, preserve science from the flames and metaphysics comes creeping back." Similarly, the difficulty that the logical positivists had with explaining the status of their own principle suggests: Throw metaphysics into the flames and logical positivism goes with it.

Contrast the positivists' account of confirmation with the account of theory choice given in chapter 5. The logical positivists and generations of confirmation theorists since have thought that the empirical value of a hypothesis could be evaluated on how well it predicted observations. I argued in contrast that the evaluation of hypotheses is much more coarse-grained, based on explanation of classes of facts. Moreover, rather than consider the verification of individual theories, I argued that theory evaluation is a comparative matter in which the best of competing explanations is chosen. If these points are correct, verification is much more complex than the positivists conceived, so that verifiability is even less likely to provide the convenient logical scalpel for excising the cancer of metaphysics from the body of science. I remarked in chapter 5 that inference to the best explanation is applicable to metaphysical theories as well as to scientific ones, and even pseudosciences such as astrology and creationism are subject to defense by arguments to the best explanation. Such arguments are weak because of the lack of evidence for them and because of the availability of better alternatives, but pseudoscientific theories can nevertheless be defended on the basis of what they explain.

Qualitatively, however, there is a noticeable difference between scientific and pseudoscientific theories. Pseudoscientific theories may appear to be highly consilient, explaining many classes of facts, but they typically do so at the cost of simplicity, as defined in chapter 5. Explanation of numerous classes of facts is achieved by a host of auxiliary hypotheses with isolated applications. Creationism provides a splendid example. We could never find a theory more consilient than the one that consists simply of the claim that what God wills happens: any event at all can be explained using the "law" that whatever God wills happens and the auxiliary hypothesis that God willed the event in question. The problem with such explanations is that a different auxiliary hypothesis is needed for each event to be explained, so that the theological theory is maximally nonsimple. (Another problem for creationism is explaining the presence of evil in the world given the assumed goodness of God.) Simpler explanations are to be preferred, even if given by less consilient theories.

Popper thought that confirmation of theories was trivially easy to come by, and that the true mark of a scientific theory is that it is capable of falsification. Like the verifiability principle, the falsifiability principle is difficult to state in a way that is neither too exclusive nor too inclusive. As Duhem (1954) argued, even scientific theories are not capable of strict falsification. For the deduction of an observation statement from a theory generally requires the use of auxiliary hypotheses, and it is always possible to reject an auxiliary hypothesis instead of the theory. As we saw in chapter 5, the consilience of a theory can often be bought at the price of decreased simplicity. In a loose sense we could say that a theory is falsified if a better explanation for its domain is found, but virtually any theory, including astrology and creationism, is falsifiable in this sense. Hence falsifiability is not the logically sufficient demarcation criterion Popper intended it to be.

Other reasons for doubting the efficacy of the falsifiability principle were discussed in chapter 8 in connection with methodological conservatism. Concern with falsification is misplaced, since higher priority should be placed on the development and comparative evaluation of research programs. Not only is falsifiability not a demarcation criterion for science; obsession with it would preclude procession beyond trivialities.

All that remains in most philosophical circles of the concern with verifiability and falsifiability is the conclusion that observations are somehow relevant to the evaluation of scientific theories, and that pseudoscientific theories are less amenable to empirical evaluation. We are not going to be able to establish a neat dividing line between science and pseudoscience on such a loose comparison. Nevertheless, in attempting to decide whether a field is scientific or pseudoscientific we can take into account, among other factors, the behavior of practitioners of the field in empirical matters. Part of the conceptual profile of science will concern empirical confirmations and disconfirmations, in contrast to pseudoscience, which is typically oblivious to such matters.

9.3. Resemblance Thinking

The conceptual profile of pseudoscience should also include use of a natural but deficient form of reasoning not used in science. I distinguish two general kinds of reasoning, called *resemblance thinking* and *correlation thinking*. Resemblance thinking infers that two things or events are causally related from the fact that they are *similar* to each other; in contrast, correlation thinking infers that two things or events are causally related from the fact that they are correlated with each other. After presenting psychological, anthropological, and historical evidence for the importance of the distinction between resemblance thinking and correlation thinking, I argue that the use of resemblance thinking is typical of such pseudosciences as astrology.

John Stuart Mill (1970, p. 501) identified as one of the most deeply rooted of all fallacies the belief "that the conditions of a phenomenon must, or at least probably will, resemble the phenomenon itself." Suppose you are asked to judge whether people with red hair are generally hot-tempered. The correlational approach would be to take a sample and count the numbers failing under the various categories of having or not having the two properties in question. Instead, most people would merely summon to mind a few examples of red-headed acquaintances and thereupon tender a judgment. Or, using resemblance thinking, they might notice a similarity between the fiery appearance of red hair and the metaphorically fiery behavior of hot-tempered people, and use this to judge that redheads are in general hot-tempered.

Correlation thinking should be construed broadly to encompass generalization from examples, statistical reasoning, and other kinds of induction. Inference to the best explanation qualifies, since it postulates causes on the basis of their ability to explain and predict observed regularities, not on the basis of similarities.

Mill as well as Jerome (1977) observed that astrology is rife with resemblance thinking. Jerome describes how astrology is based on a "principle of correspondences" or "law of analogies". For example, the reddish cast of the planet Mars leads to its association with blood, war, and aggression, while the pretty "star" Venus is associated with beauty and motherhood. Saturn, which is duller and slower than Jupiter, is associated with gloom, and (one hopes even more tenuously) with scholarship. Similarly, analogy attaches characteristics to the signs of the zodiac: Libra, represented by the scales, signifies the just and harmonious, while Scorpio resembles its namesake in being secretive and aggressive. The associations concerning the planets and signs of the zodiac are taken by astrologers as evidence of some causal influence of the heavens on the personalities and fates of individuals whose births occur at the appropriate times. Until recently, no attempt was made to determine whether there is any actual correlation between the characteristics of the signs and planets and the personalities of the people under their alleged influence.

Resemblance thinking is much more than just a quirk of astrologers. The first piece of evidence that it is a natural general method of human thinking is found in the psychological investigations of Tversky and Kahneman (1974). They maintain that people often make judgments about the relation of classes or events using a "representativeness heuristic", basing their judgments on degree of resemblance. Suppose people are asked to judge the career of the following individual.

> Steve is very shy and withdrawn, invariably helpful, but with little interest in people or in the world of reality. A meek and tidy soul, he has a need for order and structure, and a passion for detail.

Research shows that people judge the probability that Steve is, for example, a librarian by considering how similar Steve is to their stereotype of a librarian. Serious errors of judgment result from neglecting such factors as the percentage of librarians in the total population, a factor that Bayes' theorem requires us to introduce as a prior probability. Use of resemblance thinking also disposes people to neglect other important features in the estimation of probabilities, such as sample size and regression. Social psychologists Nisbett and Ross (1980) describe numerous situations in which the use of resemblance criteria leads people to make errors in attributing behavior to spurious cases.

The second piece of evidence for the pervasiveness of resemblance thinking comes from anthropology. In his celebrated *The Golden Bough*, Sir James Frazer (1964, p. 35) cites a "Law of Similarity" as one of two principles on which magic everywhere rests. This is the law that "like produces like, effect resembling cause". Frazer calls magic based on the law Homeopathic Magic, and describes such applications as injuring or destroying the image of an enemy as a way of producing actual injury. He provides numerous additional examples of homeopathic magic in many different cultures.

Richard Shweder (1977) has urged that we should understand the strange beliefs of other peoples as the result of applications of what I call resemblance thinking. For example, Zande beliefs about using fowl excrement to cure ringworm are viewed as part of a universal inclination to rely on resemblance instead of tests of correlation. Magical thinking can then be viewed, not as an especially bizarre or primitive mode of thought, but as an applicaton of a way of thinking all too natural to human beings.

The final support for the importance of the resemblance/correlation distinction comes from the historical work of Michel Foucault and Ian Hacking. Foucault (1973, p. 17) states, "Up to the end of the sixteenth century, resemblance played a constructive role in the knowledge of Western culture. It was resemblance that largely guided exegesis and the interpretation of texts; it was resemblance that organized the play of symbols, made possible knowledge of things visible and invisible, and controlled the art of representing them." According to Foucault, until the seventeenth century there was no distinction between what is seen and what is read. He quotes Paracelsus' assertion that God "has allowed nothing to remain without exterior and visible signs in the form of special marks." Knowledge is then gained by reading the signs displayed in the world, and resemblance is the primary method for this. One application is the doctrine of signatures, which guided medicine to such conclusions as that the lungs of the fox are an aid to the asthmatic, and that turmeric with its yellow color serves as a cure for jaundice. Only in the seventeenth century, with the work of Descartes, Bacon, and others, do we have the rise of correlation thinking, which seems so fundamental to us today.

Foucault's views on the dominance of resemblance thinking are confirmed by Ian Hacking's work on the emergence of probability. Hacking (1975) marks the decade around 1660 as the birth time of probability, in both its statistical aspect concerning frequencies and its epistemological aspect concerning degrees of belief. Previously, "probability" indicated approval or acceptability by intelligent people; evidence was a matter of testimony and authority, not observation or correlation; resemblance thinking sufficed to interpret God's handiwork. The new dual concept of probability was thus part of the emergence of the method of correlation thinking.

A recent example of resemblance thinking is found in a *Time* magazine article on football (*Time*, November 13, 1978, p. 112). It reports the work of a Berkeley anthropologist who argues that the sexual symbolism of the game—teammates hugging and patting each other, the quarterback receiving the ball from between the center's legs, talk of "scoring", skintight pants, and so on—suggests that football is a homosexual ceremony, serving to discharge the homoerotic impulses of players and fans. A few similarities encourage an untested causal hypothesis.

Note, however, that not all reasoning involving similarity is resemblance thinking. The detection of similarities is a pervasive feature of thought and only becomes illegitimate when the leap is made from mere similarity to causal connection. Analogies and metaphors are very important in scientific and everyday reasoning, but analogical inference is not a form of resemblance thinking. In resemblance thinking we infer from the similarity of two things or events A and B that they are causally related. Analogical inference involves similarity and causality, but in a more complicated fashion (see section 4.2.5 on analogical abduction, and 5.6 on analogy as a criterion for the best explanation). Schematically, appropriate uses of analogy can be understood as follows. We know that A and B are similar (analogous) to each other. We also know that A is causally related to C; correlation thinking would have to be the basis for this knowledge. If C is similar to D, which is near B, we might conclude by analogical inference that B might be causally related to D. Our inference is not based on any similarity between B and D, but is grounded in the known causal relation between A and C. To establish more than the presumption of a causal relation between B and D would require further correlation. More concretely, recall the use of analogical abduction to suggest a hypothesis concerning who committed a murder. The unsolved murder is seen to be similar to another murder that has been solved. The solution to the understood crime is a causal account of who committed it, and analogy serves to carry this causal account over to the unsolved case. No resemblance thinking is involved at all. Analogy here functions primarily as a heuristic device, although it may also play a subsidiary role in the validation of the existence of a causal relation between phenomena.

Resemblance thinking would be easy to implement computationally. The features of an object or kind could be represented in a framelike structure, and a program could judge degree of similarity by comparing the slots in the frame. The heuristic for making illegitimate causal judgments would be to infer a causal relation merely from the calculated similarity. Correlational heuristics for judging causal relations would have to be much more complicated, taking into account such factors as temporal relations and common causes: we should not infer a causal relation between amount of ice cream consumed and number of drownings, since the statistical correlation between them is the result of the common cause of hot days. Computational techniques for discriminating causal relations from spurious correlations have yet to be developed.

9.4. Resemblance Thinking and Pseudoscience

Because the use of resemblance thinking is so integral to astrology, it is tempting to suggest that resemblance thinking is a central feature of all pseudoscience. Resemblance thinking is also rampant in many other dubious pursuits. Graphology purports to analyze people's personality from their handwriting, maintaining, for example, that detailed symmetric doodles indicate that someone is orderly and precise. Such a correlation may well exist, but similarity rather than empirical test seems to be the basis for the assumed relation. Physiognomy holds that there is a connection between the features of the face and the character of the person, so that someone with a low forehead is deemed to be unintelligent. Physiognomy thrived for centuries without empirical test, because it "made sense" on the basis of resemblance thinking. In palmistry, a long life line on the hand is taken to predict a long life, based only on similarity rather than on any observed correlation between length of lines on the palm and length of life.

There is not, however, a perfect mesh between the resemblance/correlation distinction and the pseudoscience/science distinction. First, not all pseudoscience uses resemblance thinking. Although astrology, graphology, physiognomy, palmistry, and folk medicine revel in resemblances, pseudoscience can also be done on the basis of spurious correlations. As we saw in the last section, not all correlation indicates causation. There is a standard joke in introductory logic books about the man who successively developed massive hangovers from drinking scotch and water, gin and water, and vodka and water, then prudently decided to give up drinking water. Falling barometers do not cause storms. Thus mere attention to correlations is not sufficient to provide a scientific ground for a causal relation between objects or events. Proponents of biorhythms delight in pointing to such "confirmations" as that Elvis Presley died on a "triple low" day, and that Mark Spitz won all his Olympic gold medals while experiencing a "triple high". What I call correlation thinking involves much more than attention to selected positive instances. It requires attention also to negative instances as well as to possible alternative explanations of observed correlations.

The deans of modern pseudoscience, Immanuel Velikovsky (1965) and

Erich von Daniken (1970), both use a very rough sort of correlation thinking in support of their peculiar theories. Velikovsky uses such evidence as the coincidence among ancient myths to support his hypothesis that Venus was ejected from Jupiter about 5,000 years ago and passed near the earth before assuming its present orbit. Von Daniken also uses mythological evidence in support of his hypothesis of ancient visits by extraterrestrial beings. Both neglect alternative explanations and suffer from other problems, such as the inconsistency of Velikovsky's views with celestial mechanics; but the central objections to them do not include the use of resemblance thinking. (There do, however, seem to be a few instances, such as Velikovsky's view that the manna that supposedly nourished the ancient Hebrews during their years of wandering in the desert was carbohydrates from the tail of Venus.) Thus a field can be pseudoscientific without using resemblance thinking.

More problematically, we can look for uses of resemblance thinking that are not pseudoscientific. Consider first the methods of the humanities, especially as they concern the interpretation of texts. Literary interpretation, art appreciation, and the history of philosophy all in part involve the detection of similarities and the comparison of symbols. But this study of resemblances is not pseudoscientific because it does not purport to be scientific; connections are found, without making claims about causes and explanations. Although there is occasional use of correlation methods, as in the computer analysis of texts to establish authorship, the humanities have an important function in providing plausible interpretations; truth is another matter, one not to be reached by resemblance thinking. To take an example from the history of philosophy, the interpretation of Kant can be a philosophically important enterprise even though we may have little hope of figuring out what Kant "really" meant. Thus the humanities provide no examples of fields using resemblance thinking without being pseudoscientific: resemblance thinking is more than the recognition of similarities; it is the attribution of causality on the basis of similarities. Interpretation in the humanities does not generally involve causal attributions, so should not be counted as resemblance thinking. We should say that the humanities are nonscientific rather than pseudoscientific, since their study of similarities has a function different from the attribution of causality.

Let us now take a brief look at Freudian psychoanalysis. Freud and his followers would certainly claim that their theories are based on correlation thinking applied to many clinical observations. But controlled experiments are rare and much of Freudian theory is redolent of resemblance thinking. The penis is elevated to such symbolic importance that female resentment of male domination can be brushed away as penis envy. Compulsive neatness is attributed to problems of toilet training producing an anal retentive personality. A death instinct is hypothesized to explain human destructiveness. Nisbett and Ross (1980) note Freud's great contribution of observing that people frequently use resemblance thinking and developing the method of free association to explore their thought processes; but Freud himself seems to have fallen into resemblance thinking in propounding such doctrines as the ones mentioned. However, psychoanalysis at least attempts to use correlation thinking, and it might be argued that the psychological explanations that appear to be based on resemblance thinking arise from noting the actual associations in patients' minds; it would then be a correlational observation of peoples' use of resemblance thinking. Thus psychoanalysis, like textual interpretation, does not provide a counterexample to the claim that all disciplines that use resemblance thinking are pseudoscientific.

In sum, resemblance thinking is a pervasive aspect of human reasoning, causing much fallacious reasoning and contributing to such pseudosciences as astrology. The use of resemblance thinking is sufficient to render a discipline pseudoscientific, but pseudosciences can also be founded on incomplete or spurious correlation thinking. Nevertheless, the use of resemblance thinking belongs on the profile of pseudoscience as a typical although not universal characteristic.

9.5. Progressiveness

Thagard (1978b) proposed the following criterion for pseudoscience: "A theory which purports to be scientific is pseudoscientific if and only if (1) it has been less progressive than alternative theories over a long period of time, and faces many unsolved problems, but (2) the community of practitioners makes little attempt to develop the theory towards solutions of the problems, shows no concern for attempts to evaluate the theory in relation to others, and is selective in considering confirmations and disconfirmations." This criterion has several flaws that should be evident from the discussion so far. First, it attempts the hopeless task of providing necessary and sufficient conditions for pseudoscience. Second, it turns out to be too soft on astrology, which it was originally designed to label as pseudoscientific. For it implies that astrology could only be branded as pseudoscientific when alternative theories of personality became available with the rise of scientific psychology. Yet we saw in the last section that astrology has a feature—resemblance thinking—that marks it as pseudoscientific in a way that is independent of any historical dimension.

Although my proposed definition must therefore be abandoned, the features of pseudoscience it mentions should be incorporated into the profile of pseudoscience. The features listed under clause (2) concern the comparative evaluation of theories and have already been discussed in connection with verifiability. Clause (1), however, points to an important historical dimension of the distinction between science and pseudoscience that must now be discussed.

Velikovsky was once heard to brag that whereas physics and chemistry had gone through enormous changes, his theory of worlds in collision had survived for decades virtually unchanged. But the immutability of his theory is more suspicious than salutary. Change is a central feature of any scientific field, as new data are collected and new and better theories are discovered. In earlier chapters we saw that science progresses by developing better theories, where "better" is defined by the criteria for theory choice. Physics, for example, has progressed enormously since the time of Galileo. In the nineteenth century, the pinnacle of success was Newtonian mechanics, but in the twentieth it has been superseded by an even more consilient theory, general relativity. In contrast, astrology and creationism are hopelessly static. Astrology is virtually unchanged since the days of Ptolemy, and current practitioners show little concern with making improvements (Thagard, 1978b). Creationists undergo intellectual contortions in order to explain away the evidence for evolution, but their basic theory, that the world and its species are the result of special creation, offers no refinements over the traditional biblical story. No new classes of facts have been explained in centuries by either astrology or creationism.

Progressiveness is a historical criterion in two senses. First, assessment of progressiveness requires consideration of the record of a field over time. Second, it is sensitive to a particular historical context. Just as theory choice is comparative, considering competing explanations, so judgments of pseudoscience must take into account what alternative explanations are available. Thus astrology was not an entirely disreputable pursuit for Kepler or Newton, if they were trying to found it on correlation thinking rather than resemblance thinking; but it is unacceptable today when psychology can offer environmental and genetic explanations for people's personalities. The natural theology that flourished in early nineteenth-century Britain and attracted leading scientists such as Whewell was not contemptible. At the time, no general cosmological or biological theories were available. Darwin's theory of evolution by natural selection was a major blow to natural theology, since it provided an alternative account of how the apparent designs found in nature could have come to be. After Darwin, special creation was no longer the best explanation available for biological organization, and natural theology has been in retreat ever since. A century of advances in evolutionary theory and genetics exposes natural theology and its contemporary recrudescence, "scientific" creationism, as intellectually vapid. But remember that this was not always so: pseudoscience is a historical category.

Conceivably, a field that was at one time pseudoscientific might blossom into a science, just as chemistry rose from the ashes of the magic of alchemy. Today there are a few attempts to revive astrology using empirical methods (Gauquelin, 1969) and it cannot be ruled out *a priori* that astrology might be elevated to scientific status by use of such correlation thinking. Carlson (1985) reports on extremely thorough double-blind test of astrological predictions about personality. Astrologers failed to perform at a level better than chance, which would suggest that astrology is not only falsifiable but false, But future studies might find support for astrology. I do not think this is likely, but I raise the possibility to highlight the historical, contextual nature of judgments of pseudoscience. Contrast this with the ahistorical criteria of the logical positivists and Popper, for whom a statement could be nonscientific merely be virtue of its logical form.

9.6. Profiles of Science and Pseudoscience

To summarize the discussion of logical, psychological, and historical criteria, we can characterize science and pseudoscience by these profiles:

Science	Pseudoscience
Uses correlation thinking.	Uses resemblance thinking.
Seeks empirical confirmations and disconfirmations.	Neglects empirical matters.
Practitioners care about evaluating theories in relation to alternative theories.	Practitioners oblivious to alternative theories.
Uses highly consilient and simple theories.	Nonsimple theories: many ad hoc hypotheses.
Progresses over time: develops new theories that explain new facts.	Stagnant in doctrine and applications.

Remember that these features are not intended to be strict necessary or sufficient conditions of science or pseudoscience. But we can show that a suspect field is pseudoscientific by showing that its characteristics match those of the right side of the table better than the features on the left. Physics, chemistry, and biology fall naturally into the scientific category on the left, while astrology and creationism belong on the right. More exact conceptual profiles would arise from turning these features into rules with associated strengths, as occur in the concepts in the system PI. For example, we would have a very strong rule:

> If x is a field whose practitioners use resemblance thinking, then x is a pseudoscience.

A weaker rule would run in the other direction, providing a rough expectation:

> If x is a pseudoscience, then x has practitioners who employ resemblance thinking.

A full set of such rules would provide a more subtle means of judging a field to be scientific.

Thus the failure of the verifiability and falsifiability principles does not condemn us to relativism about the nature of science. Scientific method is not based on the strict logical procedures that the positivists and Popper advocated. Nevertheless, attention to a broader range of procedures can lead to development of principles for distinguishing science from pseudoscience and to criteria that contribute to other normative tasks of the philosophy of science.

9.7. Are the Cognitive Sciences Scientific?

At meetings of the Cognitive Science Society, one frequently hears the ironical remark, "Any field that has to call itself a science isn't." That judgment is too harsh, but it raises the question of how fields such as psychology and artificial intelligence fare according to my profiles of science and pseudoscience. (I lack the expertise to address the question of other cognitive fields, such as linguistics and neuroscience, not to mention economics or sociology.)

Consider first psychology. Cognitive psychologists certainly fare well on the criteria of using correlation thinking, since they do controlled experiments, use statistical tests, and evaluate theories on the basis of experimental results. Psychology cannot, however, make convincing claims to have achieved simple consilient theories that have developed progressively. For the past twenty years, the information processing metaphor has guided research in cognitive psychology, but there has not yet arisen a comprehensive, unifield theory that accounts for a broad range of phenomena. The best current candidate is probably Anderson's ACT* rule-based model of cognition, but he appropriately characterizes it as more of a framework providing a general pool of constructs than a theory. However, cognitive psychology certainly does not fall under the pseudoscience category either, since there are no better alternative theories available, and there is every reason to expect that psychologists would enthusiastically embrace a simple consilient theory if one were to arise. We are still awaiting the Newton or Darwin of psychology. Thus psychology is probably best characterized as a young science that lacks the development of fields such as physics and biology but is clearly more scientific than pseudoscientific.

The case of artificial intelligence is much more complicated, for we can see AI as at least three different kinds of enterprises: technological, mathematical, and quasi-experimental. The technological aspects of AI are prominent these days in the development of expert systems whose many current applications include prospecting for oil, financial management, and medical diagnosis. Such applied ventures should be neutrally counted as nonscientific rather than pseudoscientific, in the same way that manufacturing cars is not thought of as a science, even though it applies some scientific knowledge. Similarly, the activities of AI researchers concerned with such issues as algorithmic complexity are best thought of as nonscientific, since pure mathematics does not have much in common either with the features of empirical science or with those of pseudoscience as profiled above.

AI becomes more empirical when it is allied with cognitive psychology in the attempt to understand the nature of mind. Programs such as PI can be understood as ventures in theoretical cognitive psychology, intended to predict and explain observations about human thinking. In this collaboration with psychology, which I take to be the central activity of cognitive science, AI blends into psychology and inherits its characterization as a young science.

What of nonapplied, nonpsychological AI? Much work in artificial intelligence is intended neither to have direct technological application nor to constitute models of the human mind. Practitioners frequently talk of doing experiments, where what is observed is how the computer behaves when programmed in certain ways. (With complex programs, it is by no means true that "the computer only does what you tell it to do.") It seems that artificial intelligence researchers create their own phenomena, which are to be explained in terms of general principles of computational intelligence. A computational technique can be judged to be a contribution to understanding if a program performs more sophisticated tasks with it than without it. Analysis of when and how the program succeeds and fails is required to ensure that its improved performance in fact derives from the ideas being tested and not from other features of the program or domain. (I am indebted here to conversations with Bruce Buchanan.) AI is a very young field with evolving methods and standards whose relation to those of mature empirical sciences such as physics remains to be explored.

9.8. Summary

Science can be distinguished from pseudoscience by profiles that specify features typical of the two categories. These include much more than the logical matters of verification and falsification. Psychological concerns such as the use of resemblance thinking and historical issues such as progressiveness are also highly relevant to distinguishing science from pseudoscience. The resulting profiles serve to brand astrology and creationism as pseudosciences.

Chapter 10

The Process of Inquiry: Projects for Computational Philosophy of Science

The last three chapters moved progressively farther away from the descriptive, computational issues with which we began. I want now to return to similar issues, but at a much more speculative level. There is more to scientific inquiry than the procedures of problem solving, hypothesis formation, and theory evaluation discussed in earlier chapters. A full computational account of the process of scientific inquiry will need to describe in addition how problems and experiments are generated; and it will have to deal with the social dimension of science—that science is done by individuals working in collaboration. This chapter outlines two future projects for computational philosophy of science that aim at the construction of models of science rich enough to encompass its experimental and social sides. The first project is to give an integrated computational account that shows the relations of experimentation to problem solving and induction, and the second is to use ideas about parallel computation to characterize group rationality in science.

10.1. Theory and Experiment

10.1.1. The Limitations of PI
We saw in chapters 2–4 how PI simulates solving problems by a process of firing of rules and spreading activation of concepts, and how various kinds of induction—concept formation, generalization, and abduction— are triggered by the current state of activation. Figure 10.1 gives a simplified picture of PI's operation, with problem solving as the central function and various learning mechanisms triggered by it. Within the limitations already described in earlier chapters, PI suffices to describe much of scientific problem solving and theory formation. But at a higher level PI is clearly deficient in at least two respects. First, the current models says nothing about how problems arise. Like most existing AI programs for solving problems, PI requires that problems be given to it. Nothing in PI's current operation constructs or begins the solution of new problems. But problem solving is crucial to focusing the search for new theories, whose

Figure 10.1
Current operation of PI.

formation is only triggered during problem solving. So we ought to have an account of when a system should set out to solve particular problems.

A second deficiency concerns the source of observed messages in PI, which currently are just typed in by the programmer. Many scientific problems arise from observation and experiment. Darwin, for example, wondered why the observed species of animals on different islands of the Galapagos were related but different. Lavoisier wondered why things that burn increase in weight. These puzzling phenomena needed to be explained, and the attempt to explain them was part of the problem-solving process that led to new theories. But where do experiments come from? The description of PI said nothing about the source of new observations. PI does have a very simple simulated world that can pipe observations, in the form of messages, into the current state of activation; but it has no way of controlling what kinds of things it observes. The designing of experiments to produce observations is a central part of scientific inquiry, and no model of science can be complete without it.

10.1.2. Two Methodological Myths
What is the relation between theory and experiment? Most descriptions of science subscribe to one of the two following pictures of scientific practice.

> 1. the hypothetico-deductive myth, which says that scientists begin with hypotheses and then do experiments to test them, or
> 2. the inductivist myth, which says that scientists begin by doing experiments and then derive their theories from the data.

In most scientific circles, the hypothetico-deductive myth, whose foremost philosophical advocate is Popper, is dominant. Consider, for example, the standard form of papers published in the journals of the American Psychological Association. They typically begin with a statement of the hypothesis that was tested, then describe the experimental methods, and then finally discuss how the experimental results bear on the hypothesis. This form leads to compact presentation, but sometimes distorts the process by which results were compiled. In well-trod areas of investigation, it may be possible to form a sharp hypothesis and then test it. But when novel topics are being pursued, researchers in psychology and other fields cannot

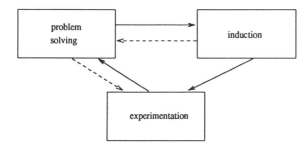

Figure 10.2
Integrated model of scientists.

always start with hypotheses sharp enough to be tested. Often some vague ideas will lead to the collection of some data, which then suggest a refinement of an existing hypothesis. Or results that are very different from what was expected may spur the abductive formation of a new hypothesis that can then be subjected to further test.

This process is too complicated to fit the inductivist myth either, since scientists do not simply begin with data and then move to theories, but are involved in a continuous loop of data collection and theory formation. Figure 10.2 contains a better overall picture of scientific inquiry. There is no favored starting point, no priority given to any of the activities of problem solving, hypothesis formation, or experimentation. Problem solving leads to various kinds of induction, including the formation of hypotheses; the need to test hypotheses leads to the design and execution of experiments; experiments generate problems to be solved, which in turn lead to new hypotheses. These three connections are shown by solid lines. In addition (see the dotted lines), the formation of hypotheses can generate new problems to be solved, if a new generalization or theory can in turn require explanation. And experimentation can be prompted directly by problem solving, for example, in the case where some simple factual information, such as the gravitational constant, is needed.

To flesh out figure 10.2's sketch of the process of inquiry, we need answers to the following six questions:

1. When and how does problem solving lead to induction, especially hypothesis formation?
2. When and how does hypothesis formation lead to experimentation?
3. When and how does experimentation generate problems to be solved?
4. When and how does induction, especially hypothesis formation, lead to problem solving?

5. When and how does problem solving lead to experimentation?

6. Is induction ever prompted directly by experimentation without mediation by problem solving?

PI furnishes at least a beginning to an answer to question (1), since it shows how induction can be triggered during problem solving. Answers to the other questions are much more problematic.

As a first approximation to an answer to question (2), we can say that hypothesis formation leads to experimentation when a new hypothesis has been formed that does not have sufficient grounds for acceptance, either because the evidence that lead to its abduction was weak or because there are alternative hypotheses that contradict it. Recall how PI performs inference to the best explanation. The presence of competing theories may prompt the construction of experiments that would provide evidence that might help to show that one theory explains more than the other. PI might therefore be enhanced by having the simulated conduction of experiments triggered by the process of inference to the best explanation. *How* such experiments are constructed is an even tougher question addressed in section 10.1.3.

To answer question (3), we must note that experiments do not always give rise to problems. If an experiment merely produces some result that fits naturally into existing knowledge, there is no reason to try to explain it. The process by which problem solving arises from experimentation would seem to be something like the following:

a. The experiment is conducted.

b. The results are checked against existing knowledge.

c. If they do not fit, then the attempt to solve the problem of explaining these results is begun.

But what does "fit" mean here? At the simplest level, it might just mean consistency. If the experimental results contradict ones previously obtained, then the problem of explaining both sets of results clearly arises. A looser sense of fit would have to do with the availability of explanations. If the experimental result is similar to ones that have already been explained by a given theory, the system should quickly check to see whether that theory also explains the new result. The check would require invoking the problem-solving procedures, but search for a new solution would be focused on the existing theory. If that search failed to find a solution, then the system would initiate full-blown problem solving that could lead to the generation of new theories. The process just described leads from experiment to problem solving via hypothesis evaluation, and so is equally relevant to question (4).

I suspect that an answer to question (5), concerning how problem solving leads to experimentation, may also require some reference to inductive procedures, although there may well be pure cases in which the attempt to solve some problem requires information that can be obtained experimentally. For example, to figure out how to put people on the moon required a precise calculation of its distance from the earth, which could be gained experimentally. As for question (6), if the assumptions concerning the pragmatics of induction that underlie PI are correct, the answer is no: Experimentation does not lead directly to hypothesis formation without some attempt at problem solving or explanation that focuses learning. In contrast, the BACON programs of Langley et al. (1987) proceed directly from data to laws using heuristics for data analysis, but their simulations of discoveries such as Kepler's laws deviate from actual historical cases (Holland et al., 1986, chapter 11).

10.1.3. Experimental Design as Problem Solving

The second part of questions (2) and (5) concerns how hypothesis formation and problem solving can lead to experimentation. For most practicing scientists, the design and conduct of experiments is their central enterprise, yet philosophers of science have had surprisingly little to tell us about it (a valuable exception is Hacking, 1983).

The design of experiments can be understood as a kind of problem solving in which, as always, analogy plays an important role. Experimental design is not directly concerned with providing explanations, so it will not lead to further hypotheses. As we saw in chapter 3, the essential components of problems are starting conditions and goals, including constraints that must not be violated. The goals of experimental design include obtaining observations that will answer the questions raised by hypothesis formation or problem solving, while practical constraints arise from the availability of facilities, materials, subjects, and so on. Experimental design is clearly a very ill-defined problem, but can become tractable in well-developed domains by the use of analogy. If the phenomena to be investigated are similar to ones that have already been studied, then the experimental techniques for the familiar phenomena can be adapted and carried over. To take an example from psychology, if we want to gain some insight into the duration of some mental process, there is a wealth of experiments using reaction times that can be taken as providing approximate solutions. Every experimental field has a set of available paradigms (in the pre-Kuhnian sense): standard experimental techniques that become the stock in trade of the researcher. A full computational model of scientific research will have to include knowledge of such techniques. It does not appear, however, that any major additions to the theory of problem solving outlined earlier would be needed to accommodate experimental design.

In artificial intelligence, work is just beginning on computational accounts of experimentation. Rajamoney, DeJong, and Faltings (1985) describe a program that works in the domain of liquids. It derives predictions about liquids from what it knows, and when the predictions contradict what is known it devises experiments to determine which of its beliefs must be changed. Friedland and Kedes (1985) have developed a system to aid in the design of experiments in molecular genetics. Shrager (1985) has written a program that simulates experimentation and hypothesis formation by people learning how to use a complex toy. No clear pattern has emerged from these nascent research programs, but the methodology promises to bring much insight into the nature of inquiry.

Figure 10.2 is guilty of exaggerating the links between hypothesis formation and experiments, since sometimes there is a fortuitous mesh of theory and experiment even though these were done independently. The background radiation discovered by Penzias and Wilson using a radio-telescope at Bell Labs proved to be a decisive piece of evidence in favor of the Big Bang theory of the origin of the universe, but the discovery of the radiation was entirely unconnected with the formation or testing of the theory (Hacking, 1983). We must not suppose, therefore, that theory formation and experimentation are always done in the service of each other.

10.1.4. An Illustration: The Extinction of the Dinosaurs

Recent work on dinosaurs illustrates the different elements of the process of inquiry just described. Wilford (1985) has chronicled the recent history of attempts to explain why dinosaurs became extinct 65 million years ago at the end of the Cretaceous period. Their extinction has inspired many abductions, to hypotheses whose postulated causes range from climatic changes to constipation. However, the hypotheses have been short on both consilience and simplicity, typically explaining little more than that the dinosaurs became extinct and requiring a host of assumptions to do so. One such hypothesis was that a comet had collided with earth, leading to the demise of the dinosaurs.

In the 1970s, the geologist Walter Alvarez and his colleagues were studying limestone in Italy, looking for rocks marking reversals in the earth's magnetic field. Serendipitously, they noticed at a level corresponding to the end of the Cretaceous period a thin layer of reddish-gray clay, barren of fossils. This is a case of data collected for purposes quite independent of the theoretical disputes to which they were eventually applied. Alvarez's physicist father, Luis, was consulted and suggested taking a measure of the amount of the rare element iridium in the clay in order to estimate the approximate time span at the Cretaceous boundary. Here we have an experiment leading to a problem and then to another experiment, with, I conjecture, some intervening hypotheses about the origin of the clay. It turned out that the clay contained an extraordinarily large amount of iridium, 30 times more than the sediment above or below it. Since iridium is several thousands times more plentiful in meteorites than in the crust of the earth, they hypothesized that its source was extraterrestrial. The attempt to explain a puzzling phenomenon—the existence of the layer of clay with high iridium content—triggered an abduction.

Suddenly the hypothesis that the dinosaurs became extinct because of collision of the earth with an extraterrestrial object was much more plausible, because the same hypothesis explained both extinction and the iridium layer. The hypothesis had become consilient! The fossil record showed that various species of dinosaurs became extinct at roughly the same time, from which it had been abduced that some cosmic collision had occurred: a collision of the planet earth with another body might have thrown up enough dust to reduce sunlight and vegetation supplies to levels below what the dinosaurs needed to survive. The same collision could have produced the iridium layer. In a detailed paper in *Science*, Alvarez et al. (1980, p. 1095) proclaimed, "In this article we present direct physical evidence for an unusual event at exactly the time of the extinctions in the planktonic realm. None of the current hypotheses adequately accounts for this evidence, but we have developed a hypothesis that appears to offer a satisfactory explanation for nearly all the available paleontological and physical evidence." The presence of high iridium content proved to occur worldwide, and eight other elements in addition to iridium were found to occur in proportions similar to those found in a typical meteorite. Thus the collision hypothesis led to much additional experimental work. Some researchers however, were not convinced that the correct explanation of the extinction of the dinosaurs had been found. They argued that the fossil record did not show that extinction had been a single cataclysmic event and that dinosaurs suffered from gradual decline independently of the cataclysm. The Alvarez group did additional experiments, both to strengthen the evidence for their view and to respond to critics (Alvarez et al., 1984). Through their efforts and those of their critics, richer and more detailed hypotheses were developed, and much new relevant evidence was collected.

Debate on the issue continues. I shall not attempt to speculate concerning the fate of the Alvarez's hypothesized explanation of dinosaur extinction, which has been introduced here merely to illustrate some of the aspects of scientific investigation. The development of ideas in this case is not compatible with either of the methodological myths discussed in section 10.1.2, but can only be understood using a much more complex, interactive model of the process of inquiry. I now consider still another kind of complexity concerning the social side of science.

10.2. Parallel Computation and Group Rationality

The account of scientific inquiry summarized in figure 10.2 finds an integrated place for experimentation, but it still provides a simplistic account of scientific inquiry. It assumes that science is essentially performed by an individual thinker who solves problems, forms hypotheses, and does experiments. Science today is performed by large communities of scientists working sometimes in collaboration, sometimes in conflict. Problem solving, hypothesis formation, and experimentation in a given field may be distributed across individuals. Different groups may be involved in the advocacy and exploration of conflicting hypotheses.

From a computational viewpoint, scientific communities can be thought of as highly parallel processors of information. Philosophical models of rationality have almost always focused on the rationality of the individual, but we shall see that group rationality may be more than a simple sum of the rationality of the individuals. To make this point, I shall first consider various advantages that recent work in computer science has found for parallel processing, and then show more particularly how viewing science as done by numerous individuals working in parallel has important philosophical consequences.

10.2.1. The Importance of Parallel Computation

It might be thought that the only computational importance of parallelism derives from speed: parallel processors operating together cannot do anything that a single processor cannot; they just do it faster. Similarly, group rationality in science might just be an aggregate of individual scientists' rationality. I shall argue, however, that parallel design of computers can offer more than just increased speed of operation: it can lead to qualitatively different means of information processing. Similarly, group rationality may require different overall standards than individual rationality.

Let us look first at parallel computation. According to Wirth (1976) and other theorists, a program should be understood as consisting of data structures and algorithms for manipulating those structures (see tutorial C). The structures and algorithms are interdependent: the algorithms must work with the data in the form given to them. In languages like Pascal, data structures are conceptually distinct from the procedures that use them, whereas in LISP procedures are themselves data structures, namely, lists. In both cases, however, it is impossible to specify algorithms without noting the kinds of structures on which they operate. Philosophers tend to assume the ubiquity of only one kind of data structure—the proposition—and only one kind of algorithm—logical reasoning. But computer science offers a wealth of structures in which data can be stored: arrays, tables, records, frames, and so on. We saw in chapter 2 that our view of the nature of thinking can be broadened considerably by allowing for the possibility of nonpropositional data structures and nonlogistic processing mechanisms.

Programming is often a matter of style. Any programmer knows that some programming tasks are much easier to do in some languages than in others. You could conceivably write AI programs in Pascal, or even assembly language, but it is much easier to design and write such symbol-manipulating programs in LISP. Thus qualitatively it is much easier to produce programs in languages that provide facilities for the appropriate kinds of data structures and algorithms. Some programming theorists even urge a kind of computational Whorf hypothesis, claiming that using a particular programming language can have a substantial effect on how problems are conceived. (Dijkstra jokes that Basic and Fortran cause permanent brain damage.)

These features of programming point to a general argument for the qualitative importance of parallel processing. Some programming tasks are much more naturally done using particular kinds of data structures and algorithms found in particular programming languages, and great gains in efficiency and ease of use can be achieved by tailoring hardware for particular programming functions. Hence in contrast to the in-principle compatibility of any program with any hardware, we find in practice that a good fit of software and hardware is indispensable, which opens the door for the potential usefulness of hardware that employs parallel processors.

In the remainder of this section, I shall try to illustrate this general lesson with specific cases concerning parallel computation. Parallel architectures offer not merely speed, but different kinds of programs that have the potential of being more reliable, more flexible, and more easily produced than programs for serial computers.

Reliability   Parallelism can engender much more natural ways of providing for system reliability than are found in serial machines. Compare, for example, the effects of removing part of the memory of a digital computer with the effect of removing a similarly small part of the human brain. In the brain, memory and processing capacity seem to be distributed over large areas, so that remaining parts can compensate for what has been removed. In contrast, removal of storage for part of a serial computer program will result eventually in a total breakdown of the program. Parallel machines such as that of Hillis (1981, p. 9) can operate much more like the human brain. A system with a few faulty cells can continue to function, since algorithms do not depend on a cell existing at a specific address. The neighbors of a cell can identify it as defective and ignore it, with performance continuing with only a slight degradation.

We can of course contrive reliability with serial computers. In the early days of computers, when failure of vacuum tubes was frequent, two computers were sometimes used in tandem, providing checking and backup for each other. But it is clearly more efficient to avoid this total duplication of resources and build some degree of reliability into each system.

Flexibility   Most philosophers and computer scientists abhor inconsistency. (Psychologists, in contrast, often enjoy it.) Popper (1965) and others have argued that an inconsistent system is worthless, since any proposition follows logically from a contradiction. Quine (1960) has urged a "principle of charity" that requires that we always interpret the utterances of others in such a was as to avoid finding them in violation of the rules of logic. "Neat" artificial intelligence researchers who see logic as the paradigm for knowledge representation (Nilsson, 1983) and similarly appalled by the havoc that inconsistency can wreak in an elegant system.

In contrast, Minsky (1974) has argued that consistency is not a paramount virtue; a sufficiently flexible system can function despite contradictions (see also Thagard, 1984). Chapter 7 contended that it is sometimes legitimate to attribute irrationality to humans, if there is an empirically supported account of what they are doing instead of following the laws of logic. Consistency then need not be a defining characteristic of an intelligent processing system.

This is especially clear from the perspective of parallel computation. Unlike a serial machine, a parallel machine does not need detailed coordination of its components. It does not matter if the information in one cell of Hillis' connection machine contradicts information in other cells, although at some point a real conflict—one that causes processing problems—may arise. Rather than imposing uniformity, different parts of a processing system can pursue different strategies for attacking problems. The alternative is to fix on a canonical set of ideas too soon, or to undergo repeated Popperian oscillations and reject well-developed sets of ideas. Parallelism is thus useful for a scruffy approach to the nature of knowledge that has room for logical contradictions.

Parallelism lends itself to audacity. With multiple hypotheses a system can afford to maintain daring but improbable hypotheses that stand little chance of being true, but that may lead to great payoffs in the unlikely event they work out. Proceeding serially, a system must tend more to look for hypotheses that are only optimal in a limited local context.

Some of the flexibility of parallelism is evident in the system PI. PI simulates parallelism by allowing the firing of any number of production rules at a single timestep, so that no strict priority of rules need be maintained. Spreading activation of concepts and the different kinds of learning also occur in parallel. The result is that the system need not concentrate on only one possible solution to a problem at a time, but can simultaneously be considering different tacks. We saw how PI simulates the discovery of the wave theory of sound but is also able at the same time to discover and explore the consequences of a particle theory.

Thus a parallel architecture more naturally gives rise to mechanisms of rational deliberation that admit flexibility in considering multiple hypotheses. Various parts of the system can work out solutions without constantly checking on what other parts of the system are doing. At some point—when external action is required—at least a partial unification must occur. How control is established is an open question; elsewhere I criticize the view that consciousness provides the needed control in humans (Thagard, 1986).

Another way in which parallelism can encourage flexibility is through the emergence, rather than the explicit programming, of important structures. Rumelhart et al. (1986) describe how schemas can be understood as emerging from much simpler connections in parallel distributed processing systems. One result is that schemas need not offer monolithic characterizations of kinds of things, but may be constructed as situations demand. A system would not store a rigid, unified schema for a restaurant, for example, but would have a set of expectations about what is likely to happen in a restaurant emerging from the parallel activity of simpler structures. Although the emphasis on emergence through parallel activity is characteristic of those like Rumelhart who favor subsymbolic "connectionist" computational models, most of the points I am making here apply just as well to symbolic parallel systems like PI.

Producibility   No processing system is created from scratch. The human mind is the product of millions of years of evolution, and design of a modern computer also has to build on ideas that already exist. My claim in this section is that parallel systems might be more "producible" in some contexts than serial ones.

Biological evolution has proceeded without any overall design, with progressively more complex information processing systems being built on top of existing ones. The current human mind-brain is a consequence of the whole evolutionary chain of mammalian development. If artificial intelligence were easier to devise, producibility might not be an issue for computers. In the early days of AI, there was much hope that programmers could directly enter into computers enough information to make them intelligent, but it is increasingly clear that this kind of spoon-feeding has limitations. Expert systems are proliferating, but each is restricted to a narrow domain. To be intelligent, computers must have some of the flexibility and learning capacity that people do. Thus parallel computation, if it brings the benefits described above, might allow intelligent machines to be produced by human designers who cannot see the whole, incredibly complex picture. Parallelism would allow greater subdivision of design tasks with no worry about all the interactions that might occur.

10.2.2. Parallelism in Scientific Communities

Thus parallelism offers many potential advantages to computation, and some of these may carry over to thinking of scientific inquiry as a collective enterprise. Scientific communities can be viewed as highly parallel systems (Kornfeld and Hewitt, 1981). Whereas individuals are generally expected to maintain consistency and coherence in their beliefs, a community can be expected to have sharply competing views. Proponents of different theories fight it out in the journals and other public forums. This kind of competition may well be better suited to the goals of scientific research than a more monolithic approach would be, since it is difficult to predict from what quarters good new ideas will come. Scientific communities require some degree of coordination to function, but they can clearly accommodate some differences in doctrine and even in method. Groups of scientists can thus have a kind of flexibility not found in individuals. Moreover, groups can also have the advantage of reliability, overcoming the aberrations of a few eccentric, incompetent, or even immoral individuals. Scientific knowledge is so complex that we cannot expect any one scientist to possess or contribute more than a tiny fraction of it, so producibility is also a gain of the social nature of science.

A simple computational model for this kind of group activity would be something like figure 10.3. Each individual reseracher would be like the one described in figure 10.2. The central executive would serve to collect and communicate information from the separate researchers. In actual science, professional journals serve much of this function, with journal editors and

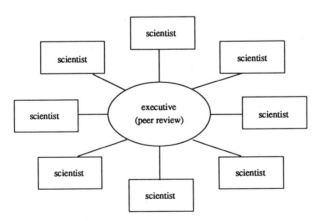

Figure 10.3
Science as parallel processing.

referees functioning to screen the results of research for what is worth looking at by other researchers. Individual scientists pursue their research through processes of problem solving, hypothesis formation, and experimentation, but share the results of their investigation through the executive. A further complicating factor is that scientists often work in teams rather than individually.

10.2.3. Group Rationality

With individuals working in parallel, we may ask what standards of rationality are appropriate (cf. Sarkar, 1983). The possibility arises that divisions of labor and method may be more efficacious in accomplishing the goal of scientific advance than the uniform alternative, in which all the individuals are methodologically similar. One current division of labor is that between theoreticians and experimenters, a division important in physics but not in current psychology. This division, however, may not have any normative significance, since it may reflect only individual differences in talents and inclinations.

A much more sensitive methodological issue concerns the question, raised in the discussion of methodological conservatism in chapter 8, of the extent to which scientists should be attached to their own hypotheses. In the parallel model of figure 10.3, we can easily imagine that different hypotheses have been discovered by different researchers. On the standard philosophical account, the attitude that each researcher has to a hypothesis of his or her own invention should be no different from the critical attitude toward hypotheses of other researchers. In real life, however, we know that people rarely live up to this standard. Scientists are as passionate as anyone else.

But perhaps we would not want it otherwise. The motivation derived from personal attachment to a hypothesis may lead to more thorough and intense research than would otherwise be done. Undoubtedly we can find cases where undue attachment to a theory led to disastrous results, excessive conservatism, or even fraud. But especially for incipient research programs, it is hard to imagine how research could be done without a degree of conviction on the part of a researcher that is greater than what would be justified by the evidence. New theories, like children, cannot always be subjected to the standards of grown-ups. Perhaps scientific research proceeds best when there is a division of labor between audacious but reckless thinkers, on the one hand, and careful but less original critics on the other. The critics would make the best journal editors, but would not necessarily be the developers of the most interesting research.

10.2.4. The Need for Experiments

How can we settle these issues about group rationality, about what methodologies are best distributed among investigators? Potentially, the question has an empirical answer, but it does not appear feasible to do a controlled experiment on human scientists, dividing them into groups with different methodologies and observing their performance. But we are not far off from being able to do computer simulations of group operations. Instead of modeling the problem-solving processes of a single individual as in PI, we could computationally model the operation of a group in which different individuals play different roles. If competing methodologies were developed explicitly enough to be programmed, we could compare a group of conservative Kuhnian scientists with a group of more critical Popperian scientists; my conjecture is that in the long run the Kuhnian group would accomplish more. Even more interesting, we could consider a mixed group with different methodological styles, encompassing the audacious, the critical, and the conservative. The experimental results might be an important contribution of computational philosophy of science to the theory of group rationality in science. At the very least, the exercise of working out the nature of such methodologies in sufficient detail to be implemented in a computational model would be highly illuminating.

10.3. Summary

Scientific inquiry cannot be simply characterized in terms of either the formation of hypotheses from data or the use of experiments to test hypotheses. The process of inquiry consists of interacting subprocesses of problem solving, theorizing, and experimentation. Future developments in computational philosophy of science will construct models of these inter-actions. We can also hope to develop still more complex parallel models that can take into account the social nature of science by considering investigators working with varying methods and motivations.

10.4. Conclusion

For some contemporary philosophers, the computational investigations in this book may only marginally count as philosophical. It is short on sharp conceptual analyses of key terms, but we have seen many reasons connected with the nature of concepts and meaning for rejecting definition as an important philosophical enterprise. Rather, this book is written in the conviction that philosophy is a theoretical enterprise that must be developed hand in hand with scientific findings, not the vagaries of common sense and imagination. In place of the folksy stories and intuitions that have been the stock-in-trade of many epistemologists, computational philosophy of science looks to the history of science, cognitive psychology, and artificial intelligence for examples, empirical constraints, and techniques. Philosophy is continuous with science, differing only in that it deals with issues that are more general, speculative, and normative than those typically found in individual sciences. The branches of philosophy concerned with reasoning are continuous with psychology and artificial intelligence. An enormous amount of work remains to be done to develop a computationally detailed, historically accurate, psychologically plausible, and philosophically defensible account of the structure and growth of scientific knowledge.

Appendix 1: Tutorials

These tutorials are intended to provide background material for the discussion in the main text. The first two, on philosophy of science and logic, are intended for readers without a background in those areas of philosophy. The third, concerned with data structures and algorithms, is for readers new to computer science. The fourth, on the notion of a schema, is designed for readers unfamiliar with recent work in cognitive psychology. References in each tutorial should provide directions for anyone interested in pursuing the issues beyond the simplifications unavoidable here.

A. Outline of the Philosophy of Science

Like most of philosophy, the philosophy of science can be traced back to Plato and Aristotle. With the rise of science in the sixteenth and seventeenth centuries, reflection expanded on the question of how experiment and hypothesis could lead to knowledge. The most influential manifesto of the new science was Francis Bacon's *Novum Organum*, first published in 1620, which formulated rules for discovering causal laws from experimental observations. Through the seventeenth and eighteenth centuries, controversies about scientific views were intermixed with controversies about methodology, for example, in debates between Cartesians and Newtonians about celestial mechanics and the appropriate role for hypotheses. Losee (1980) provides a helpful outline of the history of the philosophy of science, while Laudan (1968) provides a comprehensive bibliography.

In the first half of the nineteenth century, three major works defined the philosophy of science. In 1830, John Herschel published his *Preliminary Discourse on Natural Philosophy*, which accommodated both Baconian discovery of causal laws from observation and the use of hypotheses that go beyond what is observed. William Whewell's *Philosophy of the Inductive Sciences*, published in 1840, contained insightful discussions of the importance of scientific concepts and explanatory theories (see chapter 5). But in 1843 John Stuart Mill published the first of many editions of his *System of Logic*, which proved to be more in keeping with the empiricist temper of the times. (Empiricism is the philosophical position that knowledge comes through sense experience.)

Whereas Whewell followed Kant (1929) in emphasizing the role of the mind in providing concepts that unify observations, Mill followed Bacon in concentrating on the way in which laws could be derived from nature. Mill and Bacon recognized that there is more to the formation of causal laws than induction by simple enumeration, in which we go from noticing that all observed A's are B's to the conclusion that all A's are B's (this is similar to Mill's method of agreement). We should also apply the method of difference, in which we consider cases where the absence of A is associated with the absence of B, as well as considering the extent to which A's and B's vary together. In all such cases, though, we never go far from what is observed. Whewell, in contrast, emphasized how concepts such as "force" and "light wave", which cannot be derived directly from sense experience, play an important role in the development of powerful theories.

In the 1920s and 1930s, there emerged in Europe a school of very talented philosophers of science known as the Vienna Circle, advocating a doctrine that came to be known as "logical positivism" or "logical empiricism". It combined an empiricist epistemology (theory of knowledge) with the techniques of formal logic that had been developed by Frege and Russell (see tutorial B). Those techniques made possible a degree of rigor new to philosophy, and led, in the hands of researchers such as Carnap (1950), Reichenbach (1938), and Hempel (1965), to exact analyses of central scientific notions. According to the logical positivists, scientific theories are to be understood as sets of axioms in formal deductive systems. Theories are confirmed by deducing their consequences from the axioms, and checking to see whether the predictions hold. In contrast to earlier empiricist views such as those of Mill, this methodology is called hypothetico-deductive because it emphasizes the use of hypotheses to make predictions, rather than the derivation of laws from observations. The views of Popper (1959) evolved around the same time as those of the logical positivists, and were also hypothetico-deductive, but differed primarily in that he saw the main role of prediction to be the attempt to falsify theories, not to confirm them. The general hypothetico-deductive scheme is

> Start with hypothesis H.
> Use logic to deduce predicted observation O.
> If O is observed, then H is confirmed (Hempel), but
> if not-O is observed H is falsified (Popper).

Hempel developed in the 1940s a related account of scientific explanation that remains influential. It is called the *deductive-nomological* model, because explanation is analyzed as deduction from laws (in Greek, *nomos* means law). The general schema for explanation (Hempel 1965) is

$L_1, L_2, L_3, \ldots, L_r.$	General laws.
$C_1, C_2, C_3, \ldots, C_k.$	Statements of antecedent conditions.

E	Description of the empirical phenomenon to be explained.

Here the empirical phenomenon E is explained by showing that it follows from the antecedent conditions and the general laws. E is called the *explanandum* (plural *explananda*).

The logical positivist movement had great influence in philosophy and also in the sciences, particularly psychology, where its injunction to tie theory closely with observation fit very well with behaviorism. But in the late 1950s, critics influenced in part by the later writings of Wittgenstein (1953) began to attack some of its central tenets. Toulmin (1953) and Hanson (1958) criticized the hypothetico-deductive account of theories and argued that theory and observation were much more intertwined than empiricists allowed. In 1962, the first edition of Thomas Kuhn's *Structure of Scientific Revolutions* appeared, and it became the most influential work in the philosophy of science of the succeeding decades. Instead of neat logical theories, Kuhn talked of *paradigms*, complex conceptual schemes that govern not only how we see the world but even, at least in some of his pronouncements, how the world is. Kuhn, Feyerabend, and others used historical analyses to show that the elegant analyses of scientific theories that logical positivists offered bear little relation to scientific practice. Other criticisms of positivism came from proponents of scientific realism, the position that science is not restricted to what is observable but can achieve knowledge of what is nonobservable. Suppe (1977) provides a comprehensive account of the critique of the logical positivist view of science and some recent attempts to develop alternatives.

Today, philosophy of science is characterized by a variety of approaches. In methodology, some philosophers look more to history, others to logical analysis. In metaphysics, some are relativist, denying any notion of truth; some continue the empiricist tradition and proclaim that science is concerned with truth only with respect to what can be observed; and some are realists, attributing truth even to scientific theories. Discovery as well as justification is a topic of investigation for some philosophers. I have not attempted anything like a survey of contemporary philosophy of science, but many of these issues are discussed further in chapters of this book.

B. Formal Logic

In the late nineteenth century, the Austrian mathematician Frege developed a mathematical approach to logic, which formerly had been a largely qualitative study of various forms of reasoning. Russell and Whitehead's *Principia Mathematica*, published in the early part of this century, developed Frege's work in a more palatable formalism, so that today formal logic is an indispensable tool for philosophers and computer scientists. This tutorial gives only enough of a sketch to provide a minimal background to matters discussed in the rest of this book. Texts by Copi (1979, 1982) provide basic introductions to the notions mentioned here, and Mendelson (1964) is a much fuller discussion.

The simplest system of formal logic is propositional logic, in which formulas like **p** and **q** are used to stand for sentences such as "Paul is a philosopher" and "Quincy is a doctor". Simple formulas can be combined into more complex ones using symbols such as "&" for "and", "v" for "or", and "→" for if-then. For example, the sentence

If Paul is a philosopher, then Quincy is a doctor.

becomes

p → q.

To express negation, **not-p** is written as ∼**p**. A deduction consists of a sequence of steps, each of which is licensed by a rule of inference. Two of the most common rules of inference make it possible to draw conclusions using conditionals (if-then sentences):

Modus ponens: **p → q**
                  p
                  _____
                  Therefore **q**.

Modus tollens: **p → q**
                  not-q
                  _____
                  Therefore **not-p**.

From the conditional "If Paul is a philosopher then Quincy is a doctor" and the information that Paul is a philosopher, *modus ponens* enables you to infer that Quincy is a doctor. From the information that Quincy is not a doctor it follows by *modus tollens* that Paul is not a philosopher.

In propositional logic, statements such as "Quincy is a doctor" have to be treated as atomic wholes, but the predicate calculus, a modern version of Frege's ideas, allows further analysis. Predicate calculus distinguishes between predicates such as "is a doctor" or "is a philosopher" and constants referring to individuals such as Paul and Quincy. In the version of predicate calculus most familiar to philosophers, "Quincy is a doctor" would be formalized as **D(q)**, where "q" now stands for the individual

Quincy rather than for a proposition. Researchers in computer science tend to express this more mnemonically as **is-doctor (quincy)**. In additional to simple properties, predicates can be used to express relations between two or more things. For example, "Quincy loves Hortense" becomes **loves (quincy, hortense)**.

Predicate logic is able to formalize sentences with quantifiers such as "all" and "some" by using variables such as "x" and "y". The sentence "All doctors are rich" can be formalized as

(for-all x)(doctor(x) → rich(x))

or, more compactly, **(x)(Dx → Rx)**. The sentence "Some doctors are rich" becomes

(there-is x)(doctor(x) & rich(x));

i.e., there is some x that is both a doctor and rich. New rules of inference enable deductions to be drawn from and to quantified sentences. For example, the rule of Universal Instantiation allows the derivation of an instance from a sentence involving "all", as when **(for-all x)(doctor(x) → rich(x))** is instantiated by **doctor (quincy) → rich (quincy)**: if all doctors are rich, it follows that if Quincy is a doctor, then he is rich.

So far, I have only described the syntax of propositional and predicate logic, that is, the form of expressions and the rules of inference that operate on them. Semantics is concerned with the relations of expressions to the world. In logic, semantics concerns how the truth of complex expressions can be a function of simpler expressions. In propositional logic, it is easy to see how the truth of **p & q** is a function of the truth of **p** and **q**: **p & q** is true if and only if both **p** and **q** are true. If-then is more complicated, but logic simplifies it by specifying that **p → q** is false if **p** is true and **q** is false, but true otherwise.

Defining truth in predicate logic is more complex. An interpretation is a structure ⟨**D, I**⟩, where **D** is a set of objects and **I** is an interpretive function that provides an assignment to predicate letters and constants in a formal language. The function **I** would, for example, pick out an individual corresponding to the constant "quincy" and a set of individuals corresponding to the predicate "doctor". We can then say that **doctor(quincy)** is true just in case the assignment of **quincy** is a member of the assignment of **doctor**. The sentence **(for-all x)(doctor(x) → rich(x))** is true just in case the interpretation of **doctor** is a subset of the assignment of **rich**. An interpretation under which a set of expressions all come out true is said to be a *model* for the expressions, so this kind of semantics, due originally to Tarski (1956), is often called model-theoretic semantics.

C. Data Structures and Algorithms

A computer program is a set of instructions that produces a sequence of actions in a computer. More fully, we can say that a program consists of data structures and algorithms (Wirth, 1976; Aho, Hopcroft, and Ullman 1983). There are many different kinds of data structures. LISP, the programming language most used in artificial intelligence, is short for "LISt Processing"; its basic data structures are lists, consisting of atoms (words or numbers) enclosed in parentheses. These can range from simple lists such as

(apple banana pear peach)

to more complex structures with lists embedded in lists, as in

((fruits (banana pear peach)) (vegetables (carrot potato))).

Lists can be used to create more complex structures such as trees, stacks, and queues. A stack, for example, is a linear list in which elements are created and deleted from one end, like a stack of papers on a desk where you only look at what is on top. Lists can naturally be used to represent expressions in predicate calculus, as in the following example, slightly modified from tutorial B:

((for-all x) (doctor (x) → rich (x))).

This consists of a list with two elements, each of which is a list, the first one containing two atoms: **for-all** and **x**.

Data structures are useless without procedures that operate on them. Many useful procedures can be defined for lists, such as finding the first element of the list or what remains after the first element has been removed. Given a set of primitive procedures, more complex procedures can be defined. An *algorithm* is a procedure that operates in a sequence of well-defined steps and yields a solution. We could, for example, define a procedure for finding the second element of a list roughly as follows: remove the first element from the list and take the first element of what remains. The algorithms that can be performed depend on what data structures have been set up to work with; correlatively, the value of a data structure depends on what algorithms are available to process the information that it contains.

In current artificial intelligence, much attention is paid to the field of *knowledge representation*, which concerns ways of structuring knowledge for efficient use. Three main approaches to knowledge representation have developed (Barr and Feigenbaum, 1981). In logic programming implemented in languages such as Prolog (Clocksin and Mellish, 1981), the data structures are simplified versions of expressions in predicate calculus, and the basic algorithm is a kind of deductive proof mechanism. In rule-based systems, knowledge is expressed in production rules much like conditionals in predicate calculus:

IF x is a doctor, THEN x is rich.

The algorithms in rule-based systems match the rules against a base of knowledge and then draw conclusions in a procedural equivalent of two logical rules of inference, universal instantiation and *modus ponens*, inferring, for instance, that Quincy is rich because he is a doctor. Or they can search from desired conclusions back toward relevant information: given the goal of finding who is rich, the system can set the new subgoal of finding who is a doctor. Newell and Simon (1972) provide a classic description of the uses of rule-based systems, and Buchanan and Shortliffe (1984) describe some of the most important expert systems that have been constructed within this framework.

The third kind of knowledge representation now prevalent in AI uses the notion of a frame (Minsky, 1975). Frames are used to describe typical objects or events, using slots and values. For example, we can describe a typical banana by the frame

Banana
A-kind-of: fruit
Grown-in: tropics
Color: yellow
Length: 8 inches etc.

The A-kind-of slots establish a hierarchy: a banana is a kind of fruit that is a kind of food, and so on. Here yellow is the value of the slot for color. It is a "default" value, expressing the typical color of bananas rather than part of a definition. As Hayes (1979) has pointed out, we can translate the information in the frame into predicate calculus, or into production rules for that matter. But what is important to the selection of data structures is not just the information they contain, but the kinds of algorithms that are natural to apply to them. Much very recent work in artificial intelligence is employing hybrid representations to make possible a variety of algorithms for processing information.

A distinction is often drawn between algorithms and heuristics. A *heuristic* is a rough rule of thumb that is not guaranteed to produce a solution but stands at least some chance of helping to produce one. Algorithms, in contrast, are guaranteed to produce a solution. You know an easy algorithm for adding two long numbers together, but at best a set of rules of thumb for figuring out how to make the best roast chicken. Since we lack algorithms for performing most intelligent tasks, artificial intelligence is often said to use heuristics. It must be remembered, however, that all computer programs use algorithms at a lower level, so that the implementation of a heuristic requires the use of a host of algorithms. These are the programming procedures that are used to carry out the heuristic.

D. Schemas

Tutorial C described the artificial intelligence data structures called frames. Empirical studies in cognitive psychology have suggested that human thinking employs structures that are framelike in chunking information into useful patterns and expressing default information. In cognitive psychology, frames are more commonly referred to as schemas or "schemata". Although intense discussion of schemas has occurred only recently, the notion of a schema can be found in Bartlett (1932), and related notions occur in Head (1926) and Kant (1929). The psychological literature on schemas has become voluminous and diverse, and I shall not attempt to survey it. Useful surveys include Rumelhart (1980), Anderson (1980, chapter 5), Hastie (1981), and especially Brewer and Nakamura (1984).

Whereas frames can be given a relatively exact characterization as structures in LISP, schemas are theoretical psychological entities postulated to explain a variety of observed phenomena of human cognition, so no exact definition is to be expected. Roughly, a schema is a large, complex unit of knowledge expressing what is typical of a group of instances. By the very nature of the term, schemas involve some sort of abstraction and generalization. Schemas are posited to provide the same advantages to human cognition that frames provide to a computer. A set of schemas serves to generate a set of expectations, so that the thinker need not confront external information passively. Incoming information is processed by matching it with existing schemas, which immediately makes possible the utilization of information already acquired. For example, recognizing something as a restaurant produces a set of expectations and possible inferences using procedural mechanisms such as inheritance and defaults. Schemas, like frames, are presumably organized into complex hierarchies at progressively higher levels of abstraction.

A script (Schank and Abelson, 1977) is an important kind of schema that describes a typical sequence of events. People generally expect events in a restaurant to occur in an order much like the following: be greeted, be seated, order drinks, order food, eat, order desert, pay bill, leave. You would be very surprised if food were brought to you before you had ordered it, or if you were in a standard full-service restaurant and were asked to pay immediately after ordering. The restaurant script has other scripts embedded within it, and is itself embedded in the general frame or schema for restaurant.

Other examples of areas in which schemas have been thought to be psychologically important include category terms, such as bird, and social stereotypes, such as Irish. A schema for bird would differ from a conceptual analysis providing necessary and sufficient conditions: the point of a schema is not to define what properties belong to all and only birds, but to list properties typical of birds. Thus, a schema for bird would likely contain the default information that birds fly. The schema for the stereotypical Irishman might include a default for being Catholic. Obviously, there are potential costs as well as benefits in the use of schemas in reasoning, since error can result from careless use of default values.

The existence of such errors in human reasoning is one of the kinds of evidence that researchers have used to support claims for the psychological reality of schemas. In Brewer and Treyens (1981), subjects were asked to recall what items were in a university office in which they had been kept waiting. They often made the mistake of "recalling" that there were books in the office, even though there were none. Having a schema for university office that included a default for the presence of books would explain their error.

Schema theory also accounts for the fact that people are much better able to integrate new information about familiar topics into memory than they are able to learn unfamiliar information. To take just one example, Chiesi et al. (1979) found that people who understood baseball remembered much more new information on the topic than did nonfans. Schemas also affect the speed with which items can be recalled from memory. It should be easier to recall events that instantiate schemas and thereby are more easily accessed. A mounting list of results supports the view that the human processing system employs something like schemas to facilitate encoding and recall of information. Schemas have been postulated to have important functions in perception, discourse understanding, learning, remembering, and problem solving. Although schema theory is by no means universally accepted, the wealth of empirical applications that have been found for it provides at least a presumption that the human information processing system uses framelike structures. In addition to references already cited, see, for example, Bower, Black, and Turner (1979), Thorndyke and Hayes-Roth (1979), Cantor and Mischel (1977), Lichtenstein and Brewer (1980), Abelson (1981), and Chi, Feltovich, and Glaser (1981).

The relation between schemas and propositions is more difficult to discuss than the relation between frames and sentences in predicate calculus. Schemas are psychological entities, and there are grave problems in saying just what their structure is, how many of them there are, and how they are used. Of course, there are also great difficulties, both philosophical and psychological, in saying what a proposition is (see, for example, Gale, 1967). In the foreseeable course of empirical inquiry, there does not seem to be an experimental way of determining whether schemas have propositions as constituents. Nevertheless, the schema notion clearly has significance that is independent of the issue of whether schemas are constituted of propositions, since even if they are, they nevertheless have important emergent procedural properties. The schema, as a whole, plays a role in information processing that cannot be ascribed to unconnected, unorganized sets of propositions. Hence, despite the vagueness of the notion of a schema, there are empirical and conceptual reasons for supposing that schemas go beyond the propositional knowledge structures usually discussed by philosophers.

Appendix 2: Specification of PI

This appendix provides an outline of the structure of PI, intermediate between the general description in the text and a listing of the LISP code. The program was written by the author, based on ideas developed in collaboration with Keith Holyoak. A well-written LISP program is not like a program in Basic or Fortran that consists of a long sequence of instructions with GOTO's. Rather, like programs in more structured languages, such as Pascal and C, it consists of routines encapsulated in functions that call other functions. A good introduction to LISP including production systems is Anderson, Corbett, and Reiser (1986). The following outline of the operation of the major LISP functions in PI omits descriptions of minor functions, of which there are more than 200. Full documented code is available from the author. LISP function names are indicated in capital letters.

1. Data Structure Creation

    1.1 MAKE_RULE constructs rules whose names are LISP atoms, the property lists of which include the following features: conditions (the "if" part), consisting of a list of clauses, each of which has the same structure as the messages defined in chapter 2; actions (the "then" part); strength; status (actual or default); slot-name; activation; concepts to which the rule is attached.

    1.2 MAKE_CONCEPT constructs concepts whose names are LISP atoms, the property lists of which include the following features: superordinates, subordinates, attached rules, instances, activation.

    1.3 MAKE_PROBLEM constructs problems whose names are LISP atoms, the property lists of which include the following features: starting description, consisting of lists of messages; goals, which are also lists of messages; activation. Problems are either planning problems, where the goals are states to be reached, or explanations, where the goals are facts to be explained.

2. *Problem Solving and Explanation*

Figure A.1 outlines the problem solving and learning mechanisms in PI, showing the place in the program of most of the functions described below. The lines indicate that one function calls another: in execution of the program; EXPLAIN calls SOLVE–PROBLEM, which calls CHECK–FOR–SUCCESS, and so on.

2.1 SOLVE–PROBLEM contains the main loop of PI. In explanation problems, SOLVE–PROBLEM is called by EXPLAIN (see 2.5). Problem solving proceeds as follows:

2.1.1 Activate a given problem and the concepts from its goals and starting descriptions. Add the starting descriptions to the list of active messages.

2.1.2 Begin loop by checking whether the problem is solved, i.e., whether all the goals have been matched by active messages. If so, store the solved problem with the concepts from its starting conditions and goals. Also check whether any of the goals of the problem have been violated by projections started by EXECUTE–ACTIONS (2.2.3); if so, stop the projection.

2.1.3 Look for analogous problems. See TRIG–ANALOGY (3.1).

2.1.4 Trigger inductions. See TRIGGER (4.1).

2.1.5 Evaluate, select, and fire the best rules. See FIRE–RULES (2.2).

2.1.6 Spread activation. See CHANGE–ACTIVATION (2.3).

2.1.7 Do subgoaling. See SET–SUB–GOALS (2.4).

2.1.8 Repeat 2.1.2.

2.2 FIRE–RULES selects what rules to fire by going through the following sequence:

2.2.1 EVALUATE looks at each active rule. If a rule has all its conditions matched by active messages, then the overall value of the rule is calculated on the basis of its activation, strength, and the minimum confidence of the messages that matched the conditions. Variables in the actions are bound to values established by the match between conditions and messages.

2.2.2 SELECT–RULES uses the values calculated by EVALUATE to select the best n rules for firing, where n is an arbitrary number selected by the programmer.

2.2.3 EXECUTE–ACTIONS creates new messages out of the actions of the rules selected for firing. If an action involves a projected move, i.e., something done rather than something merely deduced, then PI starts a *projection*. (For example, search for solution of the problem of how to get from New York to Los Angeles might involve this projected action: go to Newark airport. If there

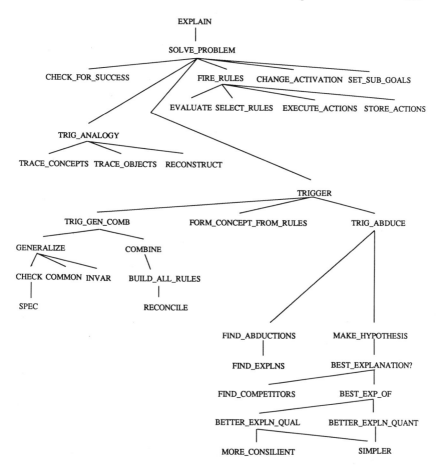

Figure A.1
Major LISP functions of PI.

are no flights at appropriate times from Newark to Los Angeles, this projection must be stopped and some other action considered.) Further inferences (such as that you are in New Jersey, if you are in Newark) are marked as depending on such a projection.

2.2.4 STORE_ACTIONS stores the new messages with the relevant concepts where they can be retrieved when the concept becomes active.

2.3 CHANGE_ACTIVATION updates the state of activation of the system. Concepts from the actions of fired rules become active. Concepts that are the subordinates or superordinates of active concepts become active. Concepts whose activation falls below a given threshold are deactivated. Messages, rules, and old problem solutions attached to active concepts become active.

2.4 SET_SUB_GOALS spreads activation backward from goals, unlike CHANGE_ACTIVATION, which spreads it forward from the starting conditions by rule firing. SET_SUB_GOALS matches the actions of active rules against the goals, and then activates the concepts from the conditions of rules that might contribute to goal solution.

2.5 EXPLAIN initiates solution of explanation problems. If what is to be explained is a set of facts (messages), it starts a problem whose goals are those facts. If what is to be explained is a rule, it starts a problem whose starting conditions are the conditions of the rule and whose goals are the actions.

3. Analogical Problem Solving

3.1 TRIG_ANALOGY triggers analogical problem solving, looking at the most active of stored problem solutions. That stored problem solution becomes the *base* for solution of the problem to be solved, the *target*.

3.2 ANALOGIZE attempts to use the base (stored problem solution) in solution of the target problem, by the following steps:

3.2.1 Find what concepts are in the base are related to what concepts in the target by TRACE_CONCEPTS (3.3).

3.2.2 Find what objects in the base are related to what objects in the target by TRACE_OBJECTS (3.4).

3.2.3 Note what effectors or hypotheses took place during the solution of the base. This information is stored by EXECUTE_ACTIONS (2.2.3) and MAKE_HYPOTHESIS (4.7.2).

3.2.4 Use these effectors or hypotheses to contribute toward a new problem solution by RECONSTRUCT (3.5).

3.3 TRACE_CONCEPTS starts with concepts from the target and

attempts to trace them back to origins in the base. FIND_ACT_ORIGINS traces back activation of a each concept C. The concepts that led to the activation of C were stored with the concept by CHANGE_ACTIVATION (2.3). FIND_ACT_ORIGINS then looks for the origins of the activating concepts and repeats until it finds a concept or concepts that were activated as part of the problem description.

3.4 TRACE_OBJECTS finds pairs of analogous objects using the pairs of analogous concepts derived by TRACE_CONCEPTS (3.3). For each concept pair, TRACE_OBJECTS attempts to find systematic relations between the objects that have the concepts.

3.5 RECONSTRUCT attempts to bring about solution of the target problem by using information from the base and the mappings constructed by TRACE_CONCEPTS (3.3) and TRACE_OBJECTS (3.4).

3.5.1 If the problem is a normal planning type, it reconstructs new subgoals based on the effectors that worked in solving the base.

3.5.2 If the problem involves explanation, it reconstructs new hypotheses based on the hypotheses that aided in providing an explanation.

3.6 If the new subgoals or hypotheses lead to a solution to the target problem, SCHEMATIZE creates an analogical schema, which is an abstract problem solution formed from the base and the target. The starting descriptions and the goals of the new schemas are abstracted from those of the base and target, using the superordinates of the relevant concepts. For example, if the concept A is used in the starting description of the base, and the concept B is used in the starting description of the target, and A and B are both a kind of C, then the concept C will be used in the starting descriptions of the new problem schema.

4. Induction

4.1 TRIGGER initiates generalization, concept formation, and abduction by calling TRIG_GEN_COMB (4.2), FORM_CONCEPT_FROM_RULES (4.6), TRIG_ABDUCE (4.3), and TRIG_ABD_GEN (4.9).

4.2 TRIG_GEN_COMB searches through the list of active messages for active concepts A and B with instances in common. If there are any, it attempts generalization that all A and B and all B are A using GENERALIZE (4.3) and conceptual combination of A and B using COMBINE (4.5).

4.3 GENERALIZE takes two concepts A and B that the active messages indicate have an instance in common and sees whether generalization is warranted by the following steps:

4.3.1 CHECK looks for counterexamples, i.e., A's that are not B's. These are found by comparing the messages (list of instances) stored with the concept A and the messages stored with B. If a counterexample is found, then the attempt to generalize is stopped; and if the generalization that all A are B has been previously formed, then the counterexample prompts specialization (see SPEC 4.4).

4.3.2 COMMON calculates the total number of instances shared by A's and B's by comparing the messages stored with A against the messages stored with B.

4.3.3 The invariability of A with respect to B is calculated by retrieving from them concepts A^* and B^* that are, respectively, the superordinates of A and B. INVAR divides the number of subordinates of A^* about which it has information concerning B^* by the total number of values of B^* those subordinates possess.

4.3.4 If the number of instances and the degree of invariability taken together pass a threshold set by the programmer, then the rule "If x is A then x is B" is formed.

Note: PI can generalize if A and B are relations, for example, forming the rule "If x loves y then y loves x." But it is not now capable of forming rules with multiple clauses, such as "All A's that are C's are B's." Rules with two clauses in their conditions can, however, be formed by a generalization followed by a specialization.

4.4 SPEC takes a rule $A \rightarrow B$ to which a counterexample has been found and forms a specialized rule $A \,\&\, C \rightarrow B$. The condition C is some "unusual" property of the object that CHECK (4.3.1) found to be A and not B, where a property is unusual if it is possessed by the object but not by other A's.

4.5 COMBINE produces a new concept by combining 2 existing ones A and B.

4.5.1 It names the new concept by hyphenation: A-B.

4.5.2 The instances of A-B are the common instances of A and B.

4.5.3 The superordinates of A-B are A and B.

4.5.4 The rules for A-B are constructed by BUILD_ALL_RULES, which considers all the rules of A and B. For each rule of A, it checks the rules of B to see if there is any potential conflict. A conflict is detected if A has a rule $A \rightarrow C$ with the same slot-name as a rule $B \rightarrow D$. In cases of conflict, RECONCILE is called to decide whether to form $A\text{-}B \rightarrow C$ or $A\text{-}B \rightarrow D$.

4.5.5 RECONCILE produces a new rule by settling the conflict by preferring actual rules over defaults, less variable rules over more variable ones, stronger rules over weaker, or by looking at active instances of objects that are A and B.

4.6 FORM_CONCEPT_FROM_RULES does a pragmatic kind of bottom-up concept formation. It forms a new concept from two rules with the same conditions and different actions: from rules A & B → C and A & B → D, it forms the concept A-B, adding to it the rules A-B → C and A-B → D, etc.

4.7 In explanation problems, TRIG_ABDUCE looks at the facts to be explained (goals) and the list of active rules to trigger abduction that in turn triggers inference to the best explanation.

4.7.1 FIND_ABDUCTIONS selects from a list of rules those that are potential explainers of a message to be explained. It uses FIND_EXPLNS to look for any rule whose action matches the message to be explained and whose conditions are not all matched by the active messages. In the simplest case, it finds a rule A → B, where B is to be explained, but it can handle relations and rules with any number of conditions.

4.7.2 MAKE_HYPOTHESIS uses the result of FIND_ABDUC-TIONS to produce new hypotheses. If all the variables in the conditions of the explanatory rule were bound by FIND_EXPLNS, it does a simple abduction. Otherwise, it does an existential abduction substituting in existential variables. It stores with the hypothesis information about what it explains and what cohypotheses were formed at the same time, and stores with what is explained information about what explains it. If the hypothesis explains more than one fact, then it is evaluated by BEST_EXPLANATION? (4.8).

4.8 BEST_EXPLANATION? can be called by abduction to evaluate a message that explains other messages, or by SOLVE_PROBLEM to evaluate rules that explain other rules.

4.8.1 FIND_COMPETITORS compiles a list of the competitors of a hypothesis H by considering what other hypotheses have been found to explain the facts that it explains. It also compiles a list of the relevant evidence. Here is the algorithm:

Let evidence = what H explains.
LOOP
Let competitors = the union of all explainers of pieces of evidence.
Let evidence = the union of evidence explained by all competitors.
Repeat loop until no new evidence is found.

4.8.2 BEST_EXP_OF picks the best explanation out of a set of competitors, selecting hypotheses by a pairwise comparison of hypotheses, first qualitatively and then quantitatively. Qualitative comparison works if one hypothesis is both more consilient and more simple than the other. Otherwise, a combined quantitative measure is used.

4.8.3 BETTER_EXPLN_QUAL qualitatively picks the better of two hypotheses, preferring one that is both more consilient and more simple, determined by MORE_CONSILIENT and SIMPLER.

4.8.4 MORE_CONSILIENT favors one hypothesis over another if what is explained by the latter is a proper subset of what is explained by the former. (What explains what was noted by MAKE_HYPOTHESIS, 4.7.2.)

4.8.5 SIMPLER compares two hypotheses on the basis of the number of cohypotheses that were formed with them, which was noted when they were formed. The formula used is

$$\text{SIMPLICITY}(H) = \frac{\text{facts explained by } H - \text{cohypotheses of } H}{\text{facts explained by } H}.$$

4.8.6 If the qualitative comparison fails, as it will if what is explained by one hypothesis is not a subset of what is explained by another, BETTER_EXPLN_QUANT does a quantitative comparison, picking the hypothesis with the highest explanation value, where

$$\text{VALUE}(H) = \text{SIMPLICITY}(H) \times \text{CONSILIENCE}(H).$$

(Here the consilience of H is just the number of facts it explains. As mentioned in chapter 5, more complicated definitions of consilience and simplicity are required to handle the varying importance of facts.)

4.9 TRIG_ABD_GEN triggers abductive rule formation by looking through the list of active messages for general hypotheses such as $H(x)$ that have played a role in explaining why $G(x)$ given $F(x)$. It then forms the rule that $F(x) \rightarrow H(x)$. (The idea here is that it is because F's are H's that they are G's.)

Obviously, features such as threshold values and precise formulas for inference to the best explanation have a substantial arbitrary component, but the implementation as a whole gives an idea of how learning can take place in the context of problem solving and how algorithms for induction can be implemented.

Appendix 3: Sample Run of PI

PI is written in FranzLISP and runs under UNIX on a Pyramid 90x computer. It has also been translated into Common LISP to run on a Sun 3/75 workstation. Here is a sample run of PI, with input in the form of concepts, rules, and problem description set up by the programmer, and output in the form of a trace of the program's execution. Plainly, the knowledge base is very impoverished and little knowledge has been given to the program beyond what enables it to spread activation from the concept of sound to the concept of wave. More realistic runs would require far more domain knowledge and more divergent paths of spreading activation, but the basic mechanisms of activation and triggering of inductive mechanisms should work the same. The run presented below does not display many of PI's mechanisms, such as analogical problem solving, spreading activation by subgoaling, generalization, and bottom-up concept formation, that have been tested on other examples.

1. Input

Here, translated into English, is the input given to PI. For simplicity, the problem of explaining why sounds reflect, propagate, and pass through each other has been stated in terms of the starting condition, **(sound ($x) true)**, and three goals: **(propagate ($x) true), (reflect ($x) true), (pass_through ($x) true)**. PI is also capable of getting the same inductive results by explaining sequentially the three rules: sounds reflect, sounds propagate, sounds pass through each other. Inference to the best explanation then evaluates the rule that sounds are waves instead of the hypothesis **(wave ($x) true)**.

Concepts with Information Provided by Programmer:

> Sound:
>> superordinates: sensation, physical_phenomenon
>> subordinates: voice, music, whistle, bang
>> rules [see below for all rules]

Propagate:
  superordinate: motion
Reflect:
  superordinate: motion
Motion:
  superordinate: change
  subordinates: propagate, reflect, pass_through
Music:
  superordinates: sound, entertainment
  subordinates: instrumental_music, singing
Instrumental_music:
  superordinate: music
  subordinates: lyre_music, flute_music
  instance: (instrumental_music (obj_a) true)
Instrument:
  superordinate: device
  subordinate: stringed instrument
Stringed_instrument:
  superordinate: instrument
  subordinate: lyre
  instance: (stringed_instrument (obj_b) true)
Move_up_down:
  superordinate: movement
  subordinate: wave, jump
Wave:
  superordinate: move_up_down
  subordinates: water_wave, hand_wave
Motion_back:
  superordinate: motion
  subordinates: reflect, bounce
Bounce:
  superordinate: motion_back
  instance: (bounce (obj_c) true)

Concepts Made without Added Structure:

  sensation, physical_phenomenon, voice, music, whistle, bang,
  entertainment, singing, device, jump, is_heard, goes_through_air,
  near, hears, echoes, is_obstructed, spread_plane, swell,
  has_crest, vibrate, movement, spread_spherically, spread_plane,
  thing, plays, instrument, pass_through, lyre_music, flute_music,
  lyre, change, person, shape, ball, pleasant, delicate.

Rules Made:

R_0_sound
  attached_concepts: (sound)
  slot: superordinate
  conditions: ((sound ($x) true))
  actions: ((sensation ($x) true))
R_1_sound
  attached_concepts: (sound)
  slot: superordinate
  conditions: ((sound ($x) true))
  actions: ((physical_phenomenon ($x) true))
R_2_propagate
  attached_concepts: (propagate)
  slot: superordinate
  conditions: ((propagate ($x) true))
  actions: ((motion ($x) true))
R_3_reflect
  attached_concepts: (reflect)
  slot: superordinate
  conditions: ((reflect ($x) true))
  actions: ((motion_back ($x) true))
R_4_instrumental_music
  attached_concepts: (instrumental_music)
  slot: superordinate
  conditions: ((instrumental_music ($x) true))
  actions: ((music ($x) true))
R_5_stringed_instrument
  attached_concepts: (stringed_instrument)
  slot: superordinate
  conditions: ((stringed_instrument ($x) true))
  actions: ((instrument ($x) true))
R_6_move_up_down
  attached_concepts: (move_up_down)
  slot: superordinate
  conditions: ((move_up_down ($x) true))
  actions: ((movement ($x) true))
R_7_wave
  attached_concepts: (wave)
  slot: superordinate
  conditions: ((wave ($x) true))
  actions: ((movement ($x) true))

R_8_bounce
    attached_concepts: (bounce)
    slot: superordinate
    conditions: ((bounce ($x) true))
    actions: ((motion_back ($x) true))
R_9_is_heard
    attached_concepts: (is_heard)
    slot: result
    conditions: ((is_heard ($x) true))
    actions: ((sound ($x) true))
R_10_sound
    attached_concepts: (sound)
    slot: transmission
    conditions: ((sound ($x) true))
    actions: ((goes_through_air ($x) true))
R_11_sound
    attached_concepts: (sound)
    slot: effect
    conditions: ((sound ($x) true) (person ($y) true) (near ($x $y) true))
    actions: ((hears ($y $x) true))
R_12_sound
    attached_concepts: (sound)
    current_value: 0
    slot: obstruction_result
    conditions: ((sound ($x) true) (is_obstructed ($x) true))
    actions: ((echoes ($x) true))
R_13_sound
    attached_concepts: (sound)
    slot: spread_shape
    conditions: ((sound ($x) true))
    actions: ((spread_spherically ($x) true))
R_14_wave
    attached_concepts: (wave)
    slot: spread_shape
    conditions: ((wave ($x) true))
    actions: ((spread_plane ($x) true))
R_15_wave
    attached_concepts: (wave)
    slot: motion_shape
    conditions: ((wave ($x) true))
    actions: ((swell ($x) true))
R_16_wave
    attached_concepts: (wave)

slot: motion
conditions: ((wave ($x) true))
actions: ((propagate ($x) true))
R_17_wave
attached_concepts: (wave)
slot: motion
conditions: ((wave ($x) true))
actions: ((has_crest ($x) true))
R_18_wave
attached_concepts: (wave)
slot: obstruction_effect
conditions: ((wave ($x) true))
actions: ((reflect ($x) true))
R_19_wave
attached_concepts: (wave)
slot: motion
conditions: ((wave ($x) true))
actions: ((pass_through ($x) true))
R_20_ball
attached_concepts: (ball)
slot: motion
conditions: ((ball ($x) true))
actions: ((propagate ($x) true))
R_21_ball
attached_concepts: (ball)
slot: motion
conditions: ((ball ($x) true))
actions: ((reflect ($x) true))
R_22_music
attached_concepts: (music)
slot: affect
conditions: ((music ($x) true))
actions: ((pleasant ($x) true))
R_23_instrument
attached_concepts: (instrument)
slot: quality
conditions: ((instrument ($x) true))
actions: ((delicate ($x) true))
R_24_instrumental_music
attached_concepts: (instrumental_music)
slot: method
conditions: ((instrumental_music ($x) true))
actions: ((instrument (%y) true) (plays (%y $x) true))

R_25_stringed_instrument
  attached_concepts: (stringed_instrument)
  slot: movement
  conditions: ((stringed_instrument ($x) true))
  actions: ((vibrate ($x) true))
R_26_vibrate
  attached_concepts: (vibrate)
  slot: move_shape
  conditions: ((vibrate ($x) true))
  actions: ((move_up_down ($x) true))
R_27_bounce
  attached_concepts: (bounce)
  slot: performer
  conditions: ((bounce ($x) true))
  actions: ((ball ($x) true))

Problem Made:

Sound_reflect:
  type: explanation
  start: ((sound ($x) true))
  goals: ((propagate ($x) true explanandum0)
         (reflect ($x) true explanandum1)
         (pass_through ($x) true explanandum2))

2. Output

Here, lightly edited for intelligibility, is the printed output of PI given the above input. At timestep 5, PI forms a ball (particle) theory of sound, which it judges to be the best explanation until timestep 9, when activation of the concept of wave leads to production of a wave theory of sound. The problem is solved once all three goals have been reached (explained). Extraneous pieces of information that do not play a significant role in this simulation, such as the degrees of confidence of the messages and degrees of activation of concepts, are omitted. Names of the hypotheses and explananda are the fourth element in messages; for example, "hypothesis1" is the name of "(wave ($x) proj_true hypothesis1)". The truth value "proj_true" stands for "projected to be true" and indicates that the hypothesis is tentative. Some messages have in fourth place the name of a hypothesis in parentheses, as in (swell ($x) proj_true (hypothesis1)); this shows that they depend on the hypothesis indicated: they are only projected to be true since they were inferred using a tentative hypothesis.

Franz Lisp, Opus 38.91
Tue Dec 2 10:56:28 EST 1986
[load /u1/pault/pi/franz.1]
[fasl /u1/pault/pi/misc.o]
[load /u1/pault/pi/begin.1]
[load /u1/pault/pi/prob.1]
[load /u1/pault/pi/prob_fire.1]
[load /u1/pault/pi/prob_spread.1]
[load /u1/pault/pi/store.1]
[load /u1/pault/pi/analog.1]
[load /u1/pault/pi/ana_schem.1]
[load /u1/pault/pi/concepts.1]
[load /u1/pault/pi/explain.1]
[load /u1/pault/pi/gen.1]
[load /u1/pault/pi/theory.1]
[load /u1/pault/pi/trig.1]
[load data/wts.1]

PI initialized.
****
Running PI with input data/wts.1.
Problem: How to explain properties of sound?

SOLVING PROBLEM: sound_reflect
STARTING FROM: ((sound ($x) true))
GOALS: ((propagate ($x) true explanandum0)
        (reflect ($x) true explanandum1)
        (pass_through ($x) true explanandum2))

PROBLEM: sound_reflect   TIMESTEP: 1
ACTIVE MESSAGES: ((sound ($x) true))
ACTIVE CONCEPTS: (propagate reflect pass_through sound)
ACTIVE RULES: nil
Triggering inductions ...
Problem not yet solved
FIRING RULES: nil

PROBLEM: sound_reflect   TIMESTEP: 2
ACTIVE MESSAGES: ((sound ($x) true))
ACTIVE CONCEPTS: (propagate reflect pass_through sound)
ACTIVE RULES: (r_13_sound r_12_sound r_11_sound
        r_10_sound r_1_sound
        r_0_sound r_3_reflect r_2_propagate)

Triggering inductions . . .
Problem not yet solved
FIRING RULES: (r_13_sound r_10_sound r_1_sound r_0_sound)
Activating concept (spread_spherically) by firing rule r_13_sound
Activating concept (goes_through_air) by firing rule r_10_sound
Activating concept (physical_phenomenon) by firing rule r_1_sound
Activating concept (sensation) by firing rule r_0_sound
Activating concept (motion) by hierarchical spread from propagate
Activating concept (motion_back) by hierarchical spread from reflect
Activating concepts (bang whistle music voice) by hierarchical spread
  from sound

PROBLEM: sound_reflect   TIMESTEP: 3
ACTIVE MESSAGES: ((sound ($x) true) (spread_spherically ($x) true)
            (goes-through_air ($x) true)
            (physical_phenomenon ($x) true)
            (sensation ($x) true))
ACTIVE CONCEPTS: (bang whistle music voice motion_back
            motion propagate
            reflect pass_through sound spread_spherically
            goes_through_air physical_phenomenon sensation)
ACTIVE RULES: (r_13_sound r_12_sound r_11_sound
            r_10_sound r_1_sound
            r_0_sound r_3_reflect r_2_propagate r_22_music)
Triggering inductions . . .
Problem not yet solved
FIRING RULES: nil
Activating concept (instrumental_music) by hierarchical spread
  from music
Activating concept (bounce) by hierarchical spread from motion_back
----

PROBLEM: sound_reflect   TIMESTEP: 4
ACTIVE MESSAGES: ((bounce (obj_c) true)
            (instrumental_music (obj_a) true)
            (sound ($x) true) (spread_spherically ($x) true)
            (goes_through_air ($x) true)
            (physical_phenomenon ($x) true)
            (sensation ($x) true))
ACTIVE CONCEPTS: (bounce instrumental_music bang whistle
            music voice
            motion_back motion propagate reflect pass_through
            sound

spread_spherically goes_through_air
physical_phenomenon
sensation)
ACTIVE RULES: (r_13_sound r_12_sound r_11_sound
r_10_sound r_1_sound
r_3_reflect r_2_propagate r_22_music
r_24_instrumental_music
r_4_instrumental_music r_27_bounce r_8_bounce)
Triggering inductions . . .
Problem not yet solved
FIRING RULES: (r_24_instrumental_music r_4_instrumental_music
r_8_bounce
r_27_bounce)
Activating concept (plays instrument) by firing rule
r_24_instrumental_music
Activating concept (ball) by firing rule r_27_bounce
Activating concepts (flute_music lyre_music) by hierarchical
spread from
instrumental_music

PROBLEM: sound_reflect   TIMESTEP: 5
ACTIVE MESSAGES: ((bounce (obj_c) true)
(instrumental_music (obj_a) true)
(music (obj_a) true) (motion_back (obj_c) true)
(sound ($x) true) (spread_spherically ($x) true)
(goes_through_air ($x) true)
(physical_phenomenon ($x) true)
(sensation ($x) true) (plays (%y obj_a) true)
(instrument (%y) true) (ball (obj_c) true))
ACTIVE CONCEPTS: (flute_music lyre_music bounce
instrumental_music bang
whistle music voice motion_back motion propagate
reflect
pass_through sound spread_spherically
goes_through_air
physical_phenomenon sensation plays instrument ball)
ACTIVE RULES: (r_21_ball r_20_ball r_23_instrument
r_13_sound r_12_sound
r_11_sound r_10_sound r_1_sound r_0_sound
r_3_reflect
r_2_propagate r_22_music r_24_instrumental_music
r_4_instrumental_music r_27_bounce r_8_bounce)

Triggering inductions ...
Simple abduction of (ball ($x) proj_true hypothesis0)
from (propagate ($x) true explanandum0) and r_20_ball
Supplementary abduction of (ball ($x) proj_true hypothesis0)
from (reflect ($x) true explanandum1) and r_21_ball
The best explanation is: hypothesis0
(ball ($x) proj_true hypothesis0)
hypothesis0 explains: (explanandum1 explanandum0)
Competing hypotheses: (hypothesis0)
Co-hypotheses: nil
Total evidence: (explanandum1 explanandum0)
Rule made: r_28_ball
(sound) - > (ball)
Abductive generalization formed from
(ball ($x) proj_true 0.3 hypothesis0)
Problem not yet solved
FIRING RULES: (r_23_instrument r_22_music r_20_ball
r_21_ball)
Activating concept (delicate) by firing rule r_23_instrument
Activating concept (pleasant) by firing rule r_22_music
Activating concept (stringed_instrument) by hierarchical spread from
instrument

PROBLEM: sound_reflect   TIMESTEP: 6
ACTIVE MESSAGES: ((stringed_instrument (obj_b) true)
(ball ($x) proj_true hypothesis0) (ball (obj_c) true)
(bounce (obj_c) true) (instrumental_music (obj_a) true)
(music (obj_a) true) (motion_back (obj_c) true)
(sound ($x) true) (spread_spherically ($x) true)
(goes_through_air ($x) true)
(physical_phenomenon ($x) true)
(sensation ($x) true) (plays (%y obj_a) true)
(instrument (%y) true) (delicate (%y) true)
(pleasant (obj_a) true)
(propagate ($x) proj_true (hypothesis0))
(reflect ($x) proj_true (hypothesis0)))
ACTIVE CONCEPTS: (stringed_instrument ball flute_music
lyre_music bounce
instrumental_music bang whistle music voice
motion_back
motion propagate reflect pass_through sound

spread_spherically goes_through_air
physical_phenomenon
sensation plays instrument delicate pleasant)
ACTIVE RULES: (r_23_instrument r_13_sound r_12_sound
  r_11_sound r_10_sound
  r_1_sound r_0_sound r_3_reflect r_2_propagate
  r_22_music
  r_24_instrumental_music r_4_instrumental_music
  r_27_bounce
  r_8_bounce r_28_ball r_21_ball r_20_ball
  r_25_stringed_instrument r_5_stringed_instrument)
Triggering inductions ...
Problem not yet solved
FIRING RULES: (r_25_stringed_instrument
  r_5_stringed_instrument r_2_propagate
  r_3_reflect)
Activating concept (vibrate) by firing rule r_25_stringed_instrument
Activating concept (lyre) by hierarchical spread from
 stringed_instrument

PROBLEM: sound_reflect TIMESTEP: 7
ACTIVE MESSAGES: ((stringed_instrument (obj_b) true)
   (ball ($x) proj_true hypothesis0)
   (ball (obj_c) true) (bounce (obj_c) true)
   (instrumental_music (obj_a) true) (music (obj_a) true)
   (motion_back (obj_c) true) (sound ($x) true)
   (spread_spherically ($x) true)
   (goes_through_air ($x) true)
   (physical_phenomenon ($x) true) (sensation ($x) true)
   (plays (%y obj_a) true) (instrument (obj_b) true)
   (instrument (%y) true) (delicate (%y) true)
   (pleasant (obj_a) true) (vibrate (obj_b) true)
   (motion_back ($x) proj_true (hypothesis0))
   (motion ($x) proj_true (hypothesis0))
   (propagate ($x) proj_true (hypothesis0))
   (reflect ($x) proj_true (hypothesis0)))
ACTIVE CONCEPTS: (lyre stringed_instrument ball flute_music
  lyre_music
  bounce instrumental_music bang whistle music
  voice motion_back motion propagate reflect
  pass_through
  sound spread_spherical goes_through_air

physical_phenomenon sensation plays instrument
delicate pleasant vibrate)
ACTIVE RULES: (r_26_vibrate r_23_instrument r_13_sound
r_12_sound r_11_sound
r_10_sound r_1_sound r_0_sound r_3_reflect
r_2_propagate
r_22_music r_24_instrumental_music
r_4_instrumental_music r_27_bounce r_8_bounce
r_28_ball r_21_ball r_20_ball
r_25_stringed_instrument
r_5_stringed_instrument)
Triggering inductions ...
Problem not yet solved
FIRING RULES: (r_23_instrument r_26_vibrate)
Activating concept (move_up_down) by firing rule r_26_vibrate
----
PROBLEM: sound_reflect   TIMESTEP: 8
ACTIVE MESSAGES: ((stringed_instrument (obj_b) true)
(ball ($x) proj_true hypothesis0)
(ball (obj_c) true) (bounce (obj_c) true)
(instrumental_music (obj_a) true) (music (obj_a) true)
(motion_back (obj_c) true) (sound ($x) true)
(spread_spherically ($x) true)
(goes_through_air ($x) true)
(physical_phenomenon ($x) true)
(sensation ($x) true) (plays (%y obj_a) true)
(instrument (obj_b) true) (instrument (%y) true)
(delicate (obj_b) true) (delicate (%y) true)
(pleasant (obj_a) true) (vibrate (obj_b) true)
(move_up_down (obj_b) true)
(motion_back ($x) proj_true (hypothesis0))
(motion ($x) proj_true (hypothesis0))
(propagate ($x) proj_true (hypothesis0))
(reflect ($x) proj_true (hypothesis0)))
ACTIVE CONCEPTS: (lyre stringed_instrument ball flute_music
lyre_music
bounce instrumental_music bang whistle music voice
motion_back motion propagate reflect pass_.through
sound
spread_spherically goes_through_air
physical_phenomenon
sensation plays instrument delicate pleasant vibrate
move_up_down)

ACTIVE RULES: (r_6_move_up_down r_26_vibrate
            r_23_instrument r_13_sound
            r_18_sound r_11_sound r_10_sound
            r_1_sound r_0_sound
            r_3_reflect r_2_propagate r_22_music
            r_24_instrumental_music r_4_instrumental_music
            r_27_bounce r_8_bounce r_28_ball r_21_ball
            r_20_ball
            r_25_stringed_instrument r_5_stringed_instrument)
Triggering inductions ...
Problem not yet solved
FIRING RULES: (r_6_move_up_down)
Activating concept (movement) by firing rule r_6_move_up_down
Activating concepts (jump wave) by hierarchical spread from
    move_up_down

PROBLEM: sound_reflect   TIMESTEP: 9
ACTIVE MESSAGES: ((stringed_instrument (obj_b) true)
            (ball ($x) proj_true hypothesis0) (ball (obj_c) true)
            (bounce (obj_c) true) (instrumental_music (obj_a) true)
            (music (obj_a) true) (motion_back (obj_c) true)
            (sound ($x) true) (spread_spherically ($x) true)
            (goes_through_air ($x) true)
            (physical_phenomenon ($x) true) (sensation ($x) true)
            (plays (%y obj_a) true) (instrument (obj_b) true)
            (instrument (%y) true) (delicate (obj_b) true)
            (delicate (%y) true) (pleasant (obj_a) true)
            (vibrate (obj_b) true) (move_up_down (obj_b) true)
            (movement (obj_b) true)
            (motion_back ($x) proj_true (hypothesis0))
            (motion ($x) proj_true (hypothesis0))
            (propagate ($x) proj_true (hypothesis0))
            (reflect ($x) proj_true (hypothesis0)))
ACTIVE CONCEPTS: (jump wave lyre stringed_instrument ball
            flute_music
            lyre_music bounce instrumental_music bang whistle
            music voice motion_back motion propagate reflect
            pass_through sound spread_spherically
            goes_through_air
            physical_phenomenon sensation plays instrument
            delicate
            pleasant vibrate move_up_down movement)

ACTIVE RULES: (r_6_move_up_down r_26_vibrate
            r_23_instrument r_13_sound
            r_12_sound r_11_sound r_10_sound r_1_sound
            r_0_sound
            r_3_reflect r_2_propagate r_22_music
            r_24_instrumental_music r_4_instrumental_music
            r_27_bounce r_8_bounce r_28_ball r_21_ball
            r_20_ball
            r_25_stringed_instrument r_5_stringed_instrument
            r_19_wave r_18_wave r_17_wave r_16_wave
            r_15_wave
            r_14_wave r_7_wave)
Triggering inductions . . .
    Simple abduction of (wave ($x) proj_true hypothesis1)
        from (propagate ($x) true explanandum0) and r_16_wave
    Supplementary abduction of (wave ($x) proj_true hypothesis1)
        from (reflect ($x) true explanandum1) and r_18_wave
    The best explanation is: hypothesis0
                    (ball ($x) proj_true hypothesis0)
        hypothesis0 explains: (explanandum1 explanandum0)
        Competing hypotheses: (hypothesis1 hypothesis0)
        Co-hypotheses: nil
        Total evidence: (explanandum1 explanandum0)
        Tied hypotheses: (hypothesis0 hypothesis1))
    Supplementary abduction of (wave ($x) proj_true hypothesis1)
        from (pass_through ($x) true nil explanandum2) and
            r_19_wave
    The best explanation is: hypothesis1
                    (wave ($x) proj_true hypothesis1)
        hypothesis1 explains: (explanandum2 explanandum1
        explanandum0)
        Competing hypotheses: (hypothesis1 hypothesis0)
        Co-hypotheses: nil
        Total evidence: (explanandum2 explanandum1 explanandum0)
Rule made: r_29_wave
    (sound) -> (wave)
    Abductive generalization formed from (wave ($x) proj_true
        hypothesis1)
Problem not yet solved
FIRING RULES: (r_19_wave r_16_wave r_18_wave r_14_wave
            r_7_wave r_15_wave)
Activating concept (spread_plane) by firing rule r_14_wave
Activating concept (swell) by firing rule r_15_wave

Activating concepts (hand_wave water_wave) by hierarchical
    spread from wave

PROBLEM: sound_reflect   TIMESTEP: 10
ACTIVE MESSAGES: ((wave ($x) proj_true hypothesis1)
            (stringed_instrument (obj_b) true)
            (ball ($x) proj_true hypothesis0)
            (ball (obj_c) true) (bounce (obj_c) true)
            (instrumental_music (obj_a) true)
            (music (obj_a) true) (motion_back (obj_c) true)
            (sound ($x) true) (spread_spherically ($x) true)
            (goes_through_air ($x) true)
            (physical_phenomenon ($x) true)
            (sensation ($x) true) (plays (%y obj_a) true)
            (instrument (obj_b) true) (instrument (%y) true)
            (delicate (obj_b) true) (delicate (%y) true)
            (pleasant (obj_a) true) (vibrate (obj_b) true)
            (move_up_down (obj_b) true) (movement (obj_b) true)
            (motion_back ($x) proj_true (hypothesis0))
            (motion ($x) proj_true (hypothesis0))
            (propagate ($x) proj_true (hypothesis0))
            (propagate ($x) proj_true (hypothesis1))
            (reflect ($x) proj_true (hypothesis0))
            (reflect ($x) proj_true (hypothesis1))
            (pass_through ($x) proj_true (hypothesis1))
            (movement ($x) proj_true (hypothesis1))
            (spread_plane ($x) proj_true (hypothesis1))
            (swell ($x) proj_true (hypothesis1)))
ACTIVE CONCEPTS: (hand_wave water_wave wave jump lyre
            stringed_instrument
            ball flute_music lyre_music bounce instrumental_music
            bang whistle music voice motion_back motion
            propagate
            reflect pass_through sound spread_spherically
            goes_through_air physical_phenomenon sensation
            plays
            instrument delicate pleasant vibrate move_up_down
            movement spread_plane swell)
ACTIVE RULES: (r_6_move_up_down r_26_vibrate
            r_23_instrument r_13_sound
            r_12_sound r_11_sound r_10_sound r_1_sound
            r_0_sound
            r_3_reflect r_2_propagate r_22_music

r_24_instrumental_music r_4_instrumental_music
r_27_bounce
r_8_bounce r_28_ball r_21_ball r_20_ball
r_25_stringed_instrument r_5_stringed_instrument
r_29_wave r_19_wave r_18_wave r_17_wave
r_16_wave
r_15_wave r_14_wave r_7_wave)
Triggering inductions ...
Conceptual combination producing: wave_sound
Concept made: wave_sound
Rule made: r_30_wave_sound
(wave_sound) -> (wave)
Rule made: r_31_wave_sound
(wave_sound) -> (sound)
Rule made: r_32_wave_sound
(wave_sound) -> (spread_spherically)
Rule made: r_33_wave_sound
(wave_sound) -> (movement)

Problem sound_reflect solved.

Tue Dec 2 10:59:42 EST 1986

References

Abelson, R. (1981). The psychological status of the script concept. *American Psychologist 36*, 715–729.

Achinstein, P. (1971). *Law and Explanation*. Oxford: Clarendon Press.

Ackerman, R. (1970). *The Philosophy of Science*. New York: Pegasus.

Aho, A., Hopcroft, J., and Ullman, J. (1983). *Data Structures and Algorithms*. Reading, MA: Addison-Wesley.

Alvarez, L., Alvarez, W., Asaro, F., and Michel, H. (1980). Extraterrestrial cause for the Cretaceous-Tertiary extinction. *Science 208*, 1095–1108.

Alvarez, W., Kaufmann, E., Surlyk, F., Alvarez, L., Asaro, F., and Michel, H. (1984). Impact theory of mass extinctions and the invertebrate fossil record. *Science 223*, 1135–1141.

Anderson, J. R. (1980). *Cognitive Psychology and Its Implications*. San Francisco: Freeman.

Anderson, J. R. (1983). *The Architecture of Cognition*. Cambridge, MA: Harvard University Press.

Anderson, J., Corbett, A., and Reiser, B. (1986). *Essential LISP*. Reading, MA: Addison-Wesley.

Ayer, A. J. (1946). *Language, Truth and Logic* (2nd edn.). New York: Dover.

Bacon, F. (1960). *The New Organon and Related Writings*. Edited by F. Anderson. Indianapolis: Bobbs-Merrill. First published 1620.

Barr, A., and Feigenbaum, E. (1981). *Handbook of Artificial Intelligence*, vol. 1. Los Altos: Kaufmann.

Bartlett, F. C. (1932). *Remembering*. Cambridge: Cambridge University Press.

Bechtel, W. (1985). Realism, instrumentalism, and the intentional stance. *Cognitive Science 9*, 473–497.

Blake, R. (1960). Theory of hypothesis among renaissance astronomers. In R. Blake, C. Ducasse, and E. H. Madden (eds.), *Theories of Scientific Method*. Seattle: University of Washington Press, pp. 22–49.

Block, N. (1986). Advertisement for a semantics for psychology. In P. French, T. Uehling, and H. Wettstein (eds.), *Midwest Studies in Philosophy, X*. Minneapolis: University of Minnesota Press, pp. 615–678.

Bower, G., Black, J., and Turner, T. (1979). Scripts in memory for text. *Cognitive Psychology 11*, 177–220.

Boyd, R. (1981). Scientific realism and naturalistic epistemology. In P. Asquith and R. Giere (eds.), *PSA 1980*, vol. 2. East Lansing, MI: Philosophy of Science Association, pp. 613–662.

Braine, M. D. S. (1978). On the relation between the natural logic of reasoning and standard logic. *Psychological Review 85*, 1–21.

Brewer, W. and Nakamura, G. (1984). The nature and function of schemas. In R. Wyer and T. Srull (eds.), *Handbook of Social Cognition*. Hillsdale, NJ: Erlbaum, pp. 119–160.

Brewer, W., and Treyens, J. (1981). Role of schemata in memory for places. *Cognitive Psychology* 13, 207–230.

Brody, B. (1972). Towards an Aristotelian theory of scientific explanation. *Philosophy of Science* 39, 20–31.

Bromberger, S. (1966). Why-questions. In R. Colodny (ed.), *Mind and Cosmos*. Pittsburgh: University of Pittsburgh Press, pp. 86–111.

Buchanan, B., and Mitchell, T. (1978). Model-directed learning of production rules. In D. Waterman and F. Hayes-Roth (eds.), *Pattern-Directed Inference Systems*. New York: Academic Press.

Buchanan, B., and Shortliffe, E. (eds.), (1984). *Rule-Based Expert Systems*. Reading, MA: Addison-Wesley.

Buchdahl, G. (1970). History of science and criteria of choice. In R. H. Steuwer (ed.), *Minnesota Studies in the Philosophy of Science*, vol. 5. Minneapolis: University of Minnesota Press, pp. 201–245.

Campbell, D. T. (1960). Blind variation and selective retention in creative thought as in other knowledge processes. *Psychological Review* 67, 380–400.

Campbell, D. T. (1974). Evolutionary epistemology. In P. Schilpp (ed.), *The Philosophy of Karl Popper*. La Salle, IL: Open Court, pp. 413–463.

Campbell, D. T. (1977). Comment on "The Natural Selection Model of Conceptual Evolution." *Philosophy of Science* 44, 502–507.

Cantor, N., and Mischel, W. (1977). Traits as prototypes: effects on recognition memory. *Journal of Personality and Social Psychology* 35, 38–48.

Carlson, S. (1985). A double-blind test of astrology. *Nature* 318, 419–425.

Carnap, R. (1928). *Der logische Aufbau der Welt*. Berlin: Welkreis-Verlag.

Carnap, R. (1950). *Logical Foundations of Probability*. Chicago: University of Chicago Press.

Cartwright, N. (1983). *How the Laws of Physics Lie*. Oxford: Clarendon Press.

Charniak, E., and McDermott, D. (1985). *Introduction to Artificial Intelligence*. Reading, MA: Addison-Wesley.

Cheng, P. W., Holyoak, K. J., Nisbett, R. E., and Oliver, L. M. (1986). Pragmatic versus syntactic approaches to training deductive reasoning. *Cognitive Psychology* 18, 293–328.

Chi, M., Feltovich, P., and Glaser, R. (1981). Categorization and representation of physics problems by experts and novices. *Cognitive Science* 5, 121–152.

Chiesi, H., Spilich, G. and Voss, J. (1979). Acquisition of domain-related information in relation to high and low domain knowledge. *Journal of Verbal Learning and Verbal Behavior* 18, 257–273.

Chomsky, N. (1972). *Language and Mind* (2nd edn.). New York: Harcourt Brace Jovanovich.

Church, A. (1949). Review of A. J. Ayer, *Language, truth, and logic*, 2nd edn. *Journal of Symbolic Logic* 14, 52–53.

Churchland, P. (1985). The ontological status of observables. In P. Churchland and C. Hooker (eds.), *Images of Science*. Chicago: University of Chicago Press, pp. 35–47.

Churchland, P., and Hooker, C. (eds.) (1985). *Images of Science*. Chicago: University of Chicago Press.

Clocksin, W., and Mellish, C. (1981). *Programming in Prolog*. Berlin: Springer-Verlag.

Cohen, L. J. (1981a). Can human irrationality be experimentally demonstrated? *Behavioral and Brain Sciences* 4, 317–331.

Cohen, L. J. (1981b). Are there any a priori constraints on the study of rationality? *Behavioral and Brain Sciences* 4, 359–367.

Copi, I. (1979). *Symbolic Logic* (5th edn.). New York: Macmillan.

Copi, I. (1982). *Introduction to Logic* (6th edn.). New York: Macmillan.

Crane, D. (1972). *Invisible Colleges: Diffusion of Knowledge in Scientific Communities*. Chicago: University of Chicago Press.

Daniels, N. (1979). Wide reflective equilibrium and theory acceptance in ethics. *Journal of Philosophy* 76, 256–282.

Daniels, N. (1980). On some methods of ethics and linguistics. *Philosophical Studies* 37, 21–36.

Daniken, E. von (1970). *Chariots of the Gods*. New York: Putnam.

Darden, L. (1983). Artificial intelligence and philosophy of science: reasoning by analogy in theory construction. In P. Asquith and T. Nickles (eds.), *PSA 1982*, vol. 2. East Lansing: Philosophy of Science Association, pp. 147–165.

Darwin, C. (1868). *The Variation of Animals and Plants under Domestication*. London: John Murray.

Darwin, C. (1903). *More Letters of Charles Darwin*. Edited by F. Darwin and A. Seward. London: John Murray.

Darwin, C. (1958). Darwin's journal. In G. de Beer (ed.), *Bulletin of the British Museum (Natural History)*. Historical Series, London, vol. 2, no. 1.

Darwin, C. (1962). *The Origin of Species* (text of 6th edn.). New York: Collier.

Darwin, C. (1969). *The Life and Letters*, 3 vols. Edited by F. Darwin. New York: Johnson Reprint Corp.

Davidson, D. (1967). Truth and meaning. *Synthese* 17, 304–323.

Dawkins, R. (1976). *The Selfish Gene*. New York: Oxford University Press.

Dennett, D. (1980). The milk of human intentionality. *Behavioral and Brain Sciences* 3, 428–430.

Dretske, F. (1985). Machines and the mental. *Proceedings and Addresses of the American Philosophical Association* 59, 23–33.

Duhem, P. (1954). *The Aim and Structure of Physical Theory*. Translated by P. Wiener. Princeton: Princeton University Press. First published 1914.

Dummett, M. (1978). *Truth and Other Enigmas*. Cambridge, MA: Harvard University Press.

Duncker, K. (1945). On problem solving. *Psychological Monographs* 58 (no. 270).

Einstein, A. (1949). Remarks concerning the essays brought together in this co-operative volume. In P. Schilpp (ed.), *Albert Einstein: Philosopher-Scientist*. La Salle, IL: Open Court, pp. 665–688.

Einstein, A., and Infeld, L. (1938). *The Evolution of Physics*. New York: Simon and Schuster.

Falkenhainer, B. (1987). Scientific theory formation through analogical inference. In P. Langley (ed.), *Proceedings of the Fourth International Workshop on Machine Learning*. Los Altos: Morgan Kaufmann, pp. 218–229.

Feigenbaum, E. and McCorduck, P. (1983). *The Fifth Generation*. Reading, MA: Addison-Wesley.

Feyerabend, P. (1965). Problems of empiricism. In R. Colodny (ed.). *Beyond the Edge of Certainty*. Pittsburgh: University of Pittsburgh Press, pp. 145–260.

Feyerabend, P. (1975). *Against Method*. London: New Left Books.

Feynman, R. (1985). *Surely You're Joking, Mr. Feynman*. New York: Bantam Books.

Fine, A. (1984). The natural ontological attitude. In J. Leplin (ed.), *Scientific Realism*. Berkeley: University of California Press, pp. 83–107.

Fodor, J. (1975). *The Language of Thought*. New York: Crowell.

Foucault, M. (1973). *The Order of Things*. New York: Vintage.

Frazer, J. (1964). *The New Golden Bough*. Edited by T. Gaster. New York: Mentor.

Frege, G. (1964). *The Basic Laws of Arithmetic*. Translated by M. Furth. Berkeley: University of California Press. First published 1893.

Frege, G. (1970). *Translations from the Philosophical Writings of Gottlob Frege*. Edited by P. Geach and M. Black. Oxford: Basil Blackwell.

Fresnel, A. (1866). *Oeuvres complètes*. Paris: Imprimerie Impériale.

Friedland, P., and Kedes, L. (1985). Discovering the secrets of DNA. *Communications of the ACM 28*, 1164–1186.

Friedman, M. (1974). Explanation and scientific understanding, *Journal of Philosophy 71*, 5–19.

Fumerton, R. (1980). Induction and reasoning to the best explanation. *Philosophy of Science 47*, 589–600.

Gale, R. (1967). Propositions, judgments, sentences, and statements. *Encyclopedia of Philosophy*. New York: Macmillan, vol. 6, pp. 494–505.

Gardner, H. (1985). *The Mind's New Science*. New York: Basic Books.

Gardner, M. (1981). *Science: Good, Bad and Bogus*. New York: Avon.

Garey, M., and Johnson, D. (1979). *Computers and Intractability*. New York: Freeman.

Gauquelin, M. (1969). *The Scientific Basis of Astrology*. Chicago: Stein and Day.

Gick, M. L., and Holyoak, K. J. (1980). Analogical problem solving. *Cognitive Psychology 12*, 306–355.

Gick, M. L., and Holyoak, K. J. (1983). Schema induction and analogical transfer. *Cognitive Psychology 15*, 1–38.

Glymour, C., Kelly, K., and Scheines, R. (1983). Two programs for testing hypotheses of any logical form. In *Proceedings of the International Machine Learning Workshop*. Urbana, IL: University of Illinois Department of Computer Science, pp. 96–98.

Goldman, A. I. (1978). Epistemics: The regulative theory of cognition. *Journal of Philosophy 75*, 509–523.

Goldman, A. I. (1986). *Cognition and Epistemology*. Cambridge, MA: Harvard University Press.

Goodman, N. (1965). *Fact, Fiction and Forecast* (2nd edn.). Indianapolis: Bobbs-Merrill.

Gregory, R. (1970). *The Intelligent Eye*. London: Weidenfeld and Nicolson.

Gruber, H. (1974). *Darwin on Man*. New York: Dutton.

Guralnik, D. (1976). *Websters New World Dictionary of the American Language* (2nd college edn). Cleveland: World Publishing.

Haack, S. (1978). *Philosophy of Logics*. Cambridge: Cambridge University Press.

Hacking, I. (1975). *The Emergence of Probability*. Cambridge: Cambridge University Press.

Hacking, I. (1983). *Representing and Intervening*. Cambridge: Cambridge University Press.

Hanson, N. R. (1958). *Patterns of Discovery*. Cambridge: Cambridge University Press.

Hanson, N. R. (1961). Is there a logic of discovery? In H. Feigl and G. Maxwell (eds.), *Current Issues in the Philosophy of Science*. New York: Holt, Rinehart and Winston, pp. 20–35.

Hanson, N. R. (1970). A picture theory of theory meaning. In M. Radner and S. Winokur (eds.). *Minnesota Studies in the Philosophy of Science*, vol. IV. Minneapolis: University of Minnesota Press, pp. 131–141.

Harman, G. (1965). The inference to the best explanation. *Philosophical Review 74*, 88–95.

Harman, G. (1967). Detachment, probability, and maximum likelihood, *Nous 1*, 404–411.

Harman, G. (1973). *Thought*. Princeton: Princeton University Press.

Harman, G. (1986). *Change in View: Principles of Reasoning*. Cambridge, MA: MIT Press/ Bradford Books.

Harman, G. (1987). (Nonsolipsistic) conceptual role semantics. In Ernest LePore (ed.), *New Directions in Semantics*. London: Academic Press, pp. 55–81.

Harvey, W. (1962). *On the Motion of the Heart and Blood in Animals*. Translated by A. Bowie. Chicago: Henry Regnery. First published 1628.

Hastie, R. (1981). Schematic principles in human memory. In E. T. Higgins, C. P. Herman, and M. P. Zanna (eds.). *Social Cognition: The Ontario Symposium on Personality and Social Psychology*. Hillsdale, NJ: Lawrence Erlbaum Associates.

Hausman, D. (1981). *Capital, Profits, and Prices: An Essay in the Philosophy of Economics*. New York: Columbia University Press.

Hausman, D. (1982). Constructive empiricism contested. *Pacific Philosophical Quarterly 63*, 21–28.

Hausman, D. (1984). Causal priority. *Nous 18*, 261–279.

Hayes, P. J. (1979). The logic of frames. In D. Metzig (ed.), *Frame Conceptions and Text Understanding*. Berlin: Walter de Gruyter, pp. 46–61.

Head, H. (1926). *Aphasia and Kindred Disorders of Speech*. Cambridge: Cambridge University Press.

Hempel, C. G. (1965). *Aspects of Scientific Explanation*. New York: The Free Press.

Herschel, J. (1830). *A Preliminary Discourse on the Study of Natural Philosophy*. London: Longman.

Hillis, D. (1981). The connection machine. A. I. Memo No. 646, Cambridge, MA: MIT Artificial Intelligence Laboratory.

Hofstadter, D. (1985). *Metamagical Themas*. New York: Basic Books.

Hofstadter, D., and Dennett D. (eds.) (1981). *The Mind's I*. New York: Basic Books.

Holland, J., Holyoak, K., Nisbett, R., and Thagard, P. (1986). *Induction: Processes of Inference, Learning, and Discovery*. Cambridge, MA: MIT Press/Bradford Books.

Holyoak, K., and Thagard, P. (1986). A computational model of analogical problem solving. In S. Vosniadou and A. Ortony (eds.), *Similarity, Analogy, and Thought* (to appear).

Holyoak, K. and Thagard, P. (1987). Analogical mapping by constraint satisfaction: a computational theory. Unpublished manuscript.

Horwich, P. (1982). *Probability and Evidence*. Cambridge: Cambridge University Press.

Hull, D. (1982). The naked meme. In H. Plotkin (ed.), *Learning, Development, and Culture*. Chichester: John Wiley, pp. 273–327.

Hume, D. (1888). *A Treatise of Human Nature*. Edited by L. A. Selby-Bigge. London: Oxford University Press. First published 1739.

Huygens, C. (1962). *Treatise on Light*. Translated by S. P. Thompson. New York: Dover. First published 1690.

Jerome, L. (1977). *Astrology Disproved*. Buffalo: Prometheus.

Johnson-Laird, P. (1983). *Mental Models*. Cambridge, MA: Harvard University Press.

Kahneman, D., and Tversky, A. (1979). Prospect theory: An analysis of decision under risk. *Econometrica 47*, 263–291.

Kant, I. (1929). *Critique of Pure Reason*. Translated by N. K. Smith. New York: St. Martins Press. First published 1787.

Kass, A. (1986). Modifying explanations to understand stories. *Proceedings of the Eighth Annual Conference of the Cognitive Science Society*. Hillsdale, NJ: Erlbaum, pp. 691–696.

Kitcher, P. (1976). Explanation, conjunction, and unification. *Journal of Philosophy 73*, 207–212.

Kitcher, P. (1981). Explanatory unification. *Philosophy of Science 48*, 507–531.

Kornfeld, W., and Hewitt, C. (1981). The scientific community metaphor. *IEEE Transactions on Systems, Man, and Cybernetics SMC-11*, 24–33.

Kuhn, T. S. (1970a). Logic of discovery or psychology of research. In I. Lakatos and A. Musgrave (eds.), *Criticism and the Growth of Knowledge*. Cambridge: Cambridge University Press, pp. 1–24.

Kuhn, T. S. (1970b). *Structure of Scientific Revolutions* (2nd edn.). Chicago: University of Chicago Press. First published 1962.

Kuhn, T. S. (1977). *The Essential Tension*. Chicago: University of Chicago Press.

Kunda, Z. (1987). Motivation and inference: self-serving generation and evaluation of causal theories. *Journal of Personality and Social Psychology 53*, 636–647.

Laird, J., Rosenbloom, P., and Newell, A. (1986). Chunking in Soar: the anatomy of a general learning mechanism. *Machine Learning 1*, 11–46.

Lakatos, I. (1970). Falsification and the methodology of scientific research programs. In I. Lakatos and A. Musgrave (eds.), *Criticism and the Growth of Knowledge*. Cambridge: Cambridge University Press, pp. 91–195.

Langley, P., Simon, H., Bradshaw, G., and Zytkow, J. (1987). *Scientific Discovery*. Cambridge, MA: MIT Press/Bradford Books.

Laudan, L. (1968). Theories of scientific method from Plato to Mach. *History of Science 7*, 1–63.

Laudan, L. (1977). *Progress and Its Problems*. Berkeley: University of California Press.

Laudan, L. (1979). Historical methodologies: an overview and manifesto. In P. Asquith and H. Kyburg (eds.), *Current Research in Philosophy of Science*. East Lansing: Philosophy of Science Association, pp. 40–54.

Laudan, L. (1981). A confutation of convergent realism. *Philosophy of Science 48*, 19–49.

Laudan, L. (1983). The demise of the demarcation problem. In R. Cohen and L. Laudan (eds.), *Physics, Philosophy, and Psychoanalysis*. Dordrecht: Reidel, pp. 111–127.

Laudan, L., Donovan, A., Laudan, R., Barker, p., Brown, H. Leplin, J., Thagard, P., and Wykstra, S. (1986). Testing methodologies against history. *Synthese 69*, 141–223.

Lavoisier, A. (1862). *Oeuvres*. Paris: Imprimerie Impériale.

Leake, D., and Owens, C. (1986). Organizing memory for explanation. *Proceedings of the Eighth Annual Conference of the Cognitive Science Society*. Hillsdale, NJ: Erlbaum, pp. 710–715.

Lehrer, K. (1974). *Knowledge*. Oxford: Clarendon Press.

Lenat, D., (1983). The role of heuristics in learning by discovery: three case studies. In R. Michalski, J. Carbonell, and T. Mitchell (eds.), *Machine Learning: An Artificial Intelligence Approach*. Palo Alto: Tioga Press.

Lichtenstein, E., and Brewer, W. (1980). Memory for goal-directed events. *Cognitive Psychology 12*, 412–445.

Lloyd, E. (1983). The nature of Darwin's support for the theory of natural selection. *Philosophy of Science 50*, 112–129.

Losee, J. (1980). *A Historical Introduction to the Philosophy of Science* (2nd ed.). Oxford: Oxford University Press.

March, J. G. (1978). Bounded rationality, ambiguity, and the engineering of choice. *Bell Journal of Economics 9*, 587–608.

Marr, D. (1982). *Vision*. San Francisco: Freeman.

Masterman, M. (1970). The nature of a paradigm. In I. Lakatos and A. Musgrave (eds.), *Criticism and the Growth of Knowledge*. Cambridge: Cambridge University Press, pp. 59–89.

McCarthy, J. (1980). Circumscription—a form of non-monotonic reasoning. *Artificial Intelligence 13*, 27–39.

McDermott, D. (1981). Artificial intelligence meets natural stupidity. In J. Haugeland (ed.), *Mind Design*. Cambridge, MA: MIT Press, pp. 143–160.

Mendelson, E. (1964). *Introduction to Mathematical Logic*. New York: Van Nostrand Reinhold.

Michalski, R., Carbonell, J., and Mitchell, T. (eds.) (1983). *Machine Learning: An Artificial Intelligence Approach*. Palo Alto: Tioga Press.

Mill, J. S. (1970). *A System of Logic* (8th edn.). London: Longman. First published 1843.

Minsky, M. (1974). A framework for representing knowledge. A.I. Memo No. 306, Cambridge, MA: MIT Artificial Intelligence Laboratory.

Minsky, M. (1975). A framework for representing knowledge. In P. H. Winston (ed.), *The Psychology of Computer Vision*. New York: McGraw-Hill, pp. 211–277.

Morris, C. (1938). *Foundations of the Theory of Signs*. Chicago: University of Chicago Press.

Nersessian, N. (1987). A cognitive-historical approach to meaning in scientific theories. In N. Nersessian (ed.), *The Process of Science: Contemporary Philosophical Approaches to Understand Scientific Practice*. Dordrecht: Martinus Nishoff, pp. 161–179.

Newell, A., and Simon, H. A. (1972). *Human Problem Solving*. Englewood Cliffs, NJ: Prentice-Hall.

Nickles, T. (ed.) (1980a). *Scientific Discovery, Logic, and Rationality*. Dordrecht: Reidel.

Nickles, T. (ed.) (1980b). *Scientific Discovery: Case Studies*. Dordrecht: Reidel.

Nilsson, N. (1983). Artificial intelligence prepares for 2001. *The AI Magazine 4(4)*, 7–14.

Nisbett, R. E., and Ross, L. (1980). *Human Inference: Strategies and Shortcomings of Social Judgment*. Englewood Cliffs, NJ: Prentice-Hall.

Overton, W. R. (1983). The decision in McLean vs Arkansas Board of Education. *Society 20(2)*, 3–12.

Passmore, J. (1968). *A Hundred Years of Philosophy*. Harmondsworth, Middlesex: Penguin.

Peirce, C. S. (1931–1958). *Collected Papers*, 8 vols. Edited by C. Hartshorne, P. Weiss, and A. Burks. Cambridge, MA: Harvard University Press.

Peng, Y., and Reggia, J. (1986). A probabilistic causal model for diagnostic problem solving. Unpublished manuscript. University of Maryland.

Perrin, C. (1986). Response to theoretical innovation in science: patterns of the chemical revolution. Paper read at Conference on Testing Theories of Scientific Change, Blacksburg, Virginia.

Piaget, J. (1970). *Genetic Epistemology*. Translated by E. Duckworth. New York: Columbia University Press.

Pople, H. (1977). The formation of composite hypotheses in diagnostic problem solving. In *Proceedings of the Fifth International Joint Conference on Artificial Intelligence*. Los Altos, CA: Kaufmann, pp. 1030–1037.

Popper, K. (1959). *The Logic of Scientific Discovery*. London: Hutchinson.

Popper, K. (1965). *Conjectures and Refutations*. New York: Basic Books.

Popper, K. (1970). Normal science and its dangers. In I. Lakatos and A. Musgrave (eds.), *Criticism and the Growth of Knowledge*. Cambridge: Cambridge University Press, pp. 51–58.

Popper, K. (1972). *Objective Knowledge*. Oxford: Oxford University Press.

Putnam, H. (1975). *Mind, Language, and Reality*. Cambridge: Cambridge University Press.

Quine, W. V. O. (1960). *Word and Object*. Cambridge, MA: MIT Press.

Quine, W. V. O. (1963). *From a Logical Point of View* (2nd edn.), New York: Harper Torchbooks.

Quine, W. V. O. (1969). *Ontological Relativity and Other Essays*. New York: Columbia University Press.

Rajamoney, S., DeJong, G., and Faltings, B. (1985). Towards a model of conceptual knowledge acquisition through directed experimentation. In *Proceedings of the Ninth International Joint Conference on Artificial Intelligence*. Palo Alto, CA: Kaufmann, pp. 688–690.

Rawls, J. (1971). *A Theory of Justice*. Cambridge, MA: Harvard University Press.

Recker, D. (1987). Causal efficacy: the structure of Darwin's argument strategy in the *Origin of Species*. *Philosophy of Science 54*, 147–175.

Reggia, J., Nau, D., and Wang, P. (1983). Diagnostic expert systems based on a set covering model. *International Journal of Man-Machine Studies 19*, 437–460.

Reichenbach, H. (1938). *Experience and Prediction*. Chicago: University of Chicago Press.

Rescher, N. (1977). *Methodological Pragmatism*. New York: New York University Press.

Resnik, M. (1985). Logic: normative or descriptive? The ethics of belief or a branch of psychology. *Philosophy of Science 52*, 221–238.

Rips, L. J. (1983). Cognitive processes in propositional reasoning. *Psychological Review 90,* 38–71.

Rock, I. (1983). *The Logic of Perception.* Cambridge, MA: MIT Press/Bradford Books.

Rorty, R. (1979). *Philosophy and the Mirror of Nature.* Princeton: Princeton University Press.

Rosch, E. (1973). On the internal structure of perceptual and semantic categories. In T. E. Moore (ed.), *Cognitive Development and the Acquisition of Language.* New York: Academic Press.

Rumelhart, D. E. (1980). Schemata: the building blocks of cognition. In R. Spiro, B. Bruce, and W. Brewer (eds.), *Theoretical Issues in Reading Comprehension.* Hillsdale, NJ: Lawrence Erlbaum, pp. 33–58.

Rumelhart, D. E., and McClelland, J. R. (1986). *Parallel Distribution Processing: Explorations in the Microstructure of Cognition,* vol. 1. Cambridge, MA: MIT Press.

Russell, B., and Whitehead, A. (1910–1913). *Principia Mathematica,* 3 vols. Cambridge: Cambridge University Press.

Salmon, W. (1966). *The Foundations of Scientific Inference.* Pittsburgh: University of Pittsburgh Press.

Samburski, S. (1973). *Physics of the Stoics.* Westport, CT: Greenwood Press.

Sarkar, H. (1983). *A Theory of Method.* Berkeley: University of California Press.

Schank, R. C. (1982). *Dynamic Memory.* Cambridge: Cambridge University Press.

Schank, R. C., and Abelson, R. P. (1977). *Scripts, Plans, Goals, and Understanding: An Inquiry into Human Knowledge Structures.* Hillsdale, NJ: Lawrence Erlbaum.

Searle, J. (1980). Minds, brains, and programs. *Behavioral and Brain Sciences 3,* 417–424.

Shrager, J. (1985). Instructionless learning: discovery of the mental model of a complex device. Unpublished doctoral dissertation, Carnegie-Mellon University, Pittsburgh.

Shweder, R. (1977). Likeness and likelihood in everyday thought: magical thinking in judgments of personality, *Current Anthropology 18,* 637–648."

Simpson, G. G. (1967). *The Meaning of Evolution* (rev. edn.). New Haven: Yale University Press.

Sklar, L. (1975). Methodological conservatism. *Philosophical Review 84,* 374–400.

Sneed, J. D. (1971). *The Logical Structure of Mathematical Physics.* Dordrecht: Reidel.

Sober, E. (1975). *Simplicity.* Oxford: Clarendon Press.

Stegmüller, W. (1979). *The Structuralist View of Theories.* New York: Springer-Verlag.

Stich, S., and Nisbett, R. E. (1980). Justification and the psychology of human reasoning. *Philosophy of Science 47,* 188–202.

Suppe, F. (1972). What's wrong with the received view on the structure of scientific theories? *Philosophy of Science 39,* 1–19.

Suppe, F. (1977). *The Structure of Scientific Theories* (2nd edn.). Urbana: University of Illinois Press.

Suppes, P. (1967). What is a scientific theory? In S. Morgenbesser (ed.), *Philosophy of Science Today.* New York: Basic Books, pp. 55–67.

Tarski, A. (1956). *Logic, Semantics, Metamathematics.* Translated by J. Woodger. Oxford: Oxford University Press.

Thagard, P. (1977a). Darwin and Whewell. *Studies in the History and Philosophy of Science 8,* 353–356.

Thagard, P. (1977b). Explanation and scientific inference. Unpublished doctoral dissertation, University of Toronto, Toronto, Ont.

Thagard, P. (1977c). The unity of Peirce's theory of hypothesis. *Transactions of the Charles S. Peirce Society 113,* 112–121.

Thagard, P. (1978a). The best explanation: criteria for theory choice. *Journal of Philosophy 75,* 76–92.

Thagard, P. (1978b). Why astrology is a pseudoscience. In P. Aquith and I. Hacking (eds.),

PSA 1978, vol. 1. East Lansing, MI: Philosophy of Science Association, pp. 223–234. (Reprinted in E. D. Klemke, R. Hollinger, and A. D. Kline (eds.), *Introductory Readings in the Philosophy of Science*. Buffalo: Prometheus Books, pp. 66–75.)

Thagard, P. (1981) Peirce on hypothesis and abduction. In K. Ketner et al. (eds.), *Proceedings of the C. S. Peirce Bicentennial International Congress*. Lubbock, Texas: Texas Tech University Press, pp. 271–274.

Thagard, P. (1984). Frames, knowledge, and inference. *Synthese 61*, 233–259.

Thagard, P. (1986). Parallel computation and the mind-body problem. *Cognitive Science 10*, 301–318.

Thagard, P. (1987). The conceptual structure of the chemical revolution. Unpublished manuscript.

Thagard, P., and Holyoak, K. (1985). Discovering the wave theory of sound: induction in the context of problem solving. *Proceedings of the Ninth International Joint Conference on Artificial Intelligence*. Los Altos: Morgan Kaufmann, 610–612.

Thagard, P., and Nisbett, R. (1983). Rationality and charity. *Philosophy of Science 50*, 250–267.

Thorndyke, P., and Hayes-Roth, B. (1979). The use of schemata in the acquisition and transfer of knowledge, *Cognitive Psychology 11*, 82–106.

Toulmin, S. (1953). *The Philosophy of Science*. London: Hutchinson.

Toulmin, S. (1972). *Human Understanding*. Princeton: Princeton University Press.

Tversky, A., and Kahneman, D. (1974). Judgment under uncertainty: heuristics and biases. *Science 185*, 1124–1131.

van Fraassen, B. (1972). A formal approach to the philosophy of science. In Colodny (ed.), *Paradigms and Paradoxes*. Pittsburgh: University of Pittsburgh Press, pp. 303–366.

van Fraassen, B. (1980). *The Scientific Image*. Oxford: Clarendon Press.

Velikovsky, I. (1965). *Worlds in Collision*. New York: Dell.

Vitruvius, (1960). *The Ten Books on Architecture*. Translated by M. H. Morgan. New York: Dover.

Whewell, W. (1967). *The Philosophy of the Inductive Sciences*. New York: Johnson Reprint Corp. First published 1840.

Wilford, J. (1985). *The Riddle of the Dinosaur*. New York: Knopf.

Wirth, N. (1976). *Algorithms + Data Structures = Programs*. Englewood Cliffs, NJ: Prentice-Hall.

Wittgenstein, L. (1953). *Philosophical Investigations*. Translated by G. E. M. Anscombe. Oxford: Blackwell.

Young, T. (1855). *Miscellaneous Works*. Edited by George Peacock. London: John Murray.

Index